ANCIENT AND MEDIEVAL
SIEGE WEAPONS

ANCIENT AND MEDIEVAL SIEGE WEAPONS

A FULLY ILLUSTRATED GUIDE TO SIEGE WEAPONS AND TACTICS

KONSTANTIN NOSSOV

ILLUSTRATED BY VLADIMIR GOLUBEV

LYONS PRESS
Guilford, Connecticut
An imprint of Globe Pequot Press

Copyright © 2005, 2012 by Konstantin Nossov

First published in Russia in 2003 as **Осадная техника: Античность и Средневековье** by Polygon Publishing House

First published in English in 2005 by Lyons Press

First Lyons Press paperback edition 2012

Lyons Press is an imprint of Globe Pequot Press.

The Library of Congress has catalogued an earlier edition as follows:

Nossov, K. (Konstantin)
    Osadnaya tekhnika Antichnosti i Srednevekov'ya.
    Ancient and medieval siege weapons / by Konstantin S. Nossov.
        p. cm.
    Includes bibliographical references and index.
    ISBN 1-59228-710-7 (trade cloth : alk. paper)
1. Siege warfare—History. 2. Sieges—History. 3. Military weapons—History—To 1500. 4. Military history, Medieval. 5. Middle Ages. I. Title.
UG443.N6813 2005
355.4'4—dc22

        2005022450

ISBN 978-0-7627-8264-2

Printed in the United States of America

10 9 8 7 6 5 4 3 2

CONTENTS

Preface to the English Edition   IX

Preface   XI

Acknowledgments   XIII

PART I. THE HISTORY OF SIEGE WARFARE

1   Ancient Egypt   3

2   Ancient Judea   9

3   Assyria   13

4   Persia   25

5   Greece   27

6   Rome   43

7   Gauls and Germanic Tribes   53

8   Byzantine Empire   57

9   The Arab World   61

10   Medieval Europe   65

PART II. SIEGE WEAPONS

11   Scaling Ladders   75

12   Mobile Sheds   81

13   Battering Rams   89

14   Borers   99

15   Siege Towers   103

16   *Sambucas*   117

17   *Agger* (Embankments)   119

18   Undermining   123

19   Ancient and Medieval Throwing Machines   133

20   Incendiary Weapons in Siege Warfare   189

21   Gunpowder and Siege Cannon   205

22 Other Siege Devices   223

PART III. METHODS OF ATTACK AND DEFENSE

23 Methods of Attack   233

24 Methods of Defense   243

25 Stratagems   253

APPENDICES

Appendix 1 Greek Measurements   259

Appendix 2 Roman Measurements   261

Appendix 3 Approximate Life Spans of Some Ancient and Medieval Authors   263

Glossary   265

Endnotes   275

Bibliography   287

Index   293

TO MY WIFE,
NATALIA ZAROSHCHINSKAYA
a clever and beautiful woman,
whose exceptional patience and invaluable assistance
made the creation of this book possible.

PREFACE
TO THE ENGLISH EDITION

Since the first edition of this book was published in 2003 (in Russian), several new excellent books on siege warfare have been released. There are the works of Duncan B. Campbell and David Nicolle, devoted respectively to the siege weapons of the ancient world and the Middle Ages. It is also necessary to note an excellent investigation by Dmitri Uvarov into medieval throwing machines, which unfortunately is not yet available in printed form. In preparing this book for a new English edition, I have supplemented the material with some facts from these works; most of the alterations have been reflected in the notes. The book has been greatly supplemented with new illustrations made by artist Vladimir V. Golubev. Since publishing the first edition, my view of some siege weapons has undergone certain changes. Therefore, in this English edition, a new treatment of some Byzantine and Arab throwing machines is given, as well as a new illustration of the "wolf" of Procopius.

In translating the book into the English language, I tried to use quotations from sources published in English-language editions. Unfortunately, however, not all sources are available in English; therefore, I sometimes had to provide my own translation of quotations from the language of the original. Although I did my best to name the English editions of primary sources, Russian and Latin editions will be found alongside. In the bibliography, I sometimes cite two different editions of the same source, if the translations differ considerably and I have made use of both versions.

To my great regret, not all first editions of contemporary foreign authors are available, even in the central Russian libraries, so I was obliged to refer to later editions whose imprints are indicated in the bibliography. In addition, some of the works by European authors have been translated into Russian, and I have not been able to find editions in their original languages. Still, I have decided to retain these references in the English edition of the book, as I think it is better to have at least some version of the work referred to rather than none at all. I would like to apologize to the reader for any inconvenience caused by having to look up references.

December 2004   Konstantin Nossov

PREFACE

The subject of this book is siege warfare and weapons in the countries of Western Europe and the Near and Middle East, from the earliest time to the end of the 15th century. The siege weapons of Medieval Russia, India, and the countries of the Far East have been examined in my other works*, so they will not be touched upon here.

The purpose of Part I, "The History of Siege Warfare," is to trace the main stages in the evolution of siege methods and weapons. Brief descriptions of individual sieges are cited here as corroboration. I did not set myself the task of describing all sieges, since this has already been superbly done elsewhere.**

Part II, "Siege Weapons," is devoted exclusively to the structure of various siege weapons and methods of using them. In this section, the reader can view reconstructions of siege engines, which have been made on the strength of descriptions and representations given in various sources.

Part III, "Methods of Attack and Defense," informs the reader, stage by stage, about the actions taken by the besiegers and the besieged, and various stratagems pertaining to sieges are also described. A "regular" planned siege as described in the book is certainly an idealized scheme, and real sieges seldom conformed to it.

Terms found in italics throughout the book are explained in the glossary.

December 2002   Konstantin Nossov

---

* Nossov, K. S., *Russkiye kreposti i osadnaya tehnika VIII–XVII vekov* (*Russian Fortresses and Siege Warfare, 8th–17th centuries*), Saint-Petersburg & Moscow, 2003; Nossov, K. S., *Zamki i kreposti Indii, Kitaya i Yaponii* (*Castles and Fortresses of India, China and Japan*), Moscow, 2001; Nossov, K.S., *Zamki Yaponii* (Castles of Japan), Saint-Petersburg, 2005)

** E.g., in such enchanting works as: Bradbury, J., *The Medieval Siege*, Woodbridge, 1992; Kern, P. B., *Ancient Siege Warfare*, London, 1999.

ACKNOWLEDGMENTS

I wish to thank artist Vladimir Golubev, who undertook the heavy burden of illustrating this book. An expert on warfare, he truly put his heart in the work, making many valuable suggestions. I am also indebted to Mikhail V. Gorelik for the materials and valuable advice he kindly offered; David Nicolle, who provided one of his photographs for the book; Duncan B. Campbell, who helped me in my quest to obtain permission to use many of the book's photographs; Marcus Cowper, editor of Ilios Publishing LLP, who introduced me to a number of very helpful people; and Christine Duffy, assistant editor at Lyons Press, who helped me clear up various questions in the course of preparing the book. I am especially grateful to Andrew V. Sarjevsky, who accompanied me on most of my travels to various parts of the world, and staunchly endured long journeys and scorching sun in search of a castle, museum, or a particular artifact. I am also deeply indebted to Natalia Zaroshchinskaya, Irina Nossova, and Marina Nossova for their inestimable assistance in the preparation of materials for the book.

PART I

THE HISTORY OF SIEGE WARFARE

The history of siege warfare is closely connected with the history of fortifications, since this type of warfare began with the building of a country's first fortifications. To completely subdue the occupied territory, one had to seize every fortress and castle in it. Although he only won a single great battle—the Battle of Hastings—William of Normandy easily managed to occupy the whole of England due to that country's lack of a developed system of castles.[1] As a rule, fortified towns and castles were situated on big rivers or road crossings. Therefore, the invading army could only pass them by making a considerable detour. This resulted in the campaign dragging on, and the undermining of its prospects of success in general, as the garrison of a fortress or a castle could make a surprise sortie and cut up the communication lines of the advancing army.

Sieges were laid much more often than decisive battles were fought. Of course, victory in a field or naval battle brought the commander greater fame, but the danger was incomparably graver, as a whole army could be lost in such a battle. Therefore, cautious commanders did not willingly enter into an open battle unless numerical superiority was manifest. During his ten-year rule, Richard I was constantly engaged in laying sieges, taking part in no more than two or three large-scale battles. Geoffrey V of Anjou conquered Normandy between 1135 and 1145 without fighting a single battle.[2]

⊙⊙⊙

ONE

ANCIENT EGYPT

We owe our knowledge of the earliest development of siege warfare in Ancient Egypt to the incised paintings of sieges found on the walls of tombs. A painting on the wall of Inti's Tomb at Deshasheh shows the level of development of siege art in the Old Kingdom (28th–23rd centuries BC). It depicts an assault by Egyptian troops on an enemy fortress, including a number of scenes of hand-to-hand battle using battle-axes and daggers. Some enemy warriors are practically pierced with arrows, which proves that even at that time the advance of storming troops was covered by mass fire from a body of Egyptian archers.

The siege of an Asian fortress by the Egyptians. Drawing from Inti's Tomb at Deshasheh. The Old Kingdom, the 5th dynasty (26th–25th centuries BC).

At the bottom of the drawing several warriors are breaching a wall or a gate with crowbars. This is not surprising, as walls made of sandstone or mud-brick were not strong enough to withstand even such primitive tools. Breaching walls with crowbars and axes is also depicted in Egyptian representations of a later period, evidence that this siege tactic was actively used.

Fortress wall of Nekheb (El Kab), like many other old Egyptian fortresses,
is built of mud-brick. Author's photograph.

In the picture we can also see a scaling ladder, applied to the wall by a warrior. It is the most ancient siege weapon, which probably appeared as soon as the first fortress walls were erected, and was widely used as early as the Old Kingdom. The scaling ladder found in a scene on the wall of Khaemweset's Tomb at Saqqara (Memphis, 6th dynasty, 25th–23rd centuries BC) is particularly interesting, as the ladder is placed on wooden disk wheels. The chariot was not yet known in Egypt at that time, so the use of a wheel was apparently know-how borrowed from some Asian tribes.

Assault on a fortress. Drawing from Amenemhat's Tomb at Beni Hasan, the Middle Kingdom,
the 12th dynasty (20th–18th centuries BC).

Our knowledge of siege warfare during the time of the Middle Kingdom (21st–18th centuries BC) is considerably richer. This was a time of overall growth for warfare in Egypt, and siege warfare also progressed significantly. Representations of siege scenes, still the main source of our knowledge about siege warfare, become more numerous during this era.

The siege tactics of this Middle Kingdom period are best represented in three scenes of fortress sieges—two in the tombs at Beni Hasan and one in the tomb of Intef at Thebes. All the drawings have much in common, indicative of the similarity of siege tactics as a whole. In all the drawings archers are hailing the besieged with arrows. Groups of warriors armed with lances, battle-axes, boomerangs, and shields are marching to their assistance. The besieged respond by shooting arrows and probably throwing stones.

The most interesting element in the drawings at Beni Hasan is the image of warriors concealed inside a protecting shed and armed with a long pole. These drawings may be considered the earliest evidence of the use of battering rams. The pole, probably with a pointed metal tip, was used for breaching the upper part of a wall. That could be done without much difficulty owing to the construction of walls in ancient Egypt: they were made of mud-brick, which crumbled easily.

Erecting a wall of mud-brick at the "Village of Pharaoh," Cairo. Such walls could be easily destroyed by picks and axes. Author's photograph.

Assault on a fortress. Drawing from Khety's Tomb at Beni Hasan,
the Middle Kingdom, the 11th dynasty (21st century BC).

The drawing in Intef's Tomb at Thebes is apparently the first evidence of the use of a mobile siege tower. The structure of the tower seems quite primitive as yet. It resembles several ladders joined together, which the attackers are climbing. However, the tower is already provided with wheels and a small bridge to enable men to pass onto the wall.

Besieging a fortress using a mobile siege tower. Drawing from Intef's Tomb
at Thebes. Middle Kingdom, the 11th dynasty (21st century BC).

The main siege weapons of the Egyptians in the period of the Old and Middle Kingdoms were bows, slings, axes, and crowbars. Throwing weapons (bows and slings) were used both by the besieged and besiegers. As to siege engines, only scaling ladders seem to have been used in the Old Kingdom. The Middle Kingdom saw the first, and most simple, battering rams and siege

The Egyptian army besieging a city. Climbing an assault ladder are Egyptian warriors covered with hand shields. In the center of the composition we can see archers and slingers; at the bottom four more walking warriors are protected by structures resembling large shields in addition to hand shields. Author's photograph.

towers, as well. An assaulting troop always advanced under the cover of a body of archers hailing the besieged with arrows and suppressing their defense.

During the New Kingdom (16th–11th centuries BC), battering rams seem to be going out of use. Thus, not a single battering ram can be found in the reliefs of the bellicose Ramses II (13th century BC)—instead, the soldiers assault walls using scaling ladders and breach the gate with their battle-axes. In 1468 BC it took Thutmose III seven months to seize the town of Megiddo.[3] These facts show that fortifications had become much more powerful by that time, and were able to successfully withstand weak Egyptian battering rams.

· TWO ·

ANCIENT JUDEA

ncient Hebrews did not invent new siege warfare techniques, nor did they use, at least
prior to the 10th century BC, siege engines invented by others. But to make up for it,
they were great masters of various battle stratagems.

The main source of information about the development of warfare in ancient Judea is the
Bible, which contains more descriptions of battles than any other Near East written document.

Having invaded Canaan (the name of the territory containing parts of today's Israel, Jordan, Syria, and Lebanon), the Hebrews found themselves in a difficult situation. Most of the
towns were well fortified, and the Hebrews were quite inexperienced in siege warfare.

Led by Joshua, the Hebrews found themselves facing the powerfully fortified town of Jericho after crossing the Jordan River. They were unable to pass by it, as the town stood in their
way; moreover, it controlled the supplies of water necessary for their military operations in
Canaan. However, it seemed absolutely impossible to seize the strongly fortified Jericho without
siege engines. The Hebrews had to resort to a clever stratagem.

First of all, Joshua sent two young men to make a reconnaissance of the terrain, as we would
say today. They stole into the house of a prostitute named Rahab, who, in exchange for her rescue after the occupation of the town by the Hebrews, agreed to assist them, and even hide them
from their persecutors.[4] Like most taverns and inns in ancient towns, Rahab's house adjoined the
town wall, and was thus of great strategic importance in itself.

According to the Bible, the siege of Jericho lasted seven days and was conducted in the following way: For six days the besieged watched a Hebrew procession going around Jericho. An
ark was carried in the middle of the procession, with seven priests marching in front and blowing seven trumpets. The priests were in their turn preceded by armed forces (probably elite
troops), and the rest followed the ark, also blowing trumpets. Nobody was allowed to utter a
sound until Joshua said: "Shout." This happened on the seventh day, and "When the trumpets
sounded, the people shouted, and at the sound of the trumpet, when the people gave a loud
shout, the wall collapsed; so every man charged straight in, and they took the city. They devoted
the city to the LORD and destroyed with the sword every living thing in it—men and women,
young and old, cattle, sheep and donkeys."[5]

All kinds of theories have been brought forward to explain the phenomena of the Jericho trumpets, beginning with the improbable suggestion that the walls could not withstand the vibration of the rhythmical marching and the sound waves from thousands of shouting people and blaring trumpets. What seems more likely is that the daily marches weakened the defenders' vigilance, thus enabling the Hebrews to mount a successful surprise attack. The Hebrews may have also managed to undermine the wall, digging to the incessant noise of the trumpets, and this resulted in its collapse.

Unfortunately, archaeologists have found very few traces of the Bible's Jericho, which would have dated back to the 13th century BC. This brings some researchers to the conclusion that there was no such siege at all. Others believe that the remains of the broken walls might have been simply washed away by waters.[6]

No less interesting is the siege of another Canaan town called Ai. According to the Bible, the town was only defended by a small number of soldiers, which inspired the Hebrews—to no purpose, however. Strictly speaking, a well-fortified town could be defended by a very small number of soldiers, on the condition that the defense was properly organized. The inhabitants of Ai were so sure of their own strength that they came out to face the approaching Israelites, and even managed to inflict heavy casualties on them in the ensuing battle.[7] The Hebrews then had to resort to cunning. At night they hid a detachment of their crack troops beyond the town, and in the morning the main bulk of their army moved to the gate of Ai again. Still more confident of their power, the inhabitants again came out to face them—to a man, as the Bible says. The Hebrews did not engage the enemy, but instead feigned retreat. When the pursuing citizens were quite far from the town, the crack troops concealed in the ambush entered the town and took it without a battle. The defenders were then gripped in a vise between the main army and the troops that occupied the town, ending in their total defeat.[8]

The seizure of Ai shows that Joshua was a skillful commander to devise such a complex maneuver as a false flight and a surprise counterattack. Nevertheless, he either did not know how to lay a regular systematic siege or could not bring himself to do it. It was probably connected with the insufficient preparedness of the army, which at that time consisted of militia. The soldiers took part in a brief campaign and then returned home, to their fields or shops. The irregulars did not undergo proper training and their discipline left much to be desired. Desertion was common.[9] The Hebrews' backwardness in siege warfare impeded their progress in future campaigns as well. They failed to capture a number of Canaanite towns, and the ones that were captured were only seized by means of cunning or treason.

It was only with the formation of a centralized state under King David (10th century BC) that Hebrew armies became capable of laying more systematic sieges, and this was primarily because they developed a professional army and used mercenaries. Militia forces continued to exist, but were only enlisted as a last resort.[10]

The Hebrews built their first large-scale siege works at the siege of the town of Abel Beth Maacah.[11] Under the supervision of King David's general, Joab, they built an embankment. The Bible states that they even tried to destroy the wall; what they used was hardly a battering ram, as even under King David's successor, Solomon, fortifications were not yet strong enough to withstand the blows of battering rams. If at that time the Hebrews had been acquainted with rams similar to those which were used by the Assyrians two centuries later, they would hardly have continued building such weak walls. An undermining seems equally improbable. It is much easier to assume that the Israelites used picks and axes to break the wall. Be that as it may, this is the first evidence of a direct breaching of a fortress wall by the Hebrews.

THREE

ASSYRIA

Further progress in siege warfare is closely connected with the rise of one of the Mesopotamian states, namely Assyria. Beginning with the rule of Tiglath-Pileser I (1115–1076 BC), Assyria became the most powerful military state in the Near East and held its superiority for five centuries—from the end of the 12th to the end of the 7th century BC.

Before that, however, under Shamshi-Adad I (1813–1781 BC), Assyria, then the city-state of Assur, experienced a short growth spurt, having attained power equal to that of Babylonia. The sons of Shamshi-Adad I failed to maintain the independence of the state and in 1757 BC acknowledged the authority of Babylonia. What is most important to us, however, is that documents which describe the siege methods of those days have been preserved since the rule of one of the sons, Ishme-Dagan I (1797–1757 BC). The documents, dating from the 18th century BC, were found in the town of Mari, situated in the upper reaches of the Euphrates. This is the first written documentation about the usage of battering rams, siege towers, sapping work, and embankments.

One of the documents tells about the use of siege towers and battering rams: ". . . I turned and laid siege to Hurara. I set against it the siege towers and battering rams and in seven days I vanquished it. Be pleased." The second document carries information about a successful use of sapping work: "As soon as I had approached the town of Qirhadat I set up siege towers. By sapping I caused its walls to collapse. On the eighth day I seized the city of Qirhadat. Rejoice."[12] Another document refers to the building of an embankment: "The town of Nilimmar that Ishme-Dagan besieged, Ishme-Dagan has now taken. As long as the siege-ramps did not reach to the heights of the top of the city wall, he could not seize the town. As soon as the siege-ramps reached the top of the wall, he gained mastery over this town."[13]

Most probably Ishme-Dagan I learned of these methods from his father, Shamshi-Adad I, who had spent some time in Babylon and had had an opportunity to study the siege warfare of the Babylonians. No representation of sieges in Mesopotamia during that time survives, however; that is why the usage of the siege methods described is not quite clear. For example, it is not apparent whether sapping work was done underground, or if the walls were broken at the foot with picks and other tools. The latter seems more probable if we take into consideration the fact that walls were often built from mud-brick and that the method had been used by the Egyptians long before. As to underground work, it demands a great deal of knowledge and experience.

The use of siege towers is not obvious either. Given the description, the towers in this case were used not to storm the walls with the help of a footbridge but rather to create a fire cover for the sappers.

Considerably more complete information about the warfare of the Assyrians has been preserved from the 9th through 7th centuries BC. Most of the surviving reliefs that represent sieges and siege weapons date from this time, when the Assyrian Empire was at the peak of its power. The Assyrians were highly skilled in the art of war, particularly in siege warfare, which became a key point in their aggressive campaigns and methods of ruling the empire. Many a siege engine was supposed to have been borrowed by the Assyrians from the Sumerians, but, like the Romans, the Assyrians surpassed the inventors of the engines in the application of the latter.

Judging by the reliefs of Ashurnasirpal II (883–859 BC), an Assyrian battering ram of the 9th century was a massive structure sitting on six wheels. Its front section contained a high tower with loopholes for archers (see plate 10). The battering ram was apparently very heavy and slow moving. Therefore, as early as the reign of Shalmaneser III (858–824 BC), it was light-

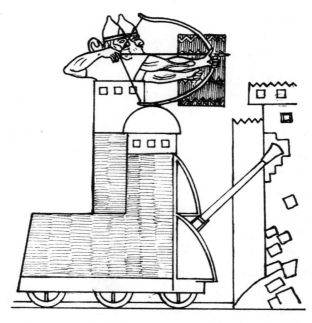

Battering ram sitting on six wheels. From the time of Ashurnasirpal II (9th century BC).

The image of an Assyrian battering ram sitting on four wheels on the
Gate of Shalmaneser III (9th century BC).

ened and placed on only four wheels. The representation of a battering ram on the Gate of Shalmaneser III allows us to assume the existence of a model without any ram-pole at all, just a cart with a pointed nose resembling a bull's head. The cart was probably loaded with stones or dirt, and driven at high speed directly at a wall or gate. Following the cart were archers who covered the working battering ram with fire. We can also see several archers in the cart itself. This structure of a battering ram was, however, apparently weaker than the one with a pendulum and a pole, which soon led to its falling into disuse—later representations of such battering rams are not found.

Sargon II (722–705 BC) increased the destructive potential of a battering ram by grouping a few rams against one section of the wall. King Sennacherib's time (705–681 BC) saw the appearance of collapsible battering rams consisting of several units. This enabled men to transfer siege engines in a string of carts and assemble them quickly on the spot. At the same time, the pole became longer, which increased the power of the ram.

The Assyrians used the battering ram in two ways. The first was to bring a ram right up to the gate, which was seen as the weakest spot of the defense. To counteract that, gates were soon flanked by towers, which hampered the use of a battering ram against them. The other more complicated way involved the building of an embankment, along which a ram could be brought right to the wall. It could be brought to the upper part of the wall, which as a rule was thinner and weaker than the foot. (Moreover, many an old fortress had a stone-laid lower part of the wall, while the upper part was made of a considerably weaker mud-brick.) To manage this, the embankment was sloped as gently as possible in order to facilitate the advance of a battering ram toward the wall. Excavations of the Hebrew town of Lachish, which the Assyrians carried by

The employment by the Assyrians of a group of battering rams against a section of a wall. Drawing from a relief of Sargon II's time (8th century BC).

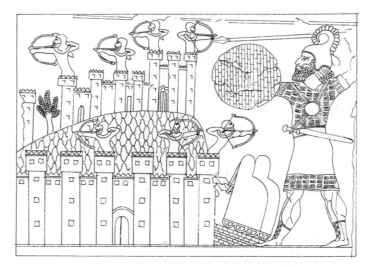

The assault on a fortress by the Assyrians. We can clearly see several battering rams attacking the fortifications simultaneously. Drawing from a relief of the time of Tiglath-Pileser III (8th century BC).

The assault on a fortress by the Assyrians, the 8th century BC.
Note the battering rams being brought up to the walls along the embankment.

storm, show that the embankment went downhill at approximately 30 degrees, growing gentler toward the summit. It was perhaps the increase in the second method of employing battering rams that led to their more lightweight construction.

The defense fought battering rams by means of chains, with which they caught the head of the log and pulled it up. The Assyrians, in their turn, detached special groups of soldiers who caught the chains with iron hooks, hanging all the weight of their bodies against the former.

Fire spelled enormous danger to siege engines, insofar as even earthen embankments had wooden frames that could be easily burned down. To protect their rams from fire, the Assyrians covered them with wet skins; however, it did not always help. Thus, in one of the reliefs (see page 18) we can see a group of soldiers in a tower sitting in the front part of a ram, pouring water down on the battering ram from long tubes. In another relief a soldier is putting out a fire by pouring water on the battering ram from a long-handled spoon.

Judging by reliefs, an Assyrian storming detachment that carried the walls by escalade consisted of both lancers and archers. The soldiers of this detachment did not wear the long armor typical of the Assyrians. Such armor would only constrain the movement of their legs, preventing them from climbing ladders as fast as was necessary. Therefore, their shortened clothing reached only as far as their knees.

The siege of a city by the Assyrians. The besieged have caught a battering ram with chains and are trying to pull it upwards, while the Assyrian warriors are trying to oppose their doing it. The besieged have probably set fire to the battering ram too, as we see the assailants pouring water from the turret. Drawing from a relief on the Gate of Shalmaneser III (9th century BC).

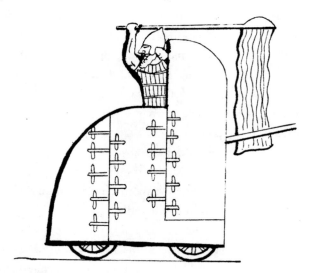

Collapsible Assyrian battering ram with a long pole. The warrior in the turret is trying to put out the fire by pouring water onto the battering ram with the help of a long spoon. The time of the rule of King Sennacherib (7th century BC).

Those storming detachments were undoubtedly well-trained elite troops. Looking closely at the reliefs, one can see that while climbing ladders, the lancers held their weapons in their hands—the lance in the right hand and the shield in the left—and the archers even managed to shoot arrows right from the ladders. In other words, these excellent soldiers of Assyrian storming troops were able to climb ladders without using their hands.

Nevertheless, even a well-trained storming detachment could hardly have fulfilled its task without a "covering force." The latter role was played by archers concealed behind large, stationary siege shields. The main task of the archers was to drive the defenders off the top of the wall, thus reducing the fire brought to bear upon the storming detachment to a minimum. The length of the shields somewhat exceeded the height of a man, and usually turned slightly inward at their upper part to secure better protection. A specially assigned soldier carried the archer's shield, holding it by the handle.

Besides archers, the Assyrians widely employed slingers and war chariots during a siege. Owing to the steep parabolic trajectory of the flight of stones launched from a sling, the slingers proved particularly effective against the defenders concealed behind the parapet of the wall. The defenders were also exposed to great danger from chariots. Assyrian war chariots rushed past the wall hailing the enemy with arrows at an unexpected angle, and just as quickly left the area under fire.[14]

Assault on an Egyptian city. Fragment of an Assyrian relief from the Palace of Ashurbanipal in Nineveh, about 645 BC. We can clearly see storm detachments of spearmen and archers climbing ladders under the cover of the fire of archers behind large stationary shields. On the left of the picture an Assyrian warrior is engaged in sapping.

The siege of a city by the Assyrians using siege shields, battering rams, and scaling ladders.
Spearmen are shown climbing the ladder without using their hands.

A number of Assyrian reliefs represent sappers working at the foot of a wall. They used such tools as crowbars, pickaxes, and borers. Gradually boring deeper and deeper into the wall, they strengthened it with wooden props lest it should fall down on them. When the deepening trenches reached the necessary size, the props were burned down, and the wall collapsed. To protect themselves from the fire from the fortress, sappers at the time of Ashurnasirpal II (884–859

An Assyrian archer hiding himself behind a siege shield.

BC) wore long armor, reaching down to the ankles, and a helmet with an aventail to protect their necks and faces. Under subsequent rulers, sappers only wore short armor, a helmet, and a fairly short, round shield; they held the latter with one hand while digging with the other. This hardly provided effective protection or made for speedy work. Therefore, under Ashurbanipal (669–630 BC), a large wattle shield was introduced for the sappers' protection. The shield curved at the top in such a way that the sapper could easily prop it against the wall, thus having both his hands free for work. The shields must have been solid enough to repel the stones thrown from the wall.

We know from reliefs and written sources that more than once, Assyrian kings led their armies into field battle, driving a chariot in front of the troops. However, in all reliefs that reproduce sieges, kings are only to be found behind the archers, providing fire support. Moreover, they always wear long armor reaching down to their ankles, which is striking proof that they had not the slightest intention of personally commanding a storm detachment. Certainly, it was a matter of prestige to a great extent; it is one thing to lead an elite force of chariots, but something completely different to place oneself at the head of an infantry detachment—even a crack one. At the same time we cannot exclude another possibility: the kings might have considered

A sapper destroying a wall at its base under the cover of a woven siege shield.

an assault to be much more dangerous than a field battle, and that was the reason why they did not take part in it.

The highly developed art of the siege in Assyria in the 7th century BC is demonstrated by the vivid description of the seizure of the Egyptian city of Memphis by Esarhaddon in 671 BC. He says: "I laid siege to Memphis, Taharqa's royal residence, and conquered it in half a day by means of mines, breaches, and assault ladders . . ."[15]

The siege of the Hebrew town of Lachish by King Sennacherib is also revealing. There is extensive evidence about this siege contained in Assyrian reliefs, the king's notes, the Bible, and archaeological findings. The town was situated on a steep mountain and was protected by powerful fortifications. High walls interspersed with square towers, and topped with crenellated battlements, encircled the town. Moreover, on the summit of the wall, the Hebrews placed wooden frames for their shields to be fixed inside, thus providing additional protection. The main gate was located close to the southwestern extremity of the town, and was to be approached along a narrow road. The outer gate was flanked by two powerful towers. Two more towers protected the inner gate, which was placed at a right angle to the outer one, so that assaulting soldiers, having penetrated through the outer gate, expose their unprotected right-hand side to enemy fire. Passing through the inner gate, storming troops found themselves in a huge square tower only to be attacked by the defenders on two sides. Finally, there was a citadel in the fortress, the last sanctuary of defense.[16]

Carrying such a powerful fortress by storm was undoubtedly an arduous task. The Assyrian king, Sennacherib himself, directed siege operations. The Assyrians pitched a camp on a height, 350 meters from the southwest angle of the town, close to the gate. Then they set about building two embankments. The bigger one went to the southwest corner of the main fortress wall, while the smaller one led to the northwest corner of the outer fortifications, in front of the main gate. On completing the erection of the embankments, the Assyrians brought battering rams up alongside them and began to breach the walls. Almost simultaneously they attacked the gate both with rams and fire. They employed no less than seven battering rams at a time. Assyrian sources also mention a sapping. No doubt the siege was an active one. Sennacherib was so proud of the seizure of Lachish that he ordered several reliefs for his royal palace at Nineveh to remind him of his deed.[17]

Notwithstanding the fact that the Assyrians used an impressive variety of siege methods, they did not always manage to carry a well-fortified fortress by storm. In such cases they resorted to a passive siege, which could last for a long time. For example, they spent three years besieging Arpad and another three years to capture Samaria. Unfortunately, we know far less about the methods of passive sieges than we do about the methods of assault. Adad-Nirari II (911–890 BC) is known to have encircled a besieged town with a ditch. At the siege of Hatarikka, the Assyrians surrounded it by a "wall higher than wall of Hatarikka" and "made a moat deeper than its moat."[18] This seems to be evidence of the fact that the Assyrians built a *circumvallation* line. At the same time, the reference to a wall that surpassed the town wall in height suggests that the Assyrians did not confine themselves to passive methods but wanted to acquire a better position for bringing fire to bear upon the enemy. The meaning of a moat deeper than the town moat is not quite clear either. Possibly, the moat was earmarked in this case not just to isolate the besieged town, but also for digging an underground gallery or draining water out of the town moat. More often than not, however, the Assyrians seemed to have confined themselves to isolating the besieged fortress by means of chariots and cavalry. The besieging troops usually stayed in a camp, surrounded by a rampart, with streets crossing at right angles—a prototype of later Roman camps.

• FOUR •

PERSIA

The foundation of the Persian Empire is associated with the name of the prominent warrior-king, Cyrus. Having taken power in Media in 559 BC, he became the ruler of the great Persian Empire, and immediately faced the necessity of besieging strong fortresses. In 546 BC, having defeated the Lydian army led by Croesus, Cyrus besieged Sardis, the capital of Lydia. The siege lasted but two weeks. According to Herodotus,[19] the city was taken thanks to Mardian Hyroiades, who had discovered an unguarded section of the fortress wall. The Lydians considered this place unapproachable because of a precipitous rock. Nevertheless, the Persians managed, probably by means of scaling ladders, to bring a large group of soldiers onto the wall, resulting in the fall of the city.

The most impressive evidence of the potential of the Persian army, however, was the siege of Babylon in 538 BC. Babylon was surrounded by a deep moat and enclosed by two rows of walls alternating with towers; it was considered impregnable. The river Euphrates flowed through the city, supplying it with water. Moreover, the Babylonians had had time to prepare for the siege and had stored provisions for years to come. Attempts to take the city by ordinary methods failed, one after another. After a protracted siege, an idea dawned upon Cyrus: as improbable as it was arduous, he wanted to divert the waters of the Euphrates.[20] Stationing a detachment in the place where the river entered the city and another one where it flowed out of it, he withdrew from the city together with the bulk of his army. He then drained the river water to a lake by means of a canal; as a result, the river became so shallow that the Persian soldiers were able to break into the city from different ends. Cyrus took chances with this assault, though; since the city walls ran along the riverbanks, the Babylonians could have trapped the Persians by closing all the gates leading to the river. The former, however, were having a good time on the occasion of a feast, obviously not expecting such a turn of events, and noticed the Persians but too late.

Not only does the siege prove that Cyrus possessed the gifts of a skilled military leader, but it also strikes one's imagination with the enormous dimensions of the undertaking. Only one who had a large labor force as well as a great number of engineers at one's disposal in the army could have run the risk of such an operation. Generally speaking, the key to the Persians' successful sieges in the course of their history lay in their capacity to arrange large-scale earthworks. Embankments and undermining were their traditional siege methods.

In his campaign against the Greeks, Cyrus's general Harpagus widely used embankments for seizing towns.[21] Telling about it, Herodotus does not mention battering rams, so one gets the impression that the assault was launched right from the embankments, which reached as far as the top of the walls. This seems unlikely. As a rule, an embankment was brought up to the wall, which was then breached by battering rams. The Persians were acquainted with siege engines as early as Cyrus's time. Xenophon[22] mentions this fact when explaining that after the seizure of Sardis, Cyrus lingered in that city to build siege engines necessary to subdue the rest of the Lydian Empire.

The Persians went on building embankments later, as well, as they did during their campaign on Cyprus around 497 BC. Excavations in the town of Paphos show that the Persians built an embankment over the ditch encircling the town. The defenders seem to have dug an underground tunnel, and tried to burn the embankment down, the latter usually having a wooden framework. A great number of missiles—dumb witnesses of a barrage of fire brought to bear upon the Persian soldiers working there—have been found on the embankment.

Undermining, however, seems to have been the most reliable method of siege warfare in the eyes of the Persians. Besieging the town of Barca, they introduced this method to the Greeks, who promptly invented a way to detect underground work and remove the threat.

> Then they besieged Barca for nine months, both digging underground passages which led to the wall and making vigorous attacks upon it. Now the passages dug were discovered by a worker of bronze with a shield covered over with bronze, who had thought of a plan as follows: carrying it round within the wall he applied it to the ground in the city, and whereas the other places to which he applied it were noiseless, at those places where digging was going on the bronze of the shield gave a sound; and the men of Barca would make a countermine there and slay the Persians who were digging mines. This then was discovered as I have said, and the attacks were repulsed by the men of Barca.[23]

According to Aeneas Tacticus,[24] this method of discovering underground work was still in use in the 4th century BC. Nevertheless, it was with the help of undermining that the town of Soli was taken by the Persians after a four-month-long siege (498 BC). Miletus, too, fell because of this use of undermining (494 BC).

• FIVE •

GREECE

Despite the fact that the Greeks were rather warlike, they had no command of siege warfare up to the 5th century BC. When attacking neighboring territory, Greek generals of that time mainly relied upon a "strategy of devastation." Siege warfare was far from perfect, and long sieges were often not worthwhile—or even turned out badly—so the enemy army had to be forced out of the town and become engaged in the field. To achieve this aim, the invading army used all of its might to inflict maximum casualties upon the agriculture of the country it wished to ruin. Crops and olive trees were taken away or destroyed; sometimes tiles were even taken off the roofs of the houses. In order to make the enemy losses as great as possible, the invasion was often undertaken just before harvest time, or at the very beginning of the process. To prevent the devastation of their country, the defenders had to leave town and become engaged in the field. Then the outcome of the war might be determined by only one battle of hoplites (the heavily armed infantry soldiers of Ancient Greece). If the defenders were too weak and preferred to seek shelter in the towns, the invading army devastated the country completely and repeated the invasion every year until the poor inhabitants were starved into surrender. So quite often it was enough just to threaten devastation to make citizens agree to peace negotiations.

Crops ripened earlier in the south of Greece than in the north, which gave Sparta an advantage over the rest of the country. The Spartans gathered the harvest and then left to devastate the states of northern Greece.[25]

The Greeks used this "strategy of devastation" for rather a long time. Even as late as the beginning of the 4th century BC, the Spartan king Agesilaus II ordered his men to root out all the trees wherever his army was advancing, thus forcing the Acarnanians to climb down their mountains and into the valleys, where they were then defeated.[26]

There were no sappers in ancient Greek armies, and obviously not enough archers and slingers, who were absolutely necessary for active siege warfare. Moreover, the army did not bring along much food, even though they brought many servants (one for each hoplite), so supplying the army was quite a problem. That is why sieges were rare, and, from the Assyrian point of view, primitive.

The most famous siege of ancient times was the legendary siege of Troy in the 12th century BC. According to Homer—who described it much later, in the 8th century BC—the siege lasted ten years, and in the end the city was taken by cunning. During the first nine years the Greeks didn't even try to blockade Troy, proven by the fact that reinforcements constantly arrived to help the defenders. The Greeks put up neither *circumvallation* nor *contravallation lines*, but instead confined themselves to digging a moat and erecting a rampart on the shore to defend their camp and ships drawn on the land. Not only were there no attempts to starve the Trojans into surrender, but not a single attack of the walls was undertaken. It was only after nine years of war that the Greeks, led by Achilles, made an attack upon the Western Gate, where Achilles was killed.

Meanwhile, the besieged were fairly active in defending the town, and from time to time, sallied out. Once the Trojans, headed by Hector, boldly attacked the besiegers' camp and nearly burned the Greek fleet down. This time the attack was again directed mainly at a gate, which Hector broke down himself with a heavy stone.

It was only by sheer cunning that the Greeks managed to seize the city. Legend[27] has it that they built a gigantic, hollow wooden horse on wheels. The best Greek soldiers, with Odysseus, king of Ithaca, at the head, concealed themselves in the horse. Then the Greeks left the horse by the walls of Troy, burned down their camp, and pretended to sail away. Acting on the advice of

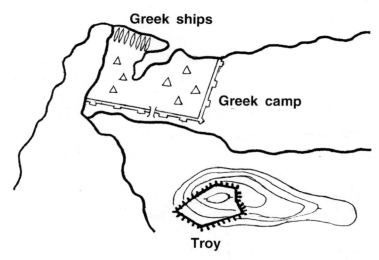

The Siege of Troy, the 12th century BC.

East curtain-wall of Troy VI and the Gate VIs. Author's photograph.

deserter Sinon, the Trojans drew the horse into the city and sat to feast. At night Sinon let the Greek soldiers out of the horse, and they killed the gate guards and opened the gate to their army.

The siege of Troy shows a lack of any knowledge of siege warfare on the side of the Greeks. True, there is an opinion that the Trojan Horse was designed as a battering ram, for the Trojans were said to have to break a part of the wall in order to bring the horse in.[28] It is, however, hard to understand why the Greeks waited until the tenth year of the war to make a battering ram.

There is another curious fact: both attacks (on Troy and the Greek camp) were made on a gate. The same tactics were used by the Greeks during the siege of Thebes, which happened a generation before the siege of Troy. As far as the legend goes, each of the seven generals led an attack upon one of the seven city gates. All of the seven generals were defeated, and six of them were killed.[29] The art of fortification was obviously leaving the art of siege behind.

The same backwardness in siege warfare was manifested by the Greeks several centuries later, in the Archaic Period (7th–6th centuries BC). However, in siege representations of that time, one can see the Greeks attacking city walls with the help of ladders. Nevertheless, more complicated technology, widely used by the contemporary Assyrians, was unknown to the Greeks.

The situation began to change in the 5th century BC. According to Herodotus,[30] during his Sicilian campaign in the 490s BC, the tyrant Hippocrates successfully besieged Callipolis,

Reconstruction of the Trojan Horse situated at the entrance of the site of Troy. Author's photograph.

Naxos, Zancle, Leontini, and a number of other "barbarian" cities. Nothing is known about the methods of besieging these cities; we only know that Hippocrates's general Gelon became famous in those sieges. Syracuse seemed to be too hard a nut to crack, and it escaped the fate of the other cities. On the whole, the Western Greeks probably had a better knowledge of siege warfare, which they might have learned from the inhabitants of the Phoenician town of Carthage. The Carthaginians were acquainted with siege warfare methods used in the Near East.

During the Greco-Persian Wars (500–449 BC), the Greeks had to maintain complete control over the occupied territories, so they had to learn how to besiege cities—otherwise their control would not have been complete. And they learned quickly.

The Greek are besieging a Phoenician city. Engraving on a silver bowl from Cyprus, the 7th century BC.

In 475 BC, probably after a long siege, the Athenians seized the city of Eion.[31] In 470 BC, the rebellious Naxos was taken hold of after three years of siege, and in 440–439 BC, they subjugated the rebel Samos, which took them nine months. The Athenians captured all those cities as a result of a blockade, and the nine-month siege of Samos was probably considered very short by their contemporaries, as Plutarch notes that Pericles—who led the Athenian troops on Samos—was very proud of his quick victory.[32]

Although those sieges were still passive in their character, they are not to be compared with the siege of Troy. Besieging Samos, the Athenians blockaded the city from the sea and surrounded it with three walls on the land.[33] According to Diodorus[34] and Plutarch,[35] they even used their siege machines (battering rams and moving covers), which "provoked astonishment by their novelty." This is the first written evidence known to us of the Greeks using battering rams. A ram-head found in Olympia dates from the first half of the 5th century BC, which proves that the Greeks were already acquainted with battering rams at that time.

In the first half of the 5th century BC, the Athenians undoubtedly surpassed all the other Greeks in siege warfare. After the Battle of Plataea (479 BC), the Persians withdrew into their camp, which was surrounded by wooden fortifications with towers. The Spartans made an attempt to seize the camp by storm, but failed because they "did not understand the art of fighting against walls." The camp was captured only with the arrival of the Athenians, who breached the wall.[36]

The Athenian army was always followed by masons and carpenters with all the necessary instruments for building siege machines.[37] The whole Athenian army, including hoplites, took

The bronze head of a battering ram found in Olympia. It is dated the first half of the 5th century BC. Note the ram heads shown on either side of the head. (Courtesy of Deutsches Archäologisches Institut Athens, Neg. No. Olympia 2800, Photographer—Herrmann)

part in it, the only exception probably being the hoplites' own servants. The latter didn't participate in action and were never mentioned as taking part in siege operations, although one can't exclude the possibility of their being used as manpower for putting up embankments, walls, and so forth. In 433 BC (or maybe a little earlier), Athenian hoplites began to receive a regular salary, which was very important for the successful accomplishment of long sieges.[38]

During the Second Peloponnesian War (435–404 BC), the Greeks became much more active in besieging towns. A typical example is the siege of Plataea, a city allied to Athens. The Spartans, besieging that city, put up an embankment and first tried to breach the wall with battering rams, and then burn down the town. The Plataeans, however, acted so skillfully that all of the Spartans' attempts led to nothing; it was only after a two-year blockade that Plataea fell.[39]

A curious fire machine was invented by Boeotians, who successfully used it for burning the Athenian camp in Delium (424 BC).[40] The machine was in fact a hollow log with a cauldron filled with lighted coals, pitch, and sulphur hanging at one end and a bellows fixed at the other. With the help of that device, the Boeotians burned the Athenians' wooden fortifications. The fire forced the defenders from the wall, giving the Boeotians an opportunity to attack. However, in that case, the Athenians' fortifications were but temporary—just a rampart strengthened by pickets and grapevine. The same type of machine seems to have been used soon after that by the Spartan general Brasidas against Lecythus, a poorly fortified fortress occupied by Athenians.[41] The latter had built a wooden tower in the place where they expected to be attacked, and they planned to put out fire from it. However, the tower didn't hold the weight of the large number of amphorae and earthenware barrels filled with water, as well as lot of stones stored there, and it broke down. Many Athenians took flight, and Brasidas seized the moment to give the command to attack.

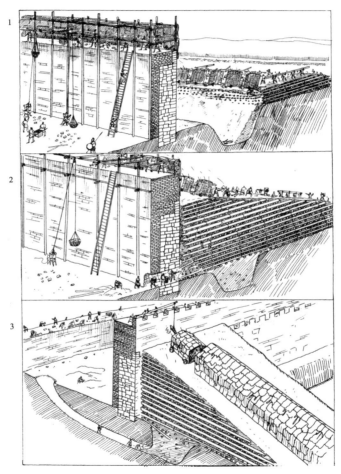

Siege operations at the walls of Plataea (the siege of 429–427 BC):
1—the Spartans are building an embankment, the Plataeans are building on a wall;
2—the Plataeans are making a hole in the wall and beginning to take earth
away from the embankment into the town;
3—the Spartans have filled up the hole in the wall, but then the Plataeans dig an
underground gallery and start taking away the earth from beneath the embankment.
They are simultaneously building a second semicircular wall beyond the first one.

Both the camp and the town were taken by storm employing new siege machines, but in both cases the fortifications were also very poor, according to Thucydides himself. Although he does not always say how this or that town fell, he almost always ascribes the fall either to a direct attack, or an absence or inadequacy of fortifications. It seems that powerful fortresses so far remained unattainable for Greek siege warfare. Direct attacks on fortifications were rather rare and mostly unsuccessful. Up to the end of the 5th century BC, blockade tactics remained the main method of laying a siege.

The defense of Greek cities was no less passive. The defenders sought shelter behind the walls in hopes that they were unassailable. It was only from there that they shot at those in attack, and we get one more proof of this in the fact that there were no secret passages (posterns) leading out of Greek fortresses that would allow the defenders to make a sortie—at least not till the end of the 5th century BC.[42]

The situation began to change dramatically at the end of the 5th and the beginning of the 4th centuries BC. The change was provoked by the events in Sicily, which was invaded by the Carthaginians in 409 BC. Well acquainted with the Near East siege weapons, the Carthaginian army surprised the Greeks with their extremely aggressive siege tactics. Thus, at the siege of Selinus, they used six gigantic siege towers and about the same number of battering rams sheathed with iron plates.

It was under the influence of Carthaginian siege technology that Dionysius I, who became the tyrant of Syracuse in 405 BC, developed his ideas of siege warfare. Dionysius I spent his life waging war with Carthage, and he became the first Greek general to widely apply the entire assortment of siege methods from as far back as the Near East empires. Those methods included active usage of various siege machines, recruiting of mercenaries, mobilization of manpower on a large scale, and resettling of the inhabitants of the occupied cities. Dionysius, however, didn't just apply what was already known. While getting Syracuse ready for defense, the engineers working for Dionysius invented the *gastraphetes*, a powerful crossbow, and predecessor of throwing machines. In comparison with the bow, the *gastraphetes* was much more powerful and had a longer range. The *gastraphetes* was soon installed on a stand and supplied with a windlass. The throwing machine was called an *oxybeles*. Both the *gastraphetes* and the first pattern of the *oxybeles* were arrow-firers—meaning they fired bolts.[43] Sometime later the *oxybeles* was adapted to shooting small stone balls.

A good idea of the siege methods used by Dionysius I is provided by the siege of Motya (398 BC), the main Carthaginian base on Sicily. The town was situated on a small island connected with the western coast of Sicily by a narrow mole (a pier or breakwater), which the defenders broke down while preparing for defense. A stone wall with twenty towers encircled the town. The wall stretched along the seashore, at some places at the very edge of the water. Larger plots of land were to be found only in the north and northeast, where the citizens had strengthened the wall by making it six meters thick. The main gate was in the northeastern part of the island, and opened on the mole. There were some more exits from the town which, according to archaeological data, were blocked by the citizens during the siege. A lead pipeline extended from the mainland to the island. The Greeks blocked that method of water supply, but the town had enough wells and containers full of water so as not to suffer from thirst during the siege.

The first thing Dionysius did was to restore and widen the mole. It was made 1.5 kilometers long and 10 meters wide in the shortest possible time. Such a large-scale operation was quite

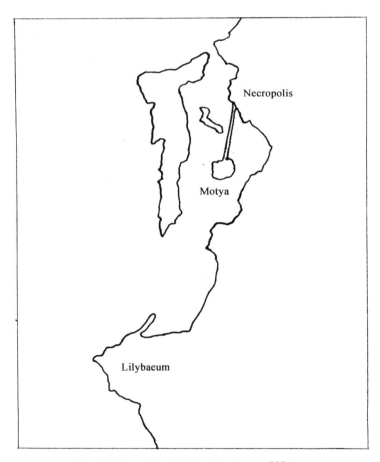

The situation of the Carthaginian town of Motya.

new to the Greeks, and shows Dionysius's ability to organize manpower much like the Assyrians or Persians used to do. True, the Assyrians, while besieging a big city, managed to seize all the small towns in the vicinity as well. Dionysius's effort to use the same tactics proved to be unsuccessful, probably due to the shortage of force at his disposal.

After the building of the mole was completed, Dionysius moved his siege towers and battering rams to the town. Confined by the small size of the island, the citizens used to build their houses higher than the town wall. Dionysius built six-story towers that rose above the town's wall and reached the tops of the houses. This seems to be the first instance of siege towers being used by the Greeks. The attack was led on the part of the wall located near the gate. Excavations revealed a great number of arrowheads, which speaks of active fire support. Apart from archers, Dionysius used recently invented *gastraphetes* and, possibly, *oxybeles*. Those arrow-firers were probably situated in the siege towers.

To combat Syracusan siege machines, the Motyans set masts supplied with rotating crossbeams on the wall. At the end of the crossbeams there were shelters for the defenders, who threw burning charred logs and oakum soaked in resin on the siege machines. Some of the Greek machines caught fire, but special fire brigades put it out. That such fire brigades were organized in his army is to Dionysius's credit if we remember the well-known fact that the Athenians, while besieging Syracuse in 416 BC, failed to put out fire and thus lost a lot of siege machines.

Acting under the cover of the fire from the towers, the battering rams breached the wall—but the siege was not over. The Motyans barricaded themselves in their houses, which were built in such a way that they formed a wall. So the Greeks drew their siege towers into the town and throwing planks from them, reached the roofs of the houses. The Motyans fought desperately. They knew well—after experiencing the typical cruelty with which the Carthaginians treated the population of captured Greek cities—that they couldn't count upon the mercy of the besiegers. The battle for houses took several days, until one night, a surprise attack by the Syracusans caused the town to fall.[44]

Thus, Dionysius I can undoubtedly be considered a revolutionary in Greek siege warfare. New siege methods soon became widespread in the Greek world. At the same time, Greek defensive tactics became more aggressive. During the siege of Himera, the besieged Greeks made a sortie, which was such a surprise for the besieging Carthaginians that, panic-stricken, their mercenaries started fighting each other rather than the Greeks.[45]

It was about the middle of the 4th century BC that the first treatise devoted to siege warfare appeared. Entitled *How to Survive under Siege*, its author is believed to be Aeneas, who much later, in the 17th century AD, was nicknamed Tacticus. Aeneas Tacticus described in detail how to organize a town emergency volunteer corps, how to stand guard and patrol, how to expose traitors and pass secret messages, and how to take other precautions, above all related to the protection of gates. The author of the treatise gives special attention to the necessity of taking away the goods stolen by the enemy, even those taken at the border when the enemy was already retreating. In general, the siege strategy described by Aeneas represents an intermediate version between the old strategy—based on meeting the enemy at the border in order to defend the fields—and the new "city" strategy, according to which the fields were to be given up and cities were to be turned into centers of defense.

Side by side with the militia, Aeneas often mentions allies and mercenaries. The latter significantly rose in number during the disruption of the Greek economy caused by the Peloponnesian War. When talking about the use of men in military operations, Aeneas makes no distinction between the citizens, the allies, and the mercenaries. Foreigners, however, enjoyed no confidence at all, proven by the fact that allied and mercenary troops were always placed separately, and the numerical superiority of the citizens of the country was strictly observed in the army.

Aeneas attached great significance to exposing traitors, and recommends a number of precautions, including the removal of the opposition chiefs,[46] relieving of debtors' condition,[47] frequent change of the guards on the wall,[48] regular change of those in command,[49] opening and inspection of all letters,[50] a ban on mass meetings,[51] and supervision of unreliable individuals and newcomers.[52] For the same purpose he recommends the use of double passwords—that is, the passwords which were to be said by both sides and accompanied by a conventional sign (for example, taking off or putting on a hat, shifting a spear from one hand to another, and so on).[53]

The treatise also suggests some ways of combating enemy siege weapons (*tortoises*, battering rams, siege towers, and undermining).[54] Aeneas, however, doesn't confine himself to passive siege methods. He also recommends surprising the enemy with sallies at the most untoward moments (e.g., when the enemy soldiers are drunk or robbing the population, or overburdened with booty[55]), and with false sorties meant to engage the enemy in a skirmish and then drawing some of them into the town and killing them there.[56] All of this demonstrates that the siege and defense tactics of the Greeks had become much more active by this period. However, countermeasures directed against siege weapons are given much less attention in the treatise than the description of the necessary guard duties, protection of gates, and precautions against traitors. The same may be said about the number of cities mentioned as having been taken in military operations. It stands no comparison with the number of the cities seized by treachery. Those facts prove that treachery and a surprise attack were still the most widespread methods of seizing a city in the 4th century BC.

Philip II (382–336 BC), the father of Alexander the Great, became a follower of Dionysius in the art of siege. He reorganized his army, turning it into a force able to wage active siege warfare. One of the first things he did as soon as he took power was to set up an engineer corps where mainly Thessalian Greeks were enrolled. In addition, Philip forbade women to follow the army on the march, and reduced the number of servants and beasts of burden. Now soldiers had to carry their luggage themselves. This had an impact on the mobility of the army as well as its ability to carry on sieges.

Not only did Philip II use all known siege methods, but he also contributed to the development of new types of throwing machines. Philip's army first had personal experience of how throwing machines functioned in the field battle against Onomarchus the Phocian (around 354 BC). Polyaenus describes how the Macedonians were drawn on under the fire of stone-projectors positioned on the mountain, encircled and put to flight.[57] This is the earliest evidence of the use of throwing machines in a field battle. The stone-projectors used by Phocians were *oxybeles*, but not yet torsion-powered.

That event made such a strong impression on Philip that he, like Dionysius before him, invited the most skilled craftsmen from all over the world. Their research led to the creation of torsion-powered throwing machines, which used the energy of twisted sinew rope. These bolt-shooting machines were much more powerful than tension-powered machines that used the energy of wood stress, like in a bow. Moreover, as Philip knew how effective slingers were during a siege, he armed his warriors with little lead balls. The latter, found in great numbers during the excavation work at Olynthus, possessed a higher accuracy and a greater destructive force than stone ones.

During the siege of Perinthus in 340 BC, Philip's army used battering rams, siege towers, throwing machines, assault ladders, and undermining.[58] Philip divided his army into several parts, which attacked the town in turn, changing frequently. As a result, fresh troops were constantly engaged, and the assault continued steadily, both day and night. Philip's siege towers were 80 cubits (about 35.5 meters) high, exceeding not only the height of the town wall but the height of all known siege towers as well. Shooting from *catapults* (torsion-powered arrow-firers) and siege towers, the Macedonians drove the defenders from the walls and then, using battering rams and undermining, brought the wall down. This, however, didn't bring victory to Philip, who had to take away his army, leaving Perinthus unseized. Byzantium played a significant role in the battle, sending *catapults* to the besieged Perinthus. His fleet being insufficient, Philip failed to block the city from the sea; as a result the defenders had something with which they could combat the Macedonian siege machines. This is, by the way, the first evidence of the use of throwing machines in defense.

Philip II improved Greek siege methods and weapons, which were later brilliantly used by his son. During his life, Alexander the Great (who reigned 336–323 BC) laid about twenty sieges, taking many towns that seemed absolutely unassailable.

Alexander had a command of all siege methods known at that time. If the circumstances demanded, the Macedonians encircled a town with *circum-* and *contravallation lines*, but a passive blockade was not to Alexander's taste. So, having encircled the Indian town of Sangala by two rows of walls, he wasn't going to waste time on a blockade. The town was attacked with the help of siege engines, throwing machines, and a sap, and was finally taken by storm.[59]

Alexander's attack on the Bactrian town called Rock of Sogdiana in 328 BC is very revealing. The city was really a fortress built on a mountain peak and protected on all sides by steep slopes. The fortress seemed so unassailable the king of Bactria had even sent his wife and daughter there for safety's sake. The defenders were so sure of their force that they not only refused to listen to the terms of surrender, but even laughed at Alexander. Then he offered an unbelievable sum of money—12 talents—to the first warrior who could climb up the mountain, and smaller sums to all those who would reach the summit, the last one getting 300 darics. Arrian writes that 300 men, who had practiced climbing during earlier sieges, took the challenge,[60] which shows how skillful the Macedonians were in siege warfare.

At night the detachment began its climb. The task was very hard; they had to drive iron dowels into the ice and crevices while it was dark, and they had to keep quiet. Thirty men fell off the precipice, but the others reached the top of the mountain. Their appearance in the fortress surprised the Bactrians and undermined their morale to such an extent that they immediately surrendered without even attempting to fight the Macedonians, even though they significantly surpassed the latter in number.

At the siege of Gaza, Alexander's army achieved something even more unbelievable. According to Arrian, Alexander fully encircled the town with an embankment that was 1,200 feet (370 meters) wide and about 250 feet (75 meters) high.[61] And this difficult siege work was completed in just two months. Even if Alexander used the local population as part of his workforce, it is rather doubtful that such a large-scale siege could have been accomplished in such a short time. He probably ordered his men to erect several separate ramps around the town so that he could attack it from different sides.[62]

By the beginning of Alexander's rule, the core of the Macedonian army consisted of heavy cavalry (Companion Cavalry) and heavy infantry (Foot Companions). Among the latter was an even more elite detachment of hypaspists ("shield-bearers"), which had probably been formed under Philip II but was first mentioned only during Alexander's era. Hypaspists were the most hardy and experienced soldiers. During battle and on the march they took the most perilous positions—on the right flank; and in the camp they served as the king's personal guard. Alexander also used hypaspists as well as other detachments of "companions" (friends) at sieges, sending them to the most dangerous places. Such use of crack detachments was not characteristic of the armies of other Greek poleis, which were rather unwilling to endanger their own hoplites in an attack on the walls, and preferred to use mercenaries for that purpose.[63]

Because of the fidelity and heroism those detachments invariably demonstrated in battle, Alexander felt that he should be the one to lead them into battle. Such practice was absolutely new, not only for the Greek world, but also for the Assyrian and Persian empires. Alexander had to pay a high price for his personal heroism: he was wounded several times, and the chest wound he received during the attack on the fortress of Multan was so serious that it almost cost him his life. His bravado, however, was never senseless. The citadel of Multan successfully defended itself until Alexander himself climbed over the wall and jumped down inside the citadel. He found himself surrounded by the enemy with only three of his comrades at his side, and it was at that moment that he was hit by an arrow. But so great was the desire of the soldiers to save their king that they climbed over the wall without any ladders, just climbing up on each other's shoulders.[64]

The most famous siege laid by Alexander the Great was the siege of Tyre in 332 BC. Tyre was situated on an island, so Alexander had to follow Dionysius's example and build a mole. During the siege, both sides widely used torsion-powered throwing machines—arrow-firers and stone-projectors. It was the first time in history that stone-throwing machines were used for breaching walls. They seem to have been invented not long before that, and Alexander was the first to use them at the siege of Halicarnassus in 334 BC. As for the Tyrians, they possessed so many *catapults* that they not only set them along the perimeter of all the town walls, but also put some of them on small ships in order to shoot at the Macedonians who were busy building the mole.

Diodorus writes that there were a great number of experienced sailors and craftsmen skilled in the building of machines in Tyre, who not only constructed throwing machines, but also invented new devices that could be used for defense. He describes one interesting structure that was a marble wheel with closely placed spokes. The wheel was rotated with the help of a device, and either broke flying arrows or threw them aside where they could do no harm.[65] This structure has never been used anywhere else, which makes us doubt Diodorus's words.

To defend themselves from the stones, the Tyrians used leather and fur sacks stuffed with seaweed, which softened the force of the strike. The defense of Tyre also gives us the first example of the use of scorching sand, which the defenders threw down on the heads of the attackers. Diodorus says that the method was invented by the Tyrians,[66] which is quite possible, as it had never before been described. Later on, softening screens and scorching sand became widely used methods of defense.

Alexander the Great built a mole on which he set siege machines—battering rams and towers. Then he took over the initiative on the sea and began to attack the town on different sides, both from the mole and the sea, and that was how he seized Tyre. In order to attack the walls from the sea, Alexander put battering rams on several ships that were tied together. It is the first time that battering rams are known to have been used for an attack from the sea.

Thus, we can see that siege warfare experienced a tremendous growth spurt during this period, thanks to the achievements of Dionysius I, Philip II, and Alexander the Great. Nevertheless, it reached the climax of its development under Demetrius I (337–283 BC). This man was so very experienced in siege warfare that he was nicknamed Poliorcetes, which means "The Besieger of Cities." His most famous siege was that of Rhodes in 305–304 BC, where Demetrius used a great number of siege machines that sparked the imagination with their variety and size. Even though he failed to seize Rhodes, one should remember that it was the most strongly fortified and powerful city in Greece.

• SIX •

ROME

Ancient Romans were no more experienced in siege warfare than the early Greeks were. A passive blockade still dominated Roman siege methods until the mid-5th century BC. True, as early as mid-6th century BC, during the rule of Servius Tullius, the Roman army saw the creation of two centuries (one century consists of about 100 soldiers) of engineers.[67] Their main task was the building of military camps and siege fortifications. That was the launching of the matchless capacity of the Romans to build engineering structures.

Siege engines (*vineae*) were first mentioned in connection with the siege of Pometia in 502 BC.[68] Unfortunately, Livy gave several versions of the same siege. While he mentions siege machinery in one version, he does not do so in the others.

Beginning with the second half of the 5th century BC, Roman siege tactics became more aggressive. In 436 BC the Romans took—by undermining—the town of Fidenae, a strong fortress supplied with everything necessary for defense. While the engineers were excavating a tunnel, the Roman troops attacked the town incessantly, day and night, in order to divert the defenders' attention. The besieged were unaware of the underground work until a Roman detachment had already entered the citadel via the tunnel.[69] The Romans also carried by escalade such towns as Labici in 417 BC and Anxur in 406 BC.[70]

The Romans, however, were still unable to get their teeth into powerful fortresses protected by high walls. The best proof is the siege of the town of Veii, which lasted from seven to ten years. It was the first siege of such duration laid by the Romans: "For the Romans, having never been accustomed to stay away from home, except in summer, and for no great length of time, and constantly to winter at home, were then first compelled by the tribunes to build forts in the enemy's country, and, raising strong works about their camp, to join winter and summer together."[71] Finally, the town fell in 396 BC after the Romans, led by Camillus, resorted to the same tactics as at the siege of Fidenae: they dug a tunnel leading into the town, while distracting the besieged by attacks on the other side of the fortress. Speaking about the beginning of the siege of Veii, Livy also mentions "the towers, the vineae, the testudines, and the other engines used in storming cities."[72] These engines, however—whether used by the Romans or not—played hardly any part in the capture of the town.

Ten years after the seizure of Veii, Camillus was preparing to take the Volsci's town of Antium for which purpose he needed, according to Livy,[73] throwing machines. If this evidence is true, it shows how swiftly throwing artillery was being spread: it was only about ten years earlier that the first arrow-firer was invented by Dionysius's engineers on Sicily.

In the course of the 4th century, the Romans learned how to lay a regular siege. At Satricum (386 BC), they began by surrounding the town with a rampart and besieging it according to the rules of military science,[74] but ended by carrying it just by escalade. At the siege of Cales in 336 BC, the Romans "constructed an *agger* [embankment] and brought up the vineae and the turrets close to the walls."[75] But they were not destined to test their machinery this time either; the town was carried by a surprise storm.

Early in the 3rd century BC the Romans invented the famous *testudo*—a formation allowing soldiers not only to protect themselves with shields on the sides but also from above; now they were completely protected from thrown missiles. Polybius compares the *testudo* with a tiled roof.[76]

The Romans first used the *testudo* in 293 BC at the siege of Aquilonia,[77] where it was directed against a town gate which had not been closed in time. Soon they became very skilled in forming a *testudo* that could easily overcome walls of moderate height; it was in this way that Heracleum was seized in 169 BC.

Thus, by the early 3rd century BC, the Romans had learned how to lay long sieges, construct *circum-* and *contravallation lines*, and build siege engines. They still experienced a grave lack of throwing artillery, and mainly relied upon passive siege methods, but the foundation had already been laid for highly developed siege warfare, which was to become a guarantee of their future victories.

In the course of the First Punic War (264–241 BC), the Romans were active in bringing their art of siege to perfection. As late as 262 BC, at a seven-month-long siege of Agrigentum, they relied only upon the use of a blockade. Polybius does not mention any Roman siege weapons used at this siege.[78] But this passive type of siege, as well as their lack of siege weapons, may have been caused by the inaccessibility of the fortress; the landscape made the use of siege engines difficult. Nevertheless, the Carthaginians had been more active in their siege of the same Agrigentum in 406 BC, employing siege towers and embankments.[79]

Only a few years after the fall of Agrigentum, the Romans were using siege weapons on a moderately larger scale. In 259 BC they carried the Sicilian town of Camarina by breaching the walls with a battering ram.[80] According to Diodorus, the Romans had received the battering rams from Syracuse.[81] However it may have been, this is the very first unquestionable evidence of the Romans' use of siege engines for breaching walls.

By the year 250 BC the Romans had seized control over almost the whole of Sicily and set about laying siege to one of the last Carthaginian strong points—the town of Lilybaeum. It was the first active and regular siege undertaken by the Romans. They had built and used embankments, siege towers, battering rams, and undermining. It is in the context of this siege that we first learn about their use of throwing machines; moreover, the latter were apparently large stone-throwing engines, as the Romans managed to breach the wall with them. The Carthaginians were no less active. They dug counter-tunnels, erected a second wall beyond the first one, and incessantly, day and night, made sorties in an effort to burn down the Romans' siege machines.[82]

By the late 3rd century BC, the Romans had already mastered the classical methods of siege warfare and were widely using various kinds of siege machines. The siege of Syracuse in 213–211 BC serves as an excellent example of siege warfare of that time. The Romans assaulted Syracuse both on land and on sea. The land forces were under the command of Appius Claudius, while the fleet was led by Marcus Claudius Marcellus. We do not know much about the land operations, as in their description of the siege, all the authors concentrate mainly on the activities of the fleet. This is quite understandable given the preponderant Roman activity here, and the first use of an engine for storming walls directly from a ship (*sambuca*). Although all their attacks were beaten off, the Romans were not to blame: they owed their defeat to the genius of one man only—Archimedes. Numerous throwing machines dispersed along the walls did not allow the

Sling bullets—dumb witnesses of the siege of Carthage by the Romans in 146 BC.
The stone balls are Punic; the lead ones, Roman. Author's photograph.

Romans to approach the latter, and even if a few ships managed to approach the wall, they were grappled by the noses with huge claws, lifted up into the air, and overturned. Finally, the Romans took Syracuse, thanks to a surprise attack and treachery.[83]

At the end of the 3rd century BC the Romans started using various tactics, which was to become most characteristic of their siege warfare in the years to come—that is, exhausting the enemy. The besieged were not allowed even a moment of quiet: one attack followed another. Meanwhile, the Romans themselves constantly brought fresh troops into the battle. In order to be able to do that, their commanders divided the army into two or three parts; while one part was engaged in fighting, another one rested. The Romans first tested this strategy at the siege of New Carthage in 209 BC,[84] then at the Spanish town of Orongis in 207 BC,[85] and the Aetolian town of Heraclea in 191 BC.[86] In the last case they first thoroughly exhausted the defenders by incessant round-the-clock attacks, and then completed their job with a stratagem. At midnight, following the sound of a trumpet, the Romans withdrew their soldiers and did not start their next attacks until morning. The Aetolians thought that the interruptions in the nightly offensive were caused by the same exhaustion that they suffered from; consequently, on hearing the trumpet, the defenders started to leave their posts without authorization and go to bed. As soon as it grew into a habit with them, the Romans undertook a surprise night attack and easily overcame the besieged, who had not had time to prepare for a defense.

During the Second Punic War (218–202 BC), a new type of military leader was formed—one who would command a battle while remaining in the rear, showing no reckless heroism. In its complete form this type was later embodied by Julius Caesar. Scipio Africanus, hero of the Second Punic War—who combined personal heroism with administrative practice—stands somewhere in between. Most brilliant commanders of the previous eras, as well as Scipio's own contemporaries, participants of the Second Punic War, considered it necessary to take personal part in all the battles, inspiring the soldiers with their own example. Alexander the Great several times found himself on the brink of death, having been cut off from his troops. Hannibal was seriously wounded on the thigh while operating a battering ram under the walls of Saguntum. Now Scipio, too, risked his life if circumstances required it. Thus, in 206 BC at the siege of Iliturgi, seeing that his soldiers were losing courage, he approached the wall and was about to climb the ladder. The soldiers, scared for their commander, renewed the assault and captured the town.[87] At the same time, Scipio realized that the main task of a commander was to direct a battle from a place of safety. The death of a commander usually led to the army fleeing in panic, so it was best for the commander to stay in the rear. Both Livy and Polybius repeatedly reproach commanders for their unwise and risky heroism. Scipio Africanus's behavior at Iliturgi, where he

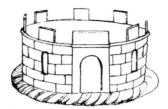 

Wreathes of reward: *corona muralis* (left) and *corona vallaris* (right).

inspired his soldiers while keeping all that was happening under control, may be considered ideal for that time.

Sieges were always looked upon as the most dangerous and arduous of military operations. It was not for nothing that when preparing for his African campaign, Scipio reviewed his legions and selected the bravest warriors, especially those who had taken part in the siege of Syracuse and so had experience in siege warfare.[88] However, even an experienced warrior would not climb a wall, exposing himself to numerous risks, without a stimulus. Therefore, soldiers who were going to storm walls were promised various rewards and a share of the booty. There were several different kinds of rewards, including praise, promotion, an increase in salary, monetary allowances, and decorations (such as silver and gold chains, *phalerae* [military award disks], etc.). The most honorable rewards were garlands: *corona muralis* for those who were the first to climb a fortress wall at the siege of a town, and *corona vallaris* for those who were the first on the rampart at an assault upon an enemy camp. At the time of the Republic, men were decorated with garlands for personal service, irrespective of their ranks, while during the Empire, these rewards became purely symbolic, and could not be awarded to anyone under the rank of centurion.

While only a few received rewards, all risked their lives. Therefore, most soldiers participated in siege operations in the hopes of pillage. In 415 BC Roman soldiers actually killed the war tribune who had promised to give them the town for pillage but had not kept his word.[89] Five years later consul Gaius Valerius Potitus refused to share the booty taken in the citadel of Carventum with the soldiers who had stormed it. The latter developed such a grudge against him that during the ovation in Rome, they abused him loudly.[90]

The regular Roman procedure of sharing booty seems to have been formed by the time of the Second Punic War. A war tribune detached men from each subdivision to collect booty; this was to be done by no more than half the soldiers while the others stood guard. At the launch of a campaign, every soldier swore to divide the spoils equally. After all the booty was taken to one place, the war tribune divided it into equal parts to be given to every soldier, including the sick, the wounded, and those absent on special missions.[91] Thus, Roman authorities endeavored to keep the army from turning into an undisciplined mob during the pillage of a town—and in most cases, they succeeded.

In spite of the considerable advances in siege warfare that they made during the Punic Wars, the Romans lagged far behind the Hellenic states in the number of throwing artillery, even as late as the beginning of the 2nd century BC. The Romans did not possess the large arsenals of throwing machines so characteristic of Greek and Carthaginian cities.[92] Most of their machines were either requisitioned by them in the neighboring towns or else built on the spot. Neither of these methods, however, could supply them with a large arsenal of artillery.

The difference between Roman and Greek siege methods can be traced by using the example of the siege of Oreus in 200 BC. The Romans laid the siege together with King Attalus of Pergamum. According to Livy:

> . . . the Romans and Attalus attacked Oreus on different sides; the former directed their assault against the citadel which faced the sea, whilst Attalus directed his towards the hollow between the two citadels where a wall separates one portion of the city from the other. And as they attacked at different points, so they employed different methods. The Romans brought their *vineae* and battering rams close up to the wall, protecting themselves with their shield-roof; the king's troops poured in a hail of missiles of every description from their *ballistae* and *catapults*. They hurled huge pieces of rock, and constructed mines and made use of every expedient which they had found useful in the former siege.[93]

The Romans were the first to penetrate into the town after their battering ram had breached a part of the wall. This shows that the Greeks' superiority in artillery did not give them material advantages as compared to the Roman siege methods.

The Roman siege of the Greek town of Ambracia in 189 BC is of considerable interest. The besiegers demonstrated a great variety here, and at the same time the scantiness of their siege methods. According to the Roman tradition, the first thing they did was build several camps, and then they began to join them by lines of *circum-* and *contravallations*. Then they set to breaching walls with battering rams—doing it at five different places simultaneously—and breaking off merlons with poles supplied with hooks. The besieged opposed them with a very active defense, making numerous sorties. After all their attacks had been beaten off, the Romans set to digging an undermining. The besieged, however, discovered what they were doing, led a countermining, and killed all Roman sappers in an underground encounter. In spite of their activity and a variety of methods, the Romans failed to take Ambracia.[94]

Roman siege warfare was perfected under Julius Caesar. He was the first Roman commander to make the artillery a regular unit in his army, even though the throwing machines transported in his wagon trains were not numerous. The sieges laid by Caesar in the course of the Gallic War (58–50 BC) demonstrate a great variety of Roman siege methods and weapons of the period; they used undermining, embankments, siege towers, *vineae*, and throwing machines, and proved themselves masters of siege field fortifications. However, the main secret of the Romans' success seems to lie in their exceptional patience and extreme perseverance in carrying on a siege.

Among the most interesting sieges are those of Avaricum and Alesia, which show not only Roman siege methods but Gallic defense methods as well. At the siege of Avaricum in 52 BC, the Romans protected themselves with *vineae*, built an embankment, and mounted siege towers on it. The Gauls responded by erecting towers on top of their wall, thus increasing the height of the latter and depriving the Romans of the advantage of a higher position. Moreover, they repeatedly made sorties and dug tunnels under the embankment, trying to burn it down. The Romans finally managed to seize the town by a surprise attack launched in the midst of a cloudburst.[95] The siege of Alesia is astonishing first of all simply because of the scale of siege work. The Romans surrounded the town with more than 22-kilometer-long *circum-* and *contravallation lines*. They had not worked in vain; it was only owing to these fortifications that they successfully repulsed an attack on two sides at a time—a sally of the besieged and an attack of the reinforcements hurrying to their rescue.[96]

If we take Caesar's word for it, Roman military activities in Gaul were marked by their mildness. This might have been explained by the fact that Gaul was looked upon as a future province, so the war was not led for annihilation as was, for example, the war against the Carthaginians. Insurgents hiding themselves behind the town walls were usually granted pardon if they had surrendered before a ram-head touched the wall. Roman demands at the capitulation of a city were also fairly modest—handing over of weapons and hostages. Moreover, Caesar often took his soldiers out of the city for the night lest they give offense to the citizens. But once the Romans had to pay for their mildness: the Aduatuci, having surrendered, concealed some of their weapons and made a treacherous sortie when the Romans had left the town for the night. The Gauls lost the battle that followed under the town walls, and the next day Caesar forcibly led his troops into the town and later sold all the inhabitants into slavery.[97]

During the Empire Period, siege methods remained the same as at the time of Julius Caesar—only now the army had even ampler possibilities of building siege fortifications and machinery. Octavian Augustus (64 BC–AD 14) carried out a substantial reorganization of the army. The Hellenic and early Roman theories and practices of warfare had been carefully studied, and the best of these tactics were chosen. The army was now accompanied by a great quantity of workers, and wagon trains carried all necessary tools and materiel. Now any war engine, as well as any field fortification, could be promptly built anywhere, even with the worst relief imaginable.

A large artillery arsenal was founded in Rome, which supplied legions with throwing machines. In the 1st century AD, one century of every legion was to be provided with one throwing machine. E. W. Marsden believes that the latter were arrow-shooting *catapults* (including *scorpions*) and stone-projecting *ballistae*. The engines differed in caliber and were handed to a legion depending on its mission.[98]

Roman sieges in the 1st century AD are known for their particular vigor and a wide use of throwing and siege engines. Thus, the Armenian fortress of Voland was seized in a mere eight hours. Tacitus writes that it was stormed on four sides with the use of scaling ladders and a *testudo* formation under an incessant fire launched from throwing machines.[99] Even more throwing machines—arrow-firers and stone-projectors, 160 engines in all—were used at the siege of Jotapata in AD 67. Here they were not only used for striking blows at live targets but also for breaching walls.[100]

During the Late Empire Period, Rome became more and more oriented to a defensive war. Fortresses and long walls, barring the barbarians' way, were built on the borders. For quite a long time these measures proved to be fairly sufficient for defense, as long as the Germans were not yet skilled enough in siege warfare.

A rather widespread opinion has it that at the time of the Late Empire, the Roman army—along with siege warfare—fell into decay, and could not compare with the Late Republic or Early Empire periods. As confirmation of this view, the following fact described by Ammianus Marcellinus is usually cited. Two of Magnentius's legions (consisting of Gauls) turned out to be quite useless in a siege war—they did not help in defense work or servicing machines—and could only make senseless sorties, rashly engaging in battle.[101] Therefore, granting that by the 4th century AD the barbarians composed an ever-growing percentage of the Roman army, the conclusion is drawn that a decreasing number of men knew how to construct and use siege weapons.

By the 4th century AD, ordinary legions were indeed no longer provided with throwing machines, so it is not surprising that common soldiers knew very little about them. Their place was taken by specialized artillery legions. Their numerical strength probably equaled the strength of an ordinary infantry legion of the time—1,000 men—and each army had one or two artillery legions attached to it.

As to a general decay of siege warfare during that period, a profound study of Ammianus Marcellinus offers numerous proofs of the opposite. At the siege of Bezabde in AD 360, the Romans employed *testudo* formations, used battering rams, and erected embankments, on which *ballistae* were mounted for bringing fire to bear upon the defenders.[102] True, the Romans had not built the big battering ram themselves; they had brought it from Carrhae, where the Persians had left it. However, apart from this battering ram, the Romans used some smaller ones, which they had apparently built on the spot. Moreover, they built battering rams during nearly every siege described by Ammianus Marcellinus. This makes us doubt that they lacked professionals for constructing siege engines.

At the siege of Aquileia in 361, the Romans not only endeavored to dig an underground tunnel and build throwing machines, but they also erected a siege tower and, mounting it on three ships, tried to storm the town walls on the side of the river. After all their attacks had been beaten off, they deprived the defenders of a water supply, having dammed water pipes and even diverted the river.[103] Those besieged by the Romans in Maiozamalcha in AD 363 were faced with throwing machines (*ballistae* and *onagers*), *tortoises*, embankments, and undermining. A battering ram breached their highest and strongest tower, and as soon as it fell down, the Romans launched a storm simultaneously on two sides while a special assault unit came out into the town from an underground tunnel.[104] In the same year at Pirisabora the Romans employed a battering ram and built a siege tower. As usual, the storm was accompanied by incessant fire brought upon the enemy from throwing machines.[105]

Ammianus Marcellinus does not usually indicate the duration of sieges, although it appears they usually lasted no longer than a period of several weeks. One gets the impression that some sieges took only a few days. Thus, Roman siege methods in the 4th century were in no way less aggressive than at the time of the Late Republic or Early Empire. Neither were siege methods and engines less multiform; they included battering rams, embankments, undermining, siege towers, throwing machines, and *testudo* formations. Therefore, we have no reason to believe that Roman siege warfare and weapons had fallen into decay by the 4th century AD.

The siege weapons of the Persians in the 4th century were much the same. Under Amida, they erected embankments, mounted *ballistae* on siege towers with an iron-bound front section, and even used war elephants,[106] "whose roar and terrible appearance are the most frightful sight that a man can imagine."[107] True, the elephants were easily turned to flight with incendiary missiles. The Byzantines resorted to an even simpler, as well as more cunning, method in beating off an attack from a Persian elephant at the defense of Edessa in 550. When an elephant approached the wall, they suspended a piglet tied on a rope from the tower. The piglet began to squeal frenziedly, and the enraged elephant turned around and attacked soldiers of his own army.[108] The Persians knew how to cover themselves with shields, *testudo* fashion—a formation they apparently borrowed from the Romans.[109]

Roman siege methods were not forgotten with the collapse of the Roman Empire. All of them were well known and widely used by the Byzantines. By the 6th century the Germans, too, had mastered these methods, as well as the siege engines. The works of Roman authors, such as Vitruvius and Vegetius, preserved their popularity and were reprinted well into the Middle Ages.

SEVEN

GAULS AND GERMANIC TRIBES

With regard to the art of siege and the defense of fortifications, both the Gallic and the Germanic tribes lagged considerably behind the Romans. Their principal tactics consisted of making a surprise raid upon the territory of a neighboring tribe or a bordering Roman province followed by no less speedy withdrawal; long sieges were not typical. According to Julius Caesar,

> . . . the Gauls' mode of besieging is the same as that of the Belgae: when after having drawn a large number of men around the whole of the fortifications, stones have begun to be cast against the wall on all sides, and the wall has been stripped of its defenders, [then], forming a *testudo*, they advance to the gates and undermine the wall: which was easily effected on this occasion; for while so large a number were casting stones and darts, no one was able to maintain his position upon the wall.[110]

This episode proves that the Gauls and Germans knew how to make an undermining and were even acquainted with the *testudo* formation, which they had probably borrowed from the Romans. As far as undermining is concerned, the Gauls were always great masters of that, "because in many places among them there are copper mines."[111] Stones were cast from slings or even by hand, as throwing machines were never employed by the Gauls.

Moreover, until the war against Caesar, the Gauls had not even known what siege engines looked like, or how to lay a "regular" siege. Thus, at the siege of Noviodunum, the Gauls easily beat off the first assault, which the Romans had made straight off the march. However, when the latter brought *vineae*, built an embankment, and began to bring up siege towers, the Gauls were frightened to such an extent that they surrendered without battle. Caesar describes it in the following words:

> The *vineae* having been quickly brought up against the town, a mound thrown up, and towers built, the Gauls, amazed by the greatness of the works, such as

they had neither seen nor heard of before, and struck also by the dispatch of the Romans, send ambassadors to Caesar respecting a surrender. . . .[112]

The same happened to the Gaulish tribe of Aduatuci. Besieged in a well-fortified town, they at first laughed loudly at the Romans erecting a siege tower. "For what purpose was so vast a machine constructed at so great a distance? With what hands, or with what strength did they, especially men of such very small stature, trust to place against their walls a tower of such great weight?" (Gauls were all tall and despised the small height of the Romans.) But as the tower approached the wall, the Aduatuci "did not believe the Romans waged war without divine aid" and begged for peace.[113]

Nevertheless, only a few years after the siege of Noviodunum, when the Romans led by Crassus besieged one of the Aquitanian towns, the Gauls tried to fight siege technique: they would make sorties and dig tunnels under the embankment and a gallery of *vineae*. Realizing, however, that these measures were having no effect, they immediately sent envoys to the Romans offering to capitulate.[114] The Gauls demonstrated as much activity at the defense of Avaricum in 52 BC, where they raised up walls, dug tunnels under the embankment, and made numerous sorties to destroy Roman siege towers and embankments.[115]

On the whole, we may conclude that by the end of the Gallic War, the Gauls no longer became panic-stricken at the sight of siege engines, and had even mastered the methods of fighting them. However, neither the Gallic nor the Germanic tribes were capable of laying a "regular" siege involving the use of sophisticated machines for a long time to come.

It was against Cicero's winter camp that the Gauls made their first attempt to lay a siege according to Roman rules. The Nervii encircled the camp in a rampart and even built towers, *falces* (poles with sickles), and *tortoises*. Caesar, however, believes that it was Roman prisoners of war who had taught them all that. The Gauls did not even have the necessary tools, and erecting earthwork fortifications, "they were forced to cut the turf with their swords, and to empty out the earth with their hands and cloaks."[116]

Up to the end of the 4th century the Germanic tribes did not know how to besiege fortresses either. They generally resorted to their favorite tactics: making a surprise raid upon bordering Roman provinces, plundering them, and promptly withdrawing to their own territory. It was very seldom that the barbarians besieged a strong point; they only did so when a fortress was sure to have decayed fortifications or insufficient garrisons. Even in such cases, however, the Germans seldom carried a siege through to successful completion. Thus, in 356 the Alemanni suddenly assaulted the fortress of Augustodunum (Autun), which had dilapidated fortifications and only a small detachment of Roman veterans to defend them. Nevertheless, this small group of veterans managed to hold on for several months, until the main forces arrived, and the Alemanni had to retire empty-handed.[117]

Ammianus Marcellinus repeatedly declares that the barbarians did not have a command of siege warfare, and considers that to be quite natural.[118] In 378, the day after a crushing defeat of the Roman troops, the Goths made an attempt to carry by assault the town of Adrianople. They did not employ any siege machines, but relied only upon a storm with the help of scaling ladders. A stone ball launched from an *onager* sowed panic, even though no one was hit. The Goths were so utterly unprepared to lay a siege that they had to pick up Roman arrows in order to have something to fire with. As a result, a few days later they were forced to retire, having suffered heavy losses, and wishing they had taken their chief's advice not to fight with walls.[119]

In the 5th century, and particularly the 6th, under the influence of Roman-Byzantine war tactics, the Germans begin to display some signs of acknowledging the rules of laying a siege with the use of various siege weapons. During that period, sieges laid by them were often successful.

As a rule, one or more fortified camps were built around a besieged town and the latter was blockaded on all sides if possible. If the offense did not have sufficient force at their disposal, only the most vital sides—the ones that allowed the enemy to make sorties or supply provisions from the outside—were blockaded.

At the siege of Rome in 537, the Goths used four battering rams, a siege tower, and scaling ladders. The barbarians did not yet have the skills necessary to use the engines; and as for the siege tower, the defenders easily stopped it, having killed all the bulls that had pulled it to the town walls, where it was left until the assault was brought to an end. After a year spent in an unavailing attempt to take Rome, the Goths had to lift the siege.[120]

A few years later, at the siege of Ariminum, the Goths again built a siege tower. This time they did not use bulls, lest it should be subject to the same fate that had befallen the one under Rome's walls, but hid inside it and set about moving it by themselves. However, the tower came to a stop, this time because the Goths had failed to fill in the moat properly, and the bunches of twigs sank under the heavy weight of the tower. The latter would move neither backward nor forward, and it was only by nightfall, and with great difficulty, that the Goths managed to bring it back to their camp.[121]

According to Procopius, the Goths were acquainted with and often used throwing machines. For instance, surrounded by the Byzantines at Mount Vesuvius, they put throwing machines on top of a high wooden tower by means of a bridge, and brought fire to bear upon the enemy from that location. Among other weapons, they used *ballistae* here, which they seem to have made by themselves.[122]

In spite of their ability to build certain kinds of siege engines, the Germanic tribes still experienced a great deal of difficulty in besieging fortresses. That is why they often destroyed fortifications of the seized towns and fortresses. Thus, the walls of Beneventum, Neapolis, Spoletium, and some other towns were razed to the ground; one-third of Rome's fortifications were also demolished after it fell.[123]

Our knowledge of Germanic defense tactics is very limited. We have reason to believe that their defense of towns and fortresses did not differ greatly from the defense methods known since ancient times, though they hardly made use of complex devices or particularly cunning stratagems. When they had sufficient force at their disposal, they willingly came out of the fortress to face the enemy in an open battle. It was considered a more honorable act than hiding oneself behind the fortress walls.

• EIGHT •

BYZANTINE EMPIRE

The Byzantines are known to have often called themselves Romans (*Romaioi*). The Byzantine Empire succeeded to all the rich inheritance of the Late Roman Empire, including the mastery of siege methods. In the 5th through 7th centuries, Byzantine siege weapons hardly differed considerably from the late Roman ones. The innovations of this time included the emergence of *Greek Fire* and a man-powered beam-sling stone-thrower. Such throwing machines had been invented in China and probably reached Europe and the Muslim East via the Avars. From the 8th century, Byzantium was oriented mainly to guerrilla-style warfare, and siege weapons were rarely used. A new wave of interest in siege machines was observed only in the 10th century, when the Byzantine Empire returned to active, large-scale military operations for a brief time. It was at that time—especially during the expeditions to Crete—that we find mention of various throwing machines (stone-projectors, *manganon*, arrow-firers, *toxoballistra*), as well as the use of battering rams and undermining.

A Byzantine author of the late 10th century wrote a treatise enumerating the following measures as being necessary at a siege:

> Tunnels should be dug underground, battering rams, *tortoises*, aforementioned *petrobolos*, wooden towers, and scaling ladders be made, hill-like embankments piled, and other siege mechanisms and necessary devices prepared, of which the ancients quite resourcefully told in their works, describing in quantity, superbly and with great use, similar inventions. For that reason we, avoiding words and descriptions, consider it inexpedient to speak of them in detail.[124]

This passage clearly shows that the Byzantines used all siege methods known at the time (such as undermining, battering rams, *tortoises*, throwing machines, siege towers, scaling ladders, embankments, and *vineae* galleries[125]); they were also well acquainted with the works and achievements of the ancients. It is also proved by the description of a siege method, earmarked for exhausting the enemy, which had been widely used by the Romans and was recommended in the treatise:

An assault upon the entire town wall should not be stopped day and night until the besieged, weakened and worn out by the continuity and strength of the fighting pressure they had to bear, covered with wounds and unable to withstand all the adversities, either . . . submit voluntarily . . . or else, having exhausted all their resources, are routed according to the laws of war.[126]

In addition to all this, the Byzantines, like the ancient Greeks, widely used the "strategy of devastation." It was recommended that an invasion on enemy territory be forestalled by dispatching, in advance, special infantry and cavalry detachments, whose task consisted of destroying crops, gardens, vineyards, and fruit-bearing trees, as well as capturing cattle. These measures were aimed at making the defenders suffer from hunger or come out of the fortresses and fight a field battle.[127]

It was recommended that the besieged town be encircled in *circumvallation* and *contravallation lines*. A *circumvallation line* (the inner one, facing the town walls) was a rampart built at a distance of two flights of an arrow from the town walls. Thus, neither arrows nor projectiles from throwing machines could reach the rampart, while siege machines were not stationed too far from the army in case it needed protection from a sudden sortie of the defenders. A *contravallation line* (the outer one) consisted of a ditch and an additional wall, if the siege was to be a long one. Detachments strong enough to counteract sorties of the defense were placed opposite all the town gates.[128] One or more fortified camps were built at a distance of 2,000 or 3,000 steps from the besieged town. There were two reasons why this distance was considered to be optimal. First, at such a distance, all the people inside the camp appeared to the besieged to be soldiers. Second, the noise of battle did not reach the camp, so one part of the army could have a rest while another part kept up an incessant attack on the besieged.[129]

To those defending a fortress, Byzantine authors recommended destroying all provisions, sowed fields, forests, and even the roofs of houses, not only near the fortress but in remote villages as well, on the threshold of the enemy approach. This was to be done in order to make the besiegers suffer from lack of food and wood, and to force them to bring in supplies from afar. Anyone who sought refuge in the fortress was instructed to bring a stock of food for no less than four months. The besieged were advised to make frequent sorties, and the troops outside the fortress were urged to keep the besiegers under constant strain.[130]

The Byzantines, however, did not confine themselves to simply borrowing their ideas about siege weapons from the ancient world, but also introduced some important innovations of their own. The most significant of them was undoubtedly *Greek Fire*—an incendiary mixture used in naval and siege warfare, invented by the Greek architect Callinicus around the 7th century. This

Greek Fire used at sea. (Skylitzes History, Cod. 5-3, N2, f.34v, Bib. Nac., Madrid)

mixture was not only used as a fire-throwing weapon, but also for complex incendiary compositions cast by throwing machines.

As early as 673, *Greek Fire* was used to burn the Arabian fleet. *Greek Fire*, which was also called "liquid," "sea," "live fire," and "Roman Fire," was first used in naval battles. For example, it played a substantial part in the defense of Constantinople in 674 and 717–718, when the Arabian fleet was again burned by it. Soon after that it became widely used in land siege warfare. It was then cast in pots or from flame-throwing siphons. It was used to destroy siege engines and burn down wooden fortifications and gates, as well as to hit the enemy in the course of an assault. For a long time *Greek Fire* remained a secret Byzantine weapon. Then, in the first half of the 9th century, it came to be used by the Muslims, and after the Crusades, it was adopted by Western Europe.

Around the middle of the 12th century, the Byzantine Empire saw the appearance of the first counterweight beam-sling stone-thrower called, like the earlier man-powered engines, *manganon*. Possibly it was the spreading of these machines that led to the strengthening of the northern section of the mainland walls of Constantinople with massive towers in the second half of the 12th century. At the end of the 12th century, we find Byzantine falling rapidly into a decline, and large throwing machines are practically no longer mentioned.

NINE

THE ARAB WORLD

From the very beginning of their triumphant expansion in the 7th century, the Arabs borrowed siege engines both from their opponents and from the peoples they conquered—mainly the Arabized Syrians, Byzantines, Iranians, and Turks. The army of the Umayyads tried to use various siege machines at the siege of Constantinople. The Umayyad caliph Marwan II was known to have had eighty stone-projectors disposed at Hims in Syria as early as the mid-8th century. At the time of the Abbasid caliphate (8th–13th centuries), throwing machines were already placed in all the important fortresses, and during each serious campaign the army was accompanied by siege weapon experts.[131] By the 12th century siege weapons had achieved material progress in Europe, and the Arabs, having acquainted themselves with these weapons during the Crusades, borrowed some of these achievements. Thus, the already existing versions of Arabian, Turkish, and Persian throwing machines were supplemented by "Frankish" (ifranji) ones. True, borrowing on the other side—by Europeans from the Arabs—was still much more frequent.

The throwing machines popular between the 7th and the 15th centuries were represented both by stone-projectors (manjaniqs) and arrow-firers (ziyar, zanburak, jarkh, and others), many of the arrow-firers being able to fire "eggs" containing an incendiary mixture as well. Up to the 12th century, stone-throwing machines were set in motion by the muscular power of the men who simultaneously pulled at ropes. It is interesting to note that light stone-throwers (arrada) placed on one supporting pillar—which could easily change the angle of firing and conduct almost circular fire—were evidently much more frequently used in the Muslim world than in Europe. Such machines were widely popular in China; they were used in the Byzantine Empire as well, but evidently never enjoyed much popularity in Europe, where bigger and more powerful structures were preferred. A most valuable Arabian source of the 12th century—the treatise written by Murda al-Tarsusi for Saladin—provides us with the first-ever description of a throwing machine that included a counterweight. It is likely that the Arabs were responsible for its invention. Because of the Arabs, the invention finds its way to China (via Syria and Iran), where these machines were called "Muslim engines" or "engines of the Western parts."

During the Crusades, throwing machines and undermining were the main siege methods employed by the Saracens. True, they were not yet experts in underground warfare in the early

12th century, which is proved by the siege of the town of Kafartab in 1115. An eyewitness found the tunnel interesting enough to describe it in much detail (see the description of the tunnel found in Chapter 18, "Undermining" p. 126). In addition, the sappers were especially invited from Khurasan (northeastern Iran). But, given all this, the tunnel had not been attacked skillfully enough—only the outer part of the wall fell in, while the inner one withstood the damage. This allows us to suppose that undermining was a comparatively new siege method in the Muslim countries at that time.[132] However, the Saracens were quick to learn, and but a few years later they were successfully using it on a large scale.

Throwing machines were readily used by Saladin. We know that he used six to eight throwing machines at the siege of Kerak and Saone; we are left only to guess, however, whether they were the old man-powered engines or the new ones with a counterweight, described by al-Tarsusi. A real expert in the application of throwing artillery was Sultan Baybars (1260–76). *Manjaniqs* played a decisive part in all of his sieges; practically on all occasions the engines had been brought from Damascus. In 1268 only two stone-throwing machines bombarded the fortress of Beaufort at the start, but toward the end of the siege there were twenty-six. The fact that money (sent from Egypt to help the campaign) was distributed among the operators of throwing machines is significant in itself. The first two machines launched a bombardment on April 4, and by April 15, the Crusaders could no longer stand up to it and offered to surrender; as true knights, they begged that women and children be allowed to go to Tyre, whereas the men would be taken prisoner. It was the arrival of throwing machines under the walls of the Crac des Chevaliers castle in 1271 that became the last inducement for the defenders to surrender.[133]

A wide use of *manjaniqs* with counterweights in the 13th and 14th centuries called for alterations in fortifications. Beginning with the 13th century, towers were brought nearer to one another; they became more solid and projected farther from the walls. Various *manjaniqs* found their way to the tops of these towers. The task of the machines was to prevent siege engines from approaching the walls. For all that, the art of siege warfare in Muslim armies considerably surpassed the art of European fortification. Sieges now took less time than before; not one Crusaders' castle withstood a siege lasting longer than six weeks. And only the most formidable of fortresses, such as Arsuf (1266), Saphet (1266), Crac des Chevaliers (1271), Margat (1285), and Acre (1291) managed to resist for six weeks. Sieges were preferably laid in summer, as a winter siege was considered almost impossible. Even Baybars, believed to be the bravest and the most experienced of besiegers, spent the winter in the citadel of Cairo, selecting another season for a campaign.[134]

Throughout the Middle Ages the Arabs were matchless experts in incendiary weapons called *naphtha*. As early as AD 630, we hear of red-hot clay balls, and in 690 of *manjaniqs* throw-

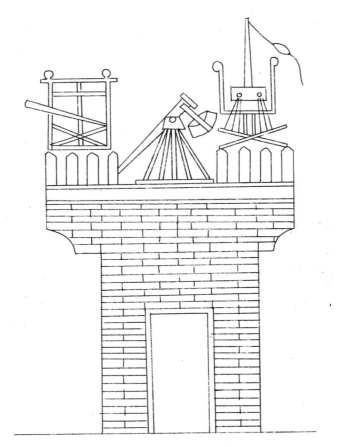

This illustration shows three throwing machines at the top of a tower. *Ziyar* is on the left; counterweight *manjaniq* is in the center; man-powered *arradah* is on the right. The manuscript "Al-Aniq fi'l-Manajaniq" was written in Egypt or Syria in 1462 but was based on earlier treatises, which have been lost.

ing burning resin incendiary balls. Incendiary arrows were used by the Muslims during the first invasion of India in 712.[135] There is a great deal of evidence of the employment of incendiary weapons in the 8th through 10th centuries as well. After the Arabian fleet was burned down by means of *Greek Fire* in 673, the Arabs promptly adopted the weapon from the Byzantines. It is possible, however, that Arabian alchemists had developed a similar composition by themselves, as the Byzantines had been able to keep it secret for a long time. In any case, as early as the first half of the 9th century, the Arabs were already using *Greek Fire*, the first after the Byzantines to do so. During the Crusades, pots of *Greek Fire* and other incendiary weapons were widely used by the Saracens, and made a strong impression on the Crusaders. In the Muslim armies there were even special detachments of *naffatun* ("naphtha troops") attached to a corps of archers.[136]

It is not clear, even today, when the Muslims first used cannon. It may even have been as early as the late 13th century, although reliable information only refers to the first half of the 14th century. Throughout the 14th century we hear of cannon being used in different places. It is possible that toward the end of the 14th century cannon began to be used by the Turks; however, all evidence before 1400 is questionable. Beyond much doubt, cannon were used by the Turks in 1424 in defending Adalia.[137] In the mid-15th century, the Turks possessed one of the most powerful cannon in the world. That was due to the Hungarian smith called Urban, who had first worked for the Byzantines but, when the latter proved unable to pay him, had defected to the side of their enemy. As a result, by the time the siege of Constantinople began in 1453, the Turks had twelve huge cannon firing (approximately) 200-kilogram balls and fifty cannon of smaller caliber firing balls of "only" 90 kilograms. Even the powerful walls of Constantinople proved helpless against these cannon.

During the siege of Constantinople the Turks used cannon together with a siege tower. True, the latter seems to have served only as a bridgehead for the archers, and did not play a role in the storm itself. At the siege of Malta in 1565, the Turks built two siege towers, which they began to move up to the walls. The defenders, however, destroyed one of them at once, firing a chain-ball (of the type used in a sea battle to damage rigging) at it, and seizing the other tower in the course of a sortie; they later used this tower against the attackers.

TEN

MEDIEVAL EUROPE

As soon as we come to analyzing siege warfare in the Middle Ages, we immediately face the problem of terminology. While ancient authors were more or less consistent in using terms related to war engines, medieval descriptions on this subject seldom—if ever—reveal any regularity. In ancient times, a great number of martial treatises were written, in which all siege weapons were described in detail. As far as Medieval Europe is concerned, we have but fictional narration about one event or another; not a single treatise on the art of war was written until the late Middle Ages. A search for adequate description is further aggravated by the fact that the authors of medieval sources were mostly monks—meaning people fairly far removed from warfare and little acquainted with military engines. One and the same engine could be called different names in different places or, vice versa, the same name could be passed from one machine to another. As a result, a huge number of names have survived, and it is often extremely difficult to associate one specific name with a concrete type of engine.

Precise conclusions as to names and their corresponding structures can only be drawn in cases where a picture of the engine has survived. It is the lack of a picture of a torsion-powered machine dating back to the 11th through 14th centuries that provoked disputes about their existence at that time, a dispute which continues to this day. Some modern researchers believe that they did exist in the Middle Ages and were analogues of antique samples (*ballistae* and *onagers*), while others tend to see a tension-powered machine (great crossbows) in the *ballista*, not a torsion-powered one. Jean Liebel has recently proven that torsion-powered arrow-firers had an absolutely new structure in the Middle Ages and were called *espringals*. (The discussion is described in detail in Chapter 19, "Ancient and Medieval Throwing Machines" p. 159)

Ancient authors like Vitruvius and Vegetius were undoubtedly well known in the Middle Ages. More than twenty manuscripts by Vegetius, dating from the 11th and 12th centuries, are to be found in the National Library in Paris alone—evidence of the significant interest in Roman warfare. Hence, it hardly seems probable that ancient siege weapons were completely forgotten and everything was invented "from naught." True, many a medieval illustration to ancient works is full of mistakes (for example, an *onager* with a "spoon" on a wheeled carriage). But on the whole we might conclude that medieval commanders were well acquainted with all the siege methods known to the Romans.

During the early Middle Ages, from the 7th to the 11th centuries, sieges of towns still prevailed over sieges of castles; the latter were insignificant in number. The most famous—though hardly the most typical—early medieval siege is that of Paris by the Vikings in 885–886. In the course of the siege, the Vikings used a great variety of siege weapons and methods, including battering rams, throwing machines, protective coverings (*mantlets*), the *testudo* formation, and fireships, as well as breaking the foot of the wall with pickaxes. They also built most machines on the spot. Despite the variety of their weapons, however, all their attacks failed. Not only were their attempts to carry the town by assault in vain, but they also could not even seize the bridgehead tower until the bridge was washed away by the stream, with only twelve defenders remaining in the tower. Moreover, during a several-months-long siege, the Vikings never took the trouble to completely blockade the town. The defenders regularly received provisions and supplies from outside, whereas famine would surely have forced them to surrender should the town have been fully blockaded.

Generally speaking, the chronicles of sieges laid by the Vikings, Franks, and other peoples of Western Europe in that period, up to the 11th century, lead us to the conclusion that the prevailing methods of capturing towns were various stratagems, surprise attacks due to guards' carelessness, and bribery. Longtime sieges were avoided, and only resorted to when it could not be helped. In the latter case the offense relied mainly on the blockade. Undoubtedly, medieval besiegers were familiar with Roman siege methods and knew how to build siege engines, but practically none of them had ever managed to lay a regular siege following Roman methods. As a rule, all storms with the use of siege machines were beaten off by the defense.

We have evidence that even before the First Crusade, man-powered beam-sling stone-throwing machines appeared in some European countries, including Spain, the south of Italy, Sicily, France, and England. In many countries, like Sicily, the south of Italy, and Spain, an Arabian influence can be clearly traced. As far back as the siege of Paris by the Vikings in 885–886, the besieged already used stone-throwing machines and a certain kind of arrow-firer. When a bolt shot out of one of these arrow-firers and ran through seven Vikings at one stroke, somebody proposed to take "the spit" to the kitchen to be roasted. However, wide use of siege weapons, and throwing machines in particular, was at that time more of an exception than the rule. The situation changed dramatically in the era of the Crusades, when the Crusaders became acquainted with the siege methods of the Byzantines and the Muslims. It was because of the Crusades that the use of *Greek Fire* became widespread in Europe. Probably the appearance of a torsion-powered arrow-firer (*espringal*) in Europe also resulted from the borrowing of a similar construction found in the Arabian arrow-firer, *ziyar*. The Crusaders also acquired a lot of experience, having to besiege truly powerful fortresses in the Holy Land. Granted all this, the Crusaders soon learned how to lay regular sieges with the use of various siege machines.

Roman, Byzantine, and Arab influences on siege warfare at the time of the efflorescence of the Middle Ages were great indeed, although the opportunities to conduct siege operations were vastly curtailed. In the first place, medieval armies differed materially from ancient ones in that they were considerably smaller. This directly affected siege methods, since siege works required such a large quantity of labor. For example, raising embankments to the walls was impossible in the Middle Ages, when a 10,000-strong army was extremely rare.

Second, recruitment was based upon the principle of feudal vassalage—where the vassals could leave their lord after about forty days. Maintenance of mercenaries was very expensive. Therefore, a longtime siege was laid only as a last resort, and only a powerful army could afford it; thus, a sustained defense provided a castle with a good chance of withstanding a siege.

Third, unlike the early Middle Ages when sieges were usually laid to towns, the period between the 12th and the 15th centuries saw castles as the main objects of sieges as a rule (the Crusades being an exception). The latter usually had powerful fortifications of short extension and were situated in places difficult to access, often in the mountains (another reason why no embankment was built onto the walls, this being simply impossible). Siege works were, therefore, far from easy. Of course, towns were also besieged in that period, but much more seldom than castles. The assailants easily overcame town walls, as a rule, but faced a powerful resistance when storming the citadel, which was in fact a castle inside a town.

Different periods of the Middle Ages saw preferences given to different siege methods and weapons. During the early Middle Ages—approximately the 7th through the 10th centuries—battering rams and undermining (in the form of breaching the wall at the foot) were very much in vogue. Siege towers, widely used as late as the 6th century, disappear and do not reappear until the 11th century, when they become popular again at the time of the Crusades. They were rather widely used between the 12th and the 14th centuries, and somewhat used up to the 16th century, probably the last time at the siege of Malta in 1565. However, although before the 14th century one can find mention of a footbridge for passing from a tower to the wall, later on, a siege tower served mostly as a bridgehead for archers or an entrance to a tunnel. Battering rams are also mentioned less frequently from the 14th century on. Now the underground tunnel, along with throwing artillery (and later on, fire artillery) becomes the favorite weapon of the besiegers from the 13th century on. Hardly a siege occurred without a tunnel, and only a moat filled with water or rocky soil rendered it impossible.

From the 11th to the 15th century, in order to blockade a castle or a town, the besiegers erected several strongholds called *bastilles*. They could be moderate-sized fortified camps or just wooden or stone towers, and they were situated in the strategically important places—usually in front of the gate where the besiegers could expect sorties or the arrival of an enemy army. *Bastilles* were sometimes built at shooting distance from the fortress structures; they were then designed for conducting constant fire against the defenders. William of Normandy built four *bastilles* to blockade Remalard in 1079. At the siege of Gironville in 1324–1325, *bastilles* were square, earthen embankments 2 meters high and having a 35-meter-long side; they were encircled in a ditch 4 meters deep and 12 to 20 meters wide. Besieging Orléans in 1428, the English erected six square *bastilles* with 30-meter-long sides. As often as not, *bastilles* acted independently if the besiegers were not able to completely blockade a fortress by connecting the *bastilles* into one blockading line.

At the end of the 12th century a new throwing machine was born in Europe. Known by the name *trebuchet*, it was a *baroballistic throwing machine*; a sling with a projectile was fixed at one end of the beam and a counterweight at the other. Moved by the force of gravity, the counterweight lowered and caused the projectile to fly at the target. Until the late 12th century, a *perrière* remained the chief stone-throwing machine. Unlike a *trebuchet*, the muscular force of people—and not a counterweight—was used in a *perrière*. The former was much more powerful, although not so rapid-firing as the latter. The new throwing machine could throw stones weighing 100 kilograms and more. If a *perrière* was principally designed for knocking down merlons and wooden galleries from the wall, a *trebuchet* could also breach the wall itself. This led to further progress in fortification: walls became thicker, the number of defense lines and towers was increased, and the towers themselves became more solid. Of course, not all the castles and fortresses were rebuilt overnight. However, those built along the new lines successfully held out against the new weapon. Thick masonry walls of a castle effectively protected the besieged from stone-throwing machines; several defense lines lessened the danger of undermining and prevented the placing of throwing machines too close to the main wall; high walls made it extremely difficult to carry them by escalade; moats filled with water stood in the way of siege towers and battering rams; and flanking towers inflicted great losses on the attackers.

As a result, the strategy of defense in the period between the beginning of the 14th century and the second quarter of the 15th century proved as a rule stronger than that of offense. Consequently, field battles were considerably rare in that period as compared with the previous or the later ones. The weaker side could hide itself behind the castle walls and in such a way avoid defeat.

This conclusion should by no means be taken as dogma. A castle was fairly often carried by open force at that time. In most cases, however, it happened because of the weakness of fortifications or insufficient garrisons. The superiority of defense was one of the factors that made it possible for minor states to exist in Medieval Europe, as well as for vassals to frequently revolt against the central authority. It was only by the late 15th century, when a victorious completion of a siege had become a question of several days and not months, that feudal disunity began to come to naught.

Early in the 14th century a weapon was born that was to revolutionize siege warfare— firearms in general, and predominantly, the cannon. The latter put an end to medieval siege machines and signified a new era in siege warfare.

At first, however, cannon were impotent against stone walls and were only used against gates, wooden fortifications, and the roofs of walls and towers. Cannon was still in the cradle at this time, and did not offer an incontestable advantage in siege warfare. Its effectiveness, range, and speed of fire were still insufficient to oust throwing artillery once and for all, so both types co-existed. The psychological effect produced by the first cannon surpassed the physical destruction they wrought. At the siege of Dortmund in 1388, cannon throwing stones 27 centimeters in

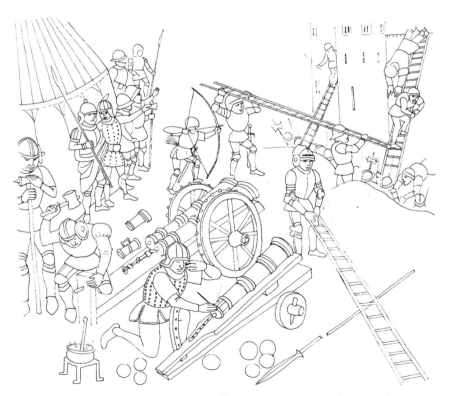

Siege with the employment of breech-loading cannon and scaling ladders, about 1470.

diameter failed to damage the walls. Twelve hundred balls were launched at the walls of the Vellexon castle in 1409, also to no avail.[138] At this time, huge cannon often served merely as a way to support the prestige of a commander, who liked to have a huge piece of artillery put in a firing position in front of a stubborn town.

Christine de Pisan recorded some interesting information concerning a weapon necessary for both the defense and offense of a castle (see Table 1).[139] The information dates from about 1408, and by comparing these data we can come to the conclusion that fortification had reached marked superiority over siege methods by this time: a garrison of no more than 200 men could successfully withstand an army of several thousand. Cannon were already widely used by both sides, although they were still on an equal footing with throwing machines. There is no doubt that serious attention was paid to undermining, which is proven by a considerable number of sappers (2,000 men). An impressive list of materiel and men, needed by the besiegers, testifies to the fact that a siege of even a small castle could only be ventured by a large military unit.

Table 1. Necessary armaments for the defense and attack on castles according to Christine de Pisan, early 15th century.

	Defense	Offense
Garrison	200	—
Carpenters	—	600
Assistant carpenters	—	600
Sappers	—	2,000
arbalète á tour (great crossbows)	6	30
Hand crossbows	48	300
Bows	20	300
Espringals (arrow-firers)	2–3	—
Spears	72	—
Battle-axes	—	400
Bricoles (*trebuchet,* or a hybrid stone-thrower)	2	—

	Defense	Offense
Couillards (*trebuchet* with two symmetrically sustained counterweights)	2	4
Engins volants (either a stone-thrower or a wall-storming machine)	—	4
Cannon	12	128
Bolts and arrows (for bows, crossbows, and arrow-firers)	37,200	262,000
Stone balls (for stone-throwers and cannon)	200	1,000 (for stone-throwers), 1,170 (for cannon)
Powder	1,000–1,500 pounds (450–675 kg)	30,000 pounds (13,500 kg)
Lead for bullets	3,000 pounds (1,350 kg)	5,000 pounds (2,250 kg)

The situation had changed dramatically by the mid-15th century. If the early 15th century is still characterized by long sieges (e.g., the siege of Rouen in 1418, which lasted six months, and that of Cherbourg in 1419, which lasted seven months), the mid-15th century sees a sharp decrease in their duration. In 1442 the siege of Dax lasted three weeks, and it took only six days to take Bourg in 1451. Only sixteen days were required to "pierce and bring down" the entire wall of Bayeux.[140] This is a direct consequence of the increase in firepower of siege cannon, and the fact that castles had become outdated, their walls unable to withstand such fire, or hold big cannon for the defense, as strong recoil loosened old walls.

By the late 15th and early 16th century, cannon had gradually ousted wooden siege engines, which had become useless and could be quickly destroyed. Both *trebuchets* and *bombards* were still used in 1475–76 at the siege of Burgos, as well as at the siege of Rhodes in 1480. The last known occasion on which *trebuchets* were used in Europe was the siege of the Muslim Malaga by Spanish troops in 1487. The body of a Muslim who had tried to kill King Ferdinand II was then cut to pieces and thrown into the town by means of a *trebuchet* (*trabuco*). By the beginning of the 16th century, throwing machines had fallen out of use, and their construction was quickly falling into oblivion, which is proven by the following curious fact: In 1521 the Spanish conquistador Cortés, while besieging the Aztec town of Tenochtitlan, ran short of powder and decided to build a *trebuchet*. As a result of the builders' inexperience, however, the machine threw a piece of rock up vertically. The latter then dropped back on the machine itself, rendering it completely useless.

PART II

SIEGE WEAPONS

Several things were needed for the construction of siege engines: skilled engineers; a considerable labor force—especially for the erection of embankments; and accessible materiel, including wood, raw hides, and so on. The position of engineer has always been an honorable and highly paid one. For instance, engineers operating the Crusaders' largest engines at Carcassonne were paid twenty-one pounds a day, but they probably remunerated the teams working under them out of this enormous sum. In 1254 a French engineer at the English court, called Jean de Mézos, was even elevated to knighthood—a unique event for that time. As to Frederick II, he valued his engineer Calamandrinus so much that he kept him chained—so it was no wonder that when he was offered freedom and a home for himself and his wife, the latter deserted to the enemy.[141] The great efforts the enemy made to destroy engineers show how highly esteemed they were; for example, we know of people rushing out into the streets in Lincoln, shouting and rejoicing when an enemy engineer was killed.[142]

Siege engines were always considered a very valuable piece of weaponry. After a siege, situation allowing, all machines were disassembled and moved to another place. For instance, it is significant that for the siege of Acre, Richard I had brought siege towers from Sicily and Cyprus, the king and his nobles personally unloading the most important parts of the towers.[143] One can judge of the value of siege machinery by the fact that the Rhodians, having sold the siege engines left behind by Demetrius Poliorcetes after an unsuccessful siege of the island, were able to build one of the Seven Wonders of the World—the famous Colossus of Rhodes—a gigantic bronze statue of Apollo, 30 meters high.

⊶∞∞⊷

• ELEVEN •

SCALING LADDERS

Scaling ladders were probably the earliest siege devices. One can see them in Egyptian tombs of the Old Kingdom (28th–22nd centuries BC). To facilitate their movement along fortress walls and for optimal accommodation, ladders were sometimes fixed on wooden disk wheels.

Successful assault against the walls of a fortress with the help of ladders depended on an exact estimation of the length of the ladder proceeding from the height of a wall. A ladder was to be high enough to reach to the top of the wall, and at the same time not to outreach the latter by too much. If a ladder was too short, the warriors could not reach the top; if it was too long, the defenders on the wall could easily push it away.

One might think the ladder could have been made longer than the height of the wall and placed at a considerable angle to the wall. No doubt, it would have been difficult for the defenders to push such a ladder away; however, in this case chances were great that the ladder would have broken down under the weight of the soldiers climbing it. Besides, ladders longer than 10 meters were unwieldy. That was the reason why an assault with the help of ladders was considered ineffective when the walls of a fortress were over 10 meters in height.

Both these facts made Polybius[144] believe that the distance between the foot of a ladder and the wall should be half the length of the ladder. Thus, knowing the height of the wall, it is easy to estimate the length of the ladder. For instance, given that a wall is 10 meters high, the bottom end of the ladder should be placed at a distance of 6 meters from the wall, while the overall length of the ladder should be about 12 meters.

That is why an individual ladder had to be built for each wall, even for each section of a wall. If a fortress had several defensive lines, it was necessary to have a stock of ladders of different lengths. For example, at the siege of Boulogne in 1351, the assailants, having captured the lower town, were unable to storm the fortifications of the upper town because their ladders proved too short.[145]

Vegetius[146] recommends two methods for the determination of the height of a fortress wall: (1) A piece of thin thread was fastened to an arrow that was shot up the wall (probably from an arrow-firer) and stuck into it. The height of the wall was then determined by the length of the thread; (2) The height of a wall was determined by the length of the shadow of the wall at sunset. The estimation was made by comparing the length of the shadow thrown by the wall with the length of the shadow thrown by a 10-foot-long pole.

The number of scaling ladders needed during a siege was immense. For instance, every two knights had one ladder between them at the siege of Jerusalem (which, in this case, meant knights along with their troops of soldiers). We have a more concrete figure for the siege of Constantinople in 1453: here, the Turks made use of 2,000 scaling ladders.[147]

Apart from wooden ladders of a fixed length, folding ladders and ladders made of rope and leather were used as well. For example, Fredegarius, a Frankish chronologist of the 7th century, writes that Franks used rope ladders. Bohemond at Antioch had a hemp ladder with hooks at both ends for fastening it at the top of a wall and at its foot.[148] Leather and rope ladders were frequently used in sudden night attacks. The ladders were thrown over the parapet of a wall with the help of long poles.

A net with hooks at the end was sometimes used instead of a rope ladder. Anonymus Byzantine says that the above method was often used by the Egyptians when assaulting fortress walls of moderate height.[149] The same author describes leather scaling ladders sewn like bellows, which inflated under the pressure of air and straightened up.[150] However, the solidity of this construction is very doubtful, even though the seams of the ladder were soaked in fat so that they did not let out the air.

One is amazed at the skill with which trained soldiers could climb scaling ladders. During the Hundred Years' War, Marshal Boucicaut demonstrated his athleticism by performing, fully armed, a somersault in the air, and then climbing to the top of a scaling ladder without using his legs, but just pulling himself up by jerks with his hands. After this demonstration, he outdid himself by shedding his armor and giving a similar performance, now using only one hand.[151] But even more impressive is the training of warriors in the assault detachments of Assyrians. If reliefs are to be believed, these soldiers climbed scaling ladders without the help of their arms; spearmen held their spears in their right hands and their shields in their left, while archers even managed to shoot arrows right from the ladder.

Besides ordinary scaling ladders, we come across quite sophisticated structures also based on ladders. Thus, Anonymus Byzantine provides a description of a ladder sitting on a wheeled platform with a boarding-bridge. The part of a bridge is played by another ladder pivoted to the first. This upper ladder was covered with boards and raised and lowered with ropes. The main ladder had steps, which protruded on either side beyond vertical posts. Holes were bored in these protuberances and ropes were run through them, which added solidity to the whole structure. In addition the lower ladder was held in place by ropes. The main ladder and the boarding-bridge were broad enough to allow three to five men, fully armed, to climb it simultaneously. The lower ladder was to be at least 0.9 meters higher than the wall. Thus, the boarding-bridge had some inclination toward the wall, which in Anonymus Byzantine's opinion made for a more courageous attack of the soldiers. Both the main ladder and the boarding-bridge were covered with hides for protection against arrows.[152]

An even more complex construction of ladders is proposed by Apollodorus.[153] The basis of his construction is formed by joined-together sections of 3.5-meter-long ladders. Such ladders were easy to carry in the train, and in case of an assault, one ladder of a given length was assembled from several such sections. A ladder of 10 meters in length was easily assembled from three sections. The upper and lower ends of the ladders were joined together, every lower ladder being broader than the upper by the thickness of the jutting ends. In assembling a longer ladder (e.g., from four sections), the ladders were laid overlapping one another for a distance of two steps and fastened together with wooden or iron bolts. The ends of the ladder were bound with strips of iron lest they should crack under their load. Moreover, the bottom, middle, and upper steps of each ladder were also bound with iron.

A ladder with a boarding bridge. A drawing from Anonymus Byzantine's book. Unfortunately, neither the original drawings of Anonymus Byzantine nor the drawings of Apollodorus and Athenaeus have been preserved. As to the drawings we see in modern editions of these authors, they were obviously made later, and in all probability, on the conjectures of later copyists. They often do not conform to the text and should be taken with a grain of salt.

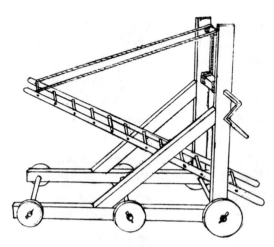

A ladder sitting on a wheeled platform, according to Valturio, 1472.

This structure of several ladders was mounted on a platform, which probably had wheels (although nothing is said about it by Apollodorus himself). Attached to the uppermost ladder was either a boarding-bridge for attacking a wall, or a long narrowing beam with a semicircular groove hollowed out inside it. This was used to pour boiling oil or water down onto the enemy (see plates 1 and 2). The beam was no less than 30 feet (8.9 meters) long and suspended not at the center but nearer the rear, or shorter end (about 2.4 meters from the end). It was operated with the help of a rope fastened to the shorter end. The rope held the whole of the beam in a horizontal position; when it was let go, the front, or longer end came down. Near the place where the beam was suspended, the groove was provided with funnels to facilitate the filling of the groove with liquid. A copper sieve, which helped to spray the liquid across a larger area, was hung at the front end. Boiling oil or water was delivered upwards by means of a rope running through a wheel attached to the upper end of the ladder. Assistants standing on the ground pulled at the ropes, bringing empty buckets down and full ones back up, thus securing a continual supply of liquid.

The soldiers climbing up the ladder found themselves in an extremely disadvantageous position. They were below the defenders and could not cover themselves fully with their shields. The besieged not only shot down at them with bows, crossbows, and slings, but also threw heavy objects on them, such as pieces of rock, logs of wood, burning barrels of resin, and boxes of stones. They also poured boiling water, hot oil, or scorching sand or quicklime down onto their heads. The effect of burning, scorching sand is depicted by Diodorus[154] in the description of the siege of Tyre:

They invented one more clever means to break down the courage of the Macedonians and subject the most courageous warriors to torture which could not be alleviated. They built copper and iron shields, put sand into them, and heated them over hot fire so that the sand became red-hot. By means of some mechanism they threw this sand at those who had fought bravest and subjected their victims to most severe suffering. The sand penetrated through the armor into the shirts, burned the body, and it could not be helped. That is why there was nobody near the sufferers begging for help to lessen their torment, and they died, going mad with horrible pain, in sufferings piteous and unquenchable.

The effect of hot oil on the Romans moving in *testudo* formation is very vividly described by Josephus[155] in an episode of the siege of Jotapata:

Whereupon they soon got it ready, being many that brought it, and what they brought being a great quantity also, and poured it on all sides upon the Romans, and threw down upon them their vessels as they were still hissing from the heat of the fire: this so burnt the Romans, that it dispersed that united band, who now tumbled down from the wall with horrid pains, for the oil did easily run down the whole body from head to foot, under their entire armor, and fed upon their flesh like flame itself, its fat and unctuous nature rendering it soon heated and slowly cooled; and as the men were cooped up in their head-pieces and breastplates, they could no way get free from this burning oil; they could only leap and roll about in their pains, as they fell down from the bridges they had laid. And as they thus were beaten back, and retired to their own party, who still pressed them forward, they were easily wounded by those that were behind them.

However, hot oil was used far less frequently than the cheaper boiling water or sand. Mariano Taccola recommends using quicklime. For lack of quicklime it is possible to use dry river sand or even dust from the street, the author says.[156]

Vegetius also describes wicker baskets filled with stones, which were balanced in the space between two merlons of a wall so that if an enemy climbing a ladder should have touched them but slightly, the stones would have come down on his head. These baskets were called *metalla* (*metella*), probably after *matella*—"chamber-pot" (soldiers' wit).[157] Sometimes the assailants were

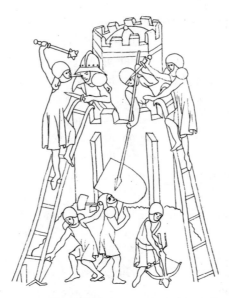

An assault involving ladders. Note the way the ladder is fixed at the bottom
by means of a driven wedge.

trapped with the help of thick linen nets, which the besieged threw over the soldiers nearest the wall and then pulled up together with the helpless prisoners inside them.[158]

It seems the favorite means of defense was the use of heavy stones. To obtain the latter, the besieged would sometimes break apart their own fortress walls or town houses (e.g., in 894 in Bergamo and in 1565 in Malta). Crema defended itself from the army of Frederick I Barbarossa by throwing red-hot iron objects with thorns down on the enemy. Parisians besieged by the Vikings poured down hot wax and tar. However, the most exotic weapon was thought of by the population of Chester. While defending their town from the Vikings in 918, they made a mixture of ale and water, boiled it in copper tubs, and then poured it down on the besiegers, whose "skin peeled off" as a result. Somewhat later they followed up their success by attacking the unhappy assailants with beehives.[159]

When the attackers neared the top of a wall, they were hit by spears and other shaft weapons. In addition, a ladder full of soldiers could always be pushed away from the wall, causing the warriors to fall to the ground or into a ditch from a great height. It was easier to push a ladder away from a wall if it was longer than required. One may be interested to know that at the siege of Pontorson during the Hundred Years' War, a ladder was pushed away from a wall by none other than a nun, Julienne, sister of Constable du Guesclin.[160]

TWELVE

MOBILE SHEDS

The simplest defensive device of the besieged was a large so-called siege shield. The earliest known representations of siege shields can be seen in Assyrian reliefs from the 9th through 7th centuries BC. Assyrian siege shields were somewhat taller than a man, and often turned in at the top. They were set firmly in the ground and held straight up with a handle, by soldiers specially intended for that purpose (shield-bearers). None of the reliefs has a representation of these shields from the front; however, they were evidently broad enough to provide cover for two or three soldiers.

The Greeks were already familiar with light and heavy wicker siege shields carried by hand. Owing to the simplicity of their manufacture, siege shields remained popular at all times. In the Middle Ages a large wooden siege shield got the name of *mantlet*, the name evidently applied both to stationary shields and mobile ones sitting on wheels. According to Mariano Taccola, siege shields were supplied with two or four wheels and secured protection at the front and, to a

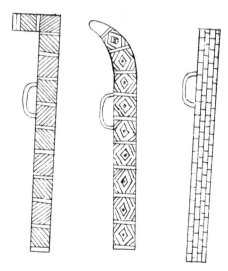

Various Assyrian siege shields for covering archers.

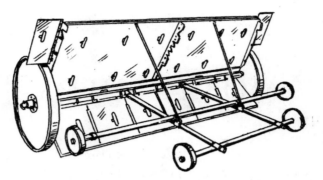

Mantlet of the 20th century. Russian model.

lesser degree, on the sides (see plate 5). Not only did they offer protection to archers, but, always moving in front of any other siege machines, protected the men and animals who set them in motion, says Taccolo.[161]

The 15th century saw the appearance of so-called large *pavises*—wooden shields almost as tall as a man, bound with leather. When stood vertically, they were kept firm in their place either with the help of a spreader bar or by being held by the handles. Some *pavises* had spikes at the bottom end to be driven into the ground. Later *pavises* had a projection, hollow inside, running vertically along the *pavis* and narrowing into a spike at the top or widening out to form a kind of cup. The facade of a *pavis* was coated with a thin layer of chalk and generously colored. It often carried a heraldic emblem or a religious inscription (e.g., "Let Virgin Mary help me." or "Let Saint George help me.") or the Biblical word "agla", composed of the initial letters of the dictum "Atha Gibbor Leolam, Adonai," meaning "Thou art strong, O Lord of Eternity." Some *pavises* were so large that two men could find shelter behind them simultaneously. Some

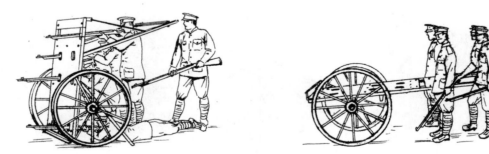

Mantlet of the 20th century. British model (ready for action and during transportation).

specimens were provided with observation windows. During a siege, *pavises*, as well as other siege shields, provided cover for shooters—archers, crossbowmen, arquebusers—whose task was to neutralize the fire coming from the besieged (see plate 4).

Wheeled shields, too heavy for warriors to carry in arms, are first found in the Greek army. The Romans called this type of shield a *pluteus*.[162] A *pluteus* was a mobile shield made of brushwood "like an arch," covered with Cilician goat shawls or hides. The structure moved on three small wheels, one of which was in the middle and the other two on either side in front. Such location of the wheels secured considerable mobility, and the *pluteus* could easily turn around in any direction. The *pluteus* usually protected archers and slingers who were trying to drive the besieged off the wall (see plate 3).

Simple sheds without wheels, carried by hand, are best known by the Latin term *vinea*. Apollodorus (the 2nd century AD) calls them *ampela*; Anonymus Byzantine (presumably the 10th century AD) named them "*tortoise* of grapevine"; and Vegetius says that *vinea* is the term used by the ancients, while at his time (about AD 400) this structure was known, in the current

Pavises. Above—German *pavises*, about 1400; below—images of pavises from the arsenal books of Emperor Maximilian I.

use of soldiers and barbarians, as "causia" (a Macedonian word for a hat with a broad brim, a cover from the sun, or a roof).[163]

Vineae were sheds about 2.4 meters wide, 2.1 meters high, and about 4.8 meters long, open on two sides. The skeleton of the structure was made of vertical poles of different lengths: the longer were 1.5 times a man's height, the shorter, the height of an average man. These vertical poles were joined by horizontal ones about 1.5 meters long. The bottom ends of the vertical poles were sharpened to go easily into the ground. The framework was covered with grapevine on top. Then the whole of a *vinea*—the front, the top, and the sides—was coated with hides, and the top covered with two layers of leathers. The hides were left to hang down loosely, which lessened the shock from the impact of missiles. A *vinea* was a fairly light structure, and the soldiers simply carried them in their hands. A considerable number of these sheds were made and put in a row, forming a roofed passage, along which the besiegers could safely approach the fortifications of the besieged (see plate 6).

Musculus was the term used by Vegetius for smaller structures evidently of a similar shape, under whose cover soldiers destroyed primitive defense works of the besieged (palisades), filled up ditches, and rammed down the earth to enable siege towers to be brought close to the walls. According to Vegetius, they received their name from a sea animal, the pilot fish. "Like the latter render help to whales . . . so do these small machines attached to big towers pave the way for their advance and make it smooth and firm."[164] Either Vegetius is mistaken or the term has changed its meaning in time. At the time of Caesar, the term *musculus* stood for sufficiently big structures resembling *tortoises* and surpassing *vineae* in solidity. Thus, at the siege of Massilia in 49 BC, the Romans built:

. . . a *musculus*, sixty feet [18 meters] long, of timber, two feet [0.6 meter] square, and to extend it from the brick tower to the enemy's tower and wall. This was the form of it: first, two beams of equal length were laid on the ground, at the distance of four feet [1.2 meters] from each other; and in them were fastened small pillars, five feet [1.5 meters] high, which were joined together by braces, with a gentle slope, on which the timber which they must place to support the roof of the musculus should be laid: upon this were laid beams, two feet [0.6 meter] square, bound with iron plates and nails. To the upper covering of the *musculus* and the upper beams, they fastened laths, four fingers square, to support the tiles which were to cover the *musculus*. The roof being thus sloped and laid over in rows in the same manner as the joists were laid on the braces, the *musculus* was covered with tiles and mortar, to secure it against fire, which might be thrown from the wall. Over the tiles hides are spread, to prevent the water let in on them by spouts from dissolving the cement of the bricks. Again, the hides were covered over with mattresses, that they might not be destroyed by fire or stones. The soldiers under the protection of the *vineae*, finish this whole work to the very tower; and suddenly, before the enemy was aware of it, moved it forward by naval machinery, by putting rollers under it, close up to the enemy's turret, so that it even touched the building.[165]

The Romans used this *musculus* for breaking the foot of a fortress tower; it proved so firm that it withstood rocks and barrels of resin and tar, which the defenders threw down from the tower. Thus we can presume that the Roman *musculus* was an analogue of the Hellenistic *digging tortoise*. It is a curious fact that the *musculus* was roofed with tiles. Covering of *tortoises* and siege towers with lead tiles is also mentioned by Philon.[166]

Complex mobile sheds, usually on wheels, were called *tortoises* (Gr: *chelone*; Lat: *testudo*) by the ancients.[167] The name owes its origin to the likeness between the machine and the animal. It is not clear whether the similarity lies in the slowness of movement or in the fact that such a structure, which has a battering ram, alternately pushes out and pulls in its "head." *Tortoises* were of different structures, and were called differently depending on their use; for instance, battering ram *tortoises* (Lat: *testudines arien-tariae*), *digging tortoises* (Lat. *testudines aggestitiae*). The structure of the battering ram and *digging tortoises*, as well as *tortoises* designed for boring, will be dealt with below in the chapters on battering rams, undermining, and borers. Here we shall be concerned with a ditch-filling *tortoise*, as well as a *tortoise* having a beak (ship's prow *tortoise*) and a willow *tortoise*.

A ditch-filling *tortoise* sat on a square base having 6.2-meter-long sides. Its height was 2.7 meters. At the front the roof projected as far as 3.5 meters beyond the body of the machine. The structure moved on four wheels that were 1.3 meters in diameter and 0.3 meter thick. According to Vitruvius, the wheels of such a *tortoise* could move not only forward or backward but also from side to side and even diagonally. However, how this was realized in practice remains a mystery: either each wheel could move like a caster in any direction, or there were several landing seats made under the wheels. The roof and sides of a *tortoise* were covered with boards, over which they placed mats made of fresh twigs. They crowned the cover with raw hides folded in two, packed with seaweed or chaff soaked in vinegar, and then sewn up (see plate 7). A defense of this kind is believed to have protected the *tortoise* not only from incendiary arrows but also from stones thrown by a *ballista*. A parapet made of planks was sometimes built on top of the *tortoise*, and the structure could be used both for filling up ditches and as an observation post. Such a *tortoise*, probably because of its heavier weight, could also be transferred on eight wheels.[168]

Ditch-filling *tortoise* with a boarding-bridge. Drawing from Anonymus Byzantine's book.

A ditch-filling *tortoise* could also be employed for crossing ditches. In this case it was provided with a boarding-bridge attached to it on a revolving axis at the front. It was raised into a vertical position with the help of ropes. The *tortoise* was brought to the edge of a ditch, then the ropes were loosened, and the boarding-bridge dropped under its own weight, forming a passage across the ditch.[169]

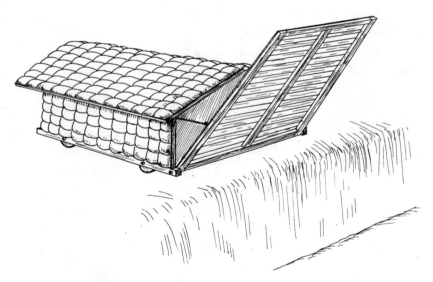

Ditch-filling *tortoise* with a boarding bridge. Reconstruction.

A *tortoise* with a beak (ship's prow *tortoise*) and a willow *tortoise*, described by Apollodorus and Anonymus Byzantine, merit special mention. Both of them are sheds without wheels, carried by hand. A beaked *tortoise* had a triangular or pentagonal framework whose acute angle was directed at the enemy (hence its name). They were built small to be easy to assemble and carry about, but they were used in great numbers. Instead of wheels, the framework was held in place by iron nails and props added to their stability (see plate 8). A willow *tortoise* looked much like a beaked one, but it was lighter than the latter. Willow *tortoises* were woven of fresh willow twigs or of tamarisk or lime-tree. Beaked and willow *tortoises* were used in storming a fortress with steep slopes, because owing to their "beak," they easily diverted stones thrown down on them. As to "mobile walls" (probably, covers like a *pluteus*) woven of willow twigs and having a rounded shape, Anonymus Byzantine recommends they be used only on absolutely smooth ground, as they cannot withstand the impact of heavy rolling objects.[170]

In the Middle Ages, *mantlets*, *vineae*, and *tortoises* were given different names, such as owl, mouse, weasel, or rat. But the pet nickname for these structures was *cat*, which they got because they could steal up to a wall like a cat.

A siege scene from Trajan's Column (Rome). In the top right hand corner we can see barrels and tree trunks being thrown down by the defenders. They are caught up by structures of vague construction, possibly ship's prow *tortoises* described by Apollodorus and Anonymus Byzantine. (TC 306–308. C. Cichorius, *Die Reliefs der Traianssäule*, Berlin, 1900. Plate CXIV. Courtesy of Verlag Walter de Gruyter & Co. GmbH)

In a 15th-century representation we can see yet another kind of cover—a wicker willow basket. It was a solely individual defensive device: a soldier put it on and moved about while wearing it (see plate 4). There was an observation window or slot in the basket, allowing the soldier to see where he was going. These baskets hardly ever became widespread. They are not mentioned either by ancient or medieval authors; only one picture of it is known, which is dated as late as the 15th century. A wicker basket could not offer sufficient defense and must have been easily penetrated with hand firearms or a powerful crossbow.

Various sheds enjoyed wide popularity in the Arab world as well. A large siege shield called a *karwah* was a framework filled with cotton and covered with hides. It was propped with slanting beams at the back and must have been fairly light, as it was easily carried by hand. Besides siege warfare, such shields were also used in field battle. Another shield of similar construction is described by al-Tarsusi. The latter calls it a *shabakah*, which was a wooden framework with rope drawn horizontally and vertically across it, like a net. This rope net was roofed with felt and hides. The entire construction was aimed at alleviating the impact of missiles. The Arabs' name for a *tortoise* was *dabbabah*, and, as elsewhere, it consisted of a wooden framework sitting on wheels and covered with boards and raw hides on top. A larger version of such a *tortoise*, covered with iron sheets and provided with a turret, was called *zahhafah*.[171]

Beginning with the second half of the 15th century, the power of firearms became so considerable that wooden siege sheds (*mantlets, vineae, tortoises*) proved absolutely useless. They were replaced by *gabions* (baskets of earth) and *fascines* (bunches of brushwood). Earthen siege works rose in importance: trenches, embankments, and ramparts for cannon batteries. Considerably later, in the early 20th century, wheeled *mantlets* enjoyed a brief revival, only now they were made of steel, not wood.

THIRTEEN

BATTERING RAMS

In its simplest form a battering ram (Gr: *krios*; Lat: *aries*) was just a massive log bound at one end with iron or copper (the binding could have the shape of a ram's head, hence the term "ram"). The log was first given a good swing by the men holding it in their arms, and then it was propelled at a wall or gate. Vitruvius ascribes the invention of this type of ram to the Carthaginians, who, with the help of a simple log that they swung in their arms, destroyed the walls of Gades (now Cadiz).[172] But there is no doubt that the battering ram appeared much earlier.

More often, however, the log was not held in the arms of soldiers, but instead was suspended with ropes or chains from a wooden frame. It was easier for the personnel to coordinate their movements this way, and thus, the effectiveness of the battering ram was increased. These frames were constructed in different ways. The simplest was invented, according to Vitruvius, by a Tyrian carpenter called Pephrasmenos, who attached a transverse crossbeam to a mast, like a balance beam.[173] A more practical structure consisted of two wooden posts inclined toward each other and fastened together at the top. Later, the battering ram was placed inside a shelter (*tortoise*)—a

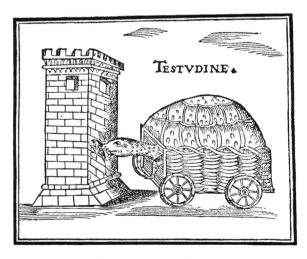

Ram-*tortoise* in action.

A most primitive battering ram. The barbarians are attacking
a Roman camp. From Trajan's Column (Rome).

wooden shed on wheels with a gabled roof. The most perfect structure was one where the batter-ing ram lay on rollers, not suspended, which provided the constant benefit of inertia and increased the penetrative power of the battering ram. Whether suspended or placed on rollers, a battering ram could be operated by hand or with the help of a windlass.

Each structure had its strong and weak points. With a battering ram placed inside a *tortoise*, the warriors who operated it were well guarded against enemy shells. However, in order to bring it up to the walls of a fortress, it was first necessary to have the ditch filled and the ground smoothed out in front of the prospective breaching location. Simpler structures were easier to deliver to the walls or gates of a fortress, but the loss of human life was incomparably heavier.

Battering rams probably appeared sometime toward the end of the third millennium BC. The earliest evidence we have of the simplest battering rams is representations of sieges of fortresses in the tombs in Beni Hasan, dating from the 21st through 18th centuries BC. In these pictures we can see a primitive battering ram—a shed with warriors hidden in it, armed with long poles. In the same pictures one can see that the walls of the fortresses were thickened at the base (talus). Talus must have appeared as an answer to battering rams. (For Egyptian representations and a more detailed discussion, see Chapter 1, "Ancient Egypt" p. 3).

Much more powerful battering rams were used by the Assyrians in the 9th through 7th centuries BC. During the reign of Ashurnasirpal II (884–859 BC), a battering ram was already a complex structure moving on six wheels. The wooden framework was about 5 meters long and 2 to 3 meters high. There was a turret in the front part of the ram, which rose about another 3 meters. The turret was crowned with a vaulted roof or a parapet, and had loopholes for archers. The battering ram proper was a log with a flattened metal head; suspended on ropes from the roof of the framework, it swung like a pendulum. A narrow ram-head was a handy weapon to destroy mud-brick or attack junctions between stone slabs of a wall, loosening the masonry. The turret served as a place for soldiers to create fire cover, in order to drive the defenders from the wall and let the battering ram work unhampered.

The weight of such battering rams must have been considerable. It is presumed that they had poles behind them and were transported by draft animals tied to the poles. Later, Assyrian kings preferred increased mobility over heavy weight. Turrets were lower, and the battering ram was positioned on four wheels. Battering rams were covered with wet raw hides against fire (see plate 10).

In the early 7th century BC, the Assyrians had collapsible battering rams consisting of several parts, so that they could be carried in the train of an army and promptly assembled on the spot. The length of the poles became longer, and the power of the battering ram increased. (For surviving Assyrian reliefs and a detailed discussion, see Chapter 3, "Assyria" p. 13)

In Greece battering rams became widespread at the time of Dionysius I, tyrant of Syracuse. Then they were actively used by Philip II, in whose army the engineer Polyidus built battering rams of different shapes. His knowledge was inherited by the famous engineers Diades and Charias, who served in the army of Alexander the Great.

Diades and Charias built ram-*tortoises* of different sizes, but their structure remained the same. A description has been found of a big *tortoise*, which was 17.7 meters long, 13.3 meters broad, and 7.1 meters high. The roof was a gabled one, and in the center of it was a four-tiered turret. The top tier of the turret contained fairly small arrow-shooting *catapults*, while in the stories below, tanks filled with water were stored against fire.[174] The battering ram, which was a rounded beam with a ram-shaped head, was suspended from the upper beam and set in motion with the help of a windlass. The whole structure was covered with raw hides (see plate 11).

Even bigger was the ram-*tortoise* built by Hegetor of Byzantium during the siege of Rhodes.[175] The *tortoise* was 18.6 meters long, 12.4 meters broad, and 10.6 meters high. It was transported on eight wheels, which were 2 meters in diameter and 0.9 meter thick. Each wheel was made of three wooden beams cut into one another, fastened together with spikes, and bound with rims of cold forging. The *tortoise* was covered with a roof made from wooden boards. It was crowned with a two-storied turret, in the bottom story of which were *catapults*, while the upper story was an open platform surrounded by a parapet assigned to two warrior watchmen (see plate 12).

In the upper part of the *tortoise* there were two rollers from which a battering ram was suspended on ropes. The ram proper was a rectangular beam about 53 meters long, thicker at the rear end and somewhat narrower toward the head. A wedge-shaped iron head was put on the beam at the front, and 4.5 meters back from the head the beam was bound with four iron rims to prevent the splitting of the wood. Moreover, the battering ram beam was bound with four ropes, each 15 centimeters thick, all down its length, and with thick chains in the center; the top was covered with raw hides. A battering ram could move in six directions: forward, backward, to the right, to the left, up, and down. All three authors assert that it could destroy a section of a wall 31 meters long and 31 meters high. However, the parameters of the *tortoise* and the length of the ropes on which the ram-beam was suspended can hardly allow such great amplitude. The most curious thing is that there was a board with a rope net fastened to the front end of the ram-beam near the head; climbing up the net, the warriors could easily reach the top of the wall. This ram-*tortoise* was attended by 100 men, and its weight was 4,000 talents (157 tons).

The size of most battering rams was doubtless much smaller than that. Moreover, Apollodorus even recommends having several small mobile *tortoises*, rather than one giant one, which would have all their drawbacks combined in it.[176]

The following requirements were to be met in building a ram-*tortoise*: The ram-beam was to be hung high enough—because the longer the ropes, the greater the swing and the force of the stroke. Consequently, a *tortoise* was to be high enough, while at the same time easy to wield and move from place to place. It was recommended that it should be twice as high as it was broad, and its length should equal its height, or be a bit less. A *tortoise* was to have a gabled roof with steep sides so that objects thrown at it should not just roll down but bounce off. At the front the roof might sometimes have a protrusion (peak) protecting the head of the battering ram against objects thrown from the wall.[177] A *tortoise* was only moved on wheels while it was being rolled to the wall. When in a stationary position, the lower beams of a *tortoise* were supported with wedges driven into the ground. Thus, some of the weight was lifted from the axles of the wheels, allowing the tortoise to be fixed to the ground. This way, it would not recoil when the battering ram attacked a target. In order to move a *tortoise* to another place, the wedges were removed and then driven in anew. The roof and often the sides of a *tortoise* were covered with layers of seaweed and raw hides against incendiary missiles of the besieged. For the same purpose, a *tortoise* was sometimes covered with up to a 7.5-centimeter-thick layer of sticky clay mixed with hair to prevent its splitting. The clay was held fast with broad-headed nails.[178]

The longer the ram-beam, the more powerful the attack. In case there was only one short beam, Apollodorus recommended not hanging it in the gravity center but instead, leaving the working front end longer; the back end should be burdened with lead weights to add balance to the structure. A beam like that would be as powerful as a long battering ram. It was also possible to assemble one long beam from two or three short ones. In this case, beams were placed between four planks nailed to them, and the whole structure was bound up with ropes. A single ram-beam was suspended with two suspension brackets; when a ram consisted of several beams, the number of suspension brackets was equal to the number of beams—i.e., one bracket to each short beam.[179] A battering ram was directed either upward at an angle to the wall—that is, the back end of a ram-beam was lower than its front end—or strictly horizontally. It was believed that a beam directed downward lost all its strength, and might even be a threat to the personnel.[180]

It seems a ram-*tortoise* seldom functioned alone; at least, some authors recommended placing behind it another, lower *tortoise* for the attending personnel, as well as two more *tortoises* behind that to ensure rear communication service.[181] However, the siege scene on the Arch of Septimius Severus shows the reverse situation—a moderate-sized ram-*tortoise* is followed by a large-sized *tortoise* for the attending personnel.

In the same relief one can clearly see that Roman ram-*tortoises* had a conventional construction, with vertical sides and a gabled roof. On the other hand, the description given by Apollodorus, and Anonymus Byzantine after him, may lead us to believe that ram-*tortoises* had

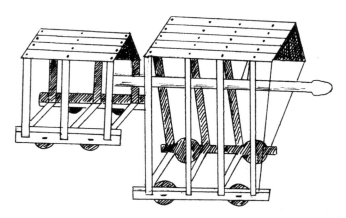

Big and small *tortoise* battering rams. Drawing from Anonymus Byzantine's book.

A siege scene from the Arch of Septimius Severus (Rome). Both the big and the small ram-*tortoises* have a construction with vertical sides and a gabled roof. It is curious that the bigger *tortoise* follows the smaller one while Apollodorus and Anonymus Byzantine describe a reverse situation—they recommend that the bigger *tortoise* with a battering ram be followed by the smaller one for the personnel attending to the battering ram.

a triangular cross section.[182] But the descriptions of both authors are so vague that they could be treated in different ways. There is not a single distinct representation of a ram-*tortoise* triangular in cross section.[183]

Unlike ordinary battering rams used for making a breach in the base or the central part of a wall, destruction of parapets called for a battering ram suspended not inside a *tortoise* but from a framework composed of ladders. Two very solid ladders were placed at an angle to one another. At the top the ladders were spanned with planking. The structure resembled a house of cards. A battering ram was hung from the roof with the help of two suspension brackets. At a distance of about 6 meters from the upper shed, another platform was made for the attending personnel. To protect these people from the missiles of the besieged, the structure was provided with a shed made of raw hides.

Besides the structure with inclined ladders, there was also one with ladders that were parallel (to one another and to the fortress wall). Both structures were not dissimilar on the whole, only in the latter instance, two battering rams were suspended to the sides of vertical posts.

When the ram-beam was rectangular in cross section and the parapet of a wall had been destroyed, the assaulting detachment could get to the top of the wall right from the beam; or, one of the sections of a ladder could be detached and thrown over onto the wall to serve as a

A battering ram for destroying the parapet of a wall. A structure of inclined ladders and one battering ram beam. Drawing from Anonymus Byzantine's book.

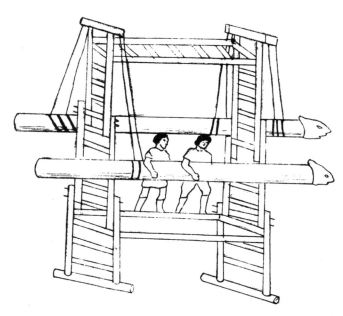

A battering ram for destroying the parapet of a wall. A structure of parallel ladders and two battering ram beams. Drawing from Anonymus Byzantine's book.

bridge for the attackers. Both Apollodorus and Anonymus Byzantine assert that the front end was spacious enough to house a single-beam—probably torsion-powered—stone-thrower (something like an *onager*), which would fire when the ram-beam was pushed forward, creating "great devastation."[184] However, a combination of a battering ram and a throwing machine in one weapon seems highly improbable.

At the time of the siege of Petra by the Byzantines (AD 550), their allies, the Sabirs, a Hunnish tribe, built a battering ram such as "neither Romans nor Persians or anybody since the creation of the world could have imagined." The main innovation was that beams and boards of a ram-*tortoise* were replaced by woven boughs. As for beams, there was only one—the ram proper. The *tortoise* was covered with hides as usual. As a result, the machine was so light that it did not need to be rolled on wheels—forty men concealed inside it could easily carry it about on their shoulders.[185] Several years later the Sabirs built similar battering rams for an attack on the fortress of Archeopolis. The fortress stood on a rock, and it was impossible to bring the ordinary type of battering rams near it.[186]

Battering rams could be placed on ships, too. Ships carrying battering rams were used for the first time by Alexander the Great during the siege of Tyre in 322 BC. A battering ram was placed on ships, which were tied together and joined by anchors. It is possible that they had a covering *tortoise* for the protection of the men who set the ram in motion.

A battering ram was the favorite siege weapon in the Middle Ages as well. It was widely used by the Anglo-Saxons during their invasion of Britain, by the Huns under Attila, and by the Byzantines and the Crusaders. Battering rams were also used in the late Middle Ages, until they were ousted by cannon and powder mining.

At first, battering rams were directed against gates—the weakest spot in a fortress for a ram. The danger was soon realized by ancient fortifiers, however, and the system of defense became more sophisticated; a fortress now had flanking towers, winding passages with several gates, and other ruses. An attack on gates became unprofitable, and battering rams were now directed against walls, especially against the angles of walls and towers, which proved to be most vulnerable to a battering ram attack. However, it was not as simple as it seemed. The fact is that walls were often built on an earthen rampart or a rock; they could have a talus, and there was usually a moat in front of them, and sometimes another, smaller, wall. To surmount these obstacles, ancient generals provided a smooth track for ram-*tortoises* by building a low embankment. Such an embankment reached up to approximately the middle of the main wall. The wall was often not so thick here as at the base, and it was easier for a battering ram to destroy it.

A battering ram was very effective against stone walls, but proved practically useless against brick ones. Owing to its softness, brick yields to pressure and weakens the force of the push. That is why a brick wall may crumble but still remain hard to breach. In view of this, a battering ram was preferable against stone walls, while brick walls were better tackled with a borer.

To fight battering rams, the defenders of a fortress threw down heavy stones or beams[187] to break the head of a battering ram, or throw off and kill the men who attended to it. Sometimes attempts were made to seize the head of a battering ram with special pincers or rope loops and pull it up. As passive defense, the besieged would let sacks of chaff down the wall to soften the pushes of a battering ram. A vivid description of methods of fighting battering rams is given by Vegetius:

> There are a lot of different means against battering rams and *falces*. Some suspend covers of mattresses and leather bellows on ropes in the places where a battering ram attacks a wall so that the stroke of the weapon, weakened by softer materials, would not break the wall. Others, catching the battering ram with a loop and having a lot of men from the wall to help them, pull it diagonally and turn it upside down together with the *tortoise*. Still others, tying iron tongues [*forfex*] with sharp teeth to pieces of rope—they call it a wolf [*lupus*]—and catching the battering ram with them, either turn it round or lift it so that it can no longer strike. Sometimes the besieged throw pedestals and marble pillars, swinging them, down the walls and squash the rams with them. But if a battering ram is strong enough to have breached a wall and, which has happened more than once, the wall falls in, the only hope left to the defenders is to pull down nearby houses inside the town and erect another wall; in case the enemy risk penetrating into the breach they will perish between the two walls.[188]

FOURTEEN

BORERS

Vitruvius ascribes the invention of borers (Gr: *trypanon*; Lat: *terebra*) to Diades, an engineer in the service of Alexander the Great. One can concur with him in this respect, as we have no evidence of borers having been used in earlier times. Borers were distinctly different from battering rams, which just broke through a wall; borers were designed for drilling holes, which led to the wall falling down. While battering rams were needed against stone walls, borers proved more efficient against brick ones.

Diades's borer was a long bed with a groove. In the groove, lying on numerous rollers, there was a sharpened log of wood about 25 meters long with an iron head. The rollers reduced friction and allowed the log to move faster. Next to the groove were two windlasses, which were used to set the log in motion. The entire structure was placed in a *tortoise* of bow-shaped wooden beams covered on top with raw hides as protection against fire[189] (see plate 13).

Apollodorus and Anonymus Byzantine give descriptions of another type of a borer.[190] An iron rod 1.5 meters long and as thick as a finger served as the drill of this borer. Forged to its end was an iron plate about 22 by 15 centimeters, narrowing toward the point. The borer was inserted into a wooden cylinder, which was set in motion with the help of a rope or a crosspiece (levels placed crosswise, like in the case of a windlass). The cylinder widened at the end forming a head, which revolved in a special socket. From behind, the entire structure was propped by

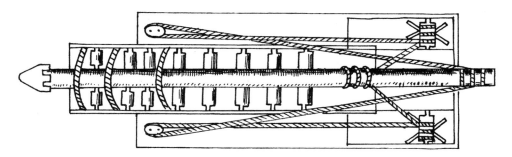

A borer sitting on a row of rollers. Drawing from Athenaeus Mechanicus's book.

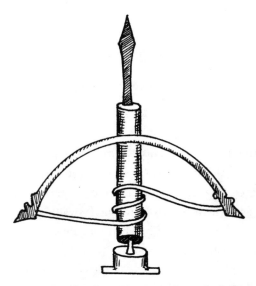

A borer. Drawing from Anonymus Byzantine's book.

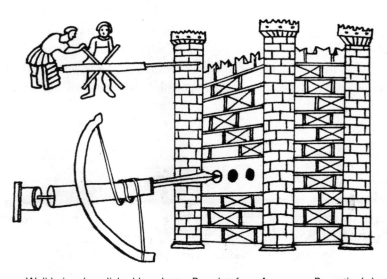

Wall being demolished by a borer. Drawing from Anonymus Byzantine's book.

a support, which moved together with the borer. On the evidence of the authors, such a borer strongly resembled one used by common drillers.

During a siege these borers were operated under the cover of *tortoises*, coated with a layer of clay, or siege shields. The holes in the wall were drilled upward at an acute angle to the wall, the idea being that the debris should empty out of the holes by itself while the borer rested firmly in the ground. Moreover, the inclination initiated the subsidence of a wall, as well as its falling in on the outside. It was recommended that the holes be distributed evenly on a line at a distance of 1.25 feet (37 centimeters) from one another, not at the very foot of a wall but about 3 feet (89 centimeters) up it, so that the debris did not hinder further boring (see plate 14).

Having been bored, the hole was filled with rods of dry wood saturated with sulphur or pitch. These rods, not more than 5.5 centimeters thick, were round, not rectangular, in cross section, so that some space was left between them, and so they burned better. The rods were to be driven into the holes at a depth of one foot (30 centimeters), not to the whole length; the lower rods were to be longer than the upper ones in order to make the fire flame up and gain strength from the wind. The rods were designed to prevent the wall's falling in ahead of time.

After the first row of holes was drilled and filled up, additional holes were to be drilled at intervals between them; in this case, the holes were drilled at an angle to the right and to

Blowing flames by bellows and burning down props in the holes made by a borer. As a result the wall falls in. Drawing from Anonymus Byzantine's book.

Borer according to a 14th-century treatise.

the left so that all the holes were interconnected. The second row of holes was filled with rods, dry chips, and splinters of wood; then all of these combustibles were ignited. In calm weather when the fire spread poorly, the recommendation was to blow the flames with bellows through hollow reed stems. If a wall would not fall in after the props had burned down, Anonymus Byzantine recommended using a battering ram. The thrust of a battering ram alone against brick walls was barely enough to cause a crack to appear (as it did in the case of stone walls), but if the wall had already been weakened by well-placed holes, a battering ram could indeed cause it to fall in.

• FIFTEEN •

SIEGE TOWERS

The earliest image of a siege tower found in Intef's Tomb at Thebes dates back to the 21st century BC. In Assyrian documents, siege towers are mentioned in the 18th century BC, although it is not precisely known what they were like at that time. Not a single Assyrian relief of the 9th through the 7th centuries BC has been found that shows a siege tower with sufficient exactitude. One is inclined to think that when it comes to structure, the Assyrian siege towers were not unlike early large battering rams.

The Greeks became acquainted with siege towers in the course of the Carthaginian invasion of Sicily in the late 5th century BC. Only a few years later, Sicilian Greeks under the leadership of Dionysius I were themselves actively using mobile siege towers (Gr: *phoretoi pyrgoi*; Lat: *turres ambulatoriae*). At the siege of Motya in 398 BC they built six-story towers, which brought them final victory over the besieged. In Eastern Greece this new siege weapon won popularity owing to Philip II (382–336 BC). His son Alexander the Great also made active use of various siege engines built for him by two engineers, Diades and Charias. Diades left us a treatise containing a description of the mechanism of various siege machines, including siege towers. This work has not survived to present time, but excerpts from it have endured in the works of Vitruvius,[191] Athenaeus,[192] and Anonymus Byzantine.[193]

Diades's siege towers were of three sizes: ten-, fifteen-, and twenty-story ones. The ten-story tower was 60 cubits (about 26.6 meters) high, the fifteen-story reached 90 cubits (39.9 meters) in height, and the twenty-story tower was as high as 120 cubits (53.2 meters). The structure was the same; the only difference was in the length, breadth, and thickness of the beams. Each tier had a circular gallery and was provided with windows. The base of the tower was square, each side of a ten-story tower being 17 cubits (7.5 meters) long, and that of a twenty-story tower, 24 cubits (10.6 meters). The towers narrowed toward the top—the area of the upper platform being one-fifth that of the base. The narrowing of a tower toward the top added stability to the structure, and evidently was a rule without exception for the engineers both of antiquity and the Middle Ages.

However, the narrowing of a tower alone was not enough to guarantee its stability. Also of importance was the correlation between the height of a tower and the size of its base. For instance,

Diades's twenty-story tower, the base of which was less than one-fifth of its height, must have been rather unstable. Demetrius Poliorcetes's tower, which he used at the siege of Rhodes in 305–304 BC, appears to have been more practical. The base of this nine-story tower was 22 meters wide, its top was 9 meters wide, and the height of the tower reached 44.5 meters.[194] Thus, the base was about half the height. According to Plutarch, Demetrius's tower "did not sway or rock to and fro when in motion, but stood straight and firm on its base, moving along with a deafening squeak and crash, inspiring awe in the hearts of spectators, but filling their eyes with involuntary glee."[195] But it seems not all towers were this steady. At least, Apollodorus recommends giving additional firmness to a tower by fixing it in place with tight rope fastened at the corners on top and halfway up the tower and tied to wooden or iron stakes driven into the ground.[196] It seems they tried to consolidate a tower with a stretcher whenever it was not in motion.

The biggest mobile siege towers were called *helepolis* (from Gr: *helein*—"take," and *polis*—"city, town"; hence, "city-taker"). The epithet "big" giving but subjective estimation, we shall use this term as a synonym for all kinds of siege towers.[197]

On the whole the structure of siege towers,[198] except in detail, probably remained the same throughout the centuries. Relatively short beams, whose length, width, and thickness varied according to the height of a tower, were used in the construction of towers. For example, a ten-story (60 cubits high) tower had 22.2-centimeter-thick beams at the bottom and 14.8-centimeter-thick beams at the top. Beams for a twenty-story (120 cubits high) tower were to be about one foot (29.6 centimeters) at the bottom.[199] All beams, both horizontal and vertical, were placed two to three in a row, which contributed to the steadiness of the structure, and should one beam break, it would be held by the remaining one or two beams. Regardless of the fact that the towers narrowed toward the top, all the vertical beams were placed strictly at 90 degrees to the surface of the earth.[200] The narrowing of the tower was secured by lessening the length of the horizontal beams, and, correspondingly, the area of every next floor. The height of every story was not the same either. For example, the first story of a twenty-story tower was 7.5 cubits (3.3 meters) high, the second to the fifth stories, 5 cubits (2.2 meters) high, and the others were only 4 cubits and 2 palms (1.9 meters) high.[201]

There was often a gallery built around each story as protection against incendiary missiles and to facilitate the putting out of a fire (see plate 15). For instance, Diades's twenty-story tower had a gallery 3 cubits (1.3 meters) wide. Communication between the stories was by staircases placed diagonally inside the tiers. Two staircases were sometimes built—one to get up, the other down.

The towers of Diades and Charias sat on six or eight wheels, while towers having less than ten stories could have but four wheels. Demetrius's tower at Rhodes, however, moved on eight

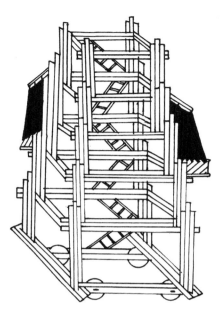

The structure of a siege tower. Drawing from Anonymus Byzantine's book.

wooden wheels (nearly one meter in diameter), bound with iron bands. The axes of a *helepolis*'s wheels could be shifted and placed at 90-degree angles to each other. Athenaeus also recommends that a revolving wheel be put before a siege tower, as well as ram-*tortoises* and other mobile engines. With the help of this wheel, the machine could change its direction, which added to its mobility and made it more difficult for the besieged to hit it.[202]

Hellenistic gigantism is believed to have been succeeded by Roman practicality. Indeed, the tallest Roman siege tower we know of was one used at the siege of Masada in AD 73. It was 60 cubits high (about 26.6 meters), which corresponds to the smallest ten-story tower of Diades. Even so, it is believed that the height of the tower was proven by the relief; the town of Masada stood on top of a mountain. There is also mention of a ten-story tower at the time of Caesar. But the Romans preferred using towers from 15 meters (the siege of Jotapata, AD 67) to 22.2 meters high (the siege of Jerusalem, AD 70). In all cases the Romans only used siege towers to suppress enemy fire from a high position.[203]

According to Vegetius, however, the Romans mainly used siege towers of three sizes: those having a long side of the base measuring 30 feet (8.9m); one that measured 40 feet (11.8 meters), and sometimes 50 feet (14.8 meters). Unfortunately, he does not indicate the exact number of stories in siege towers, confining himself to saying that "they surpassed, in height, not only the walls of the city but towers as well."[204] If we compare the indicated parameters with the respective parameters of Diades's towers, we will see that the length of the base of the first of these towers exceeds the corresponding size of the base of a ten-story tower of Diades's, and the length of the side of the latter (14.8 meters) exceeds the respective dimension for even a twenty-story tower of Diades's. We are only to guess whether Roman towers were lower and broader at the base, or whether there existed, in the period of the Roman Empire, multistory towers similar to Hellenistic ones.

Vegetius goes on to say that a siege tower also housed a battering ram and an assaulting bridge. The author points out three main levels in a siege tower: a battering ram occupied the lower stories, an assaulting bridge (*exostra*) was in the center, and the upper stories housed javelin-throwers and slingers. Apparently, light throwing machines, about which we read in Josephus, must have been placed here as well. Communication between the floors was by means of numerous stairways; the towers themselves moved on "many wheels" (meaning more than four, probably).[205]

Transfer of siege towers was accomplished by the muscle power of men or animals. At the siege of Rhodes, Demetrius selected 3,400 strong men to set the towers in motion. A tower was pushed from within, and on the outside from behind; all the same, there was not enough space for more than 1,200 men. Either Diodorus is mistaken, or those 3,400 men were divided into three shifts. A tower was sometimes set in motion with the help of a big windlass placed on the first floor of the tower.[206] When the circumstances favored it, a tower was likely to be pulled by oxen. The army of the Persian king Cyrus is believed to have been the first to use oxen for moving a siege tower in the mid-6th century BC. They tied the oxen to a special beam in such a way that they could move in a rank. Later, it probably became a common method of transfer of siege towers.

There were two ways of bringing a siege tower to its destination: putting draft cattle ahead of it, and letting them pull it up to the wall; or, having the tower and the animals move in opposite directions—the tower toward the wall and the animals away from it. In the latter case, a pair of short poles with a system of pulleys fixed on them was driven into the ground by the wall. The animals moved away from the wall, pulling at the rope that was pushed through the pulleys, thereby bringing the tower up to the wall. The latter method was certainly preferable, but more labor intensive. For instance, at the siege of Rome in AD 537, the Goths chose the simpler way, putting the oxen ahead of the tower. The defenders of the city were quick to take advantage of this and promptly killed all the oxen. The siege tower stopped, never reaching the wall.

Siege towers could be operated from the sea, too. In this case they were installed on two cargo ships standing alongside and fastened to each other. It was a risky business, however; the whole structure was easily broken and overturned during a storm or even a strong wind, which only raised the morale of the besieged. Therefore, Athenaeus, echoed by Anonymus Byzantine,

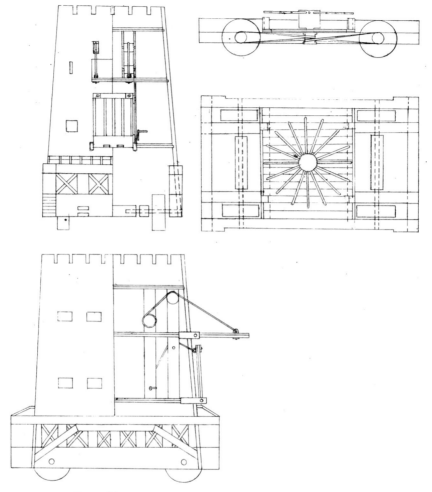

Siege tower according to Biton; it is set in motion by a windlass. E. W. Marsden's reconstruction.

recommended supplying ships with special struts and increasing the dead load of the construction so as to prevent the leaning of the towers. As the ships approached the walls, the towers were to be straightened with the help of ropes and pulley-blocks.[207] Obviously sea *helepolis* were to have a considerably longer assaulting bridge as compared with land ones.

It took from several days to several months to build a siege tower, depending on the amount of essential materials and labor on hand. In all cases, when circumstances allowed, towers were preferably disassembled into several pieces and moved from one place to another in a wagon

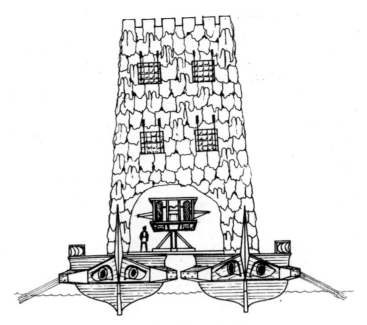

Helepolis positioned on ships.

train. This method involved certain difficulties. For instance, twenty-six carts were needed for the transportation of one siege tower at the time of the Hundred Years' War. It took Edward I thirty carts to transfer a *helepolis* of wood and hides to Stirling.[208]

Incendiary missiles and balls sent from throwing machines (or, later, from cannon) spelled the worst kind of danger for siege towers. To protect a tower from fire and missiles, it was bound with boards and covered with raw hides in such a way that the hides did not fit close to the boards but hung loosely, thus weakening the force of a strike. Loosely hanging mats were used for the same purpose; they either replaced the hides or were used alongside the latter. Hides were to hang tails-down so that when water was poured down on them, it flowed down the whole structure and put out the fire. In addition, nails with large, protruding heads were pounded into the boards, and the space between the nail heads and the boards was coated with clay. Sometimes sacks filled with vinegar-moistened chaff, or nets filled with wet moss or seaweed, were hung outside a tower.[209] A tower was occasionally bound with iron or bronze plates and roofed with lead tiles;[210] this was expensive, however. Evidently, iron sheets were used more often; we know of several such instances, including Demetrius Poliorcetes's tower at the siege of Rhodes, Roman towers at the siege of Jotapata, and the siege tower of the Persians at the siege of Amida.

The question of how many sides of a siege tower were covered with boards, hides, and metal sheets remains in dispute. There is no direct answer found in any source. On the one hand, it may seem pointless to cover a tower from the rear side, as it was not likely to be attacked there. Besides, an open rear part of the tower allowed the commander to keep an eye on what was going on inside it. On the other hand, in cases where serious damage was inflicted on the front part of the tower, Philon recommended turning it around, with the whole side to the enemy, and then repairing it. This allows us to suppose that towers *were* covered on all sides, as otherwise, even if a tower was to face the enemy with its side, an open rear part may have found itself under fire from a flank.[211]

All of the above devices prevented incendiary arrows from burning a tower, and to some degree, weakened the force of the missiles' impact. If inflammation had already taken place, the fire was put out by pouring water down on it from the upper stories, or, the more preferable mixture of water and vinegar. Water was supplied to the upper stories of a tower with the help of bullock intestines, and onto the roof with the help of joined perforated reed elbows. Water was pumped through these original water pipes from a leather bellows below.[212]

A siege tower offered many advantages to the besiegers. They could pass from its upper stories onto the walls by throwing over an assaulting bridge. Throwing machines could be mounted

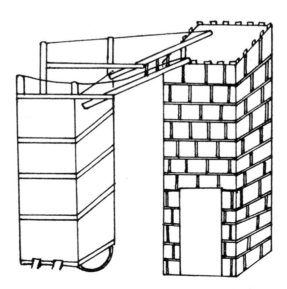

A siege tower with a boarding-bridge thrown over to the fortress tower.
Drawing from Apollodorus's book.

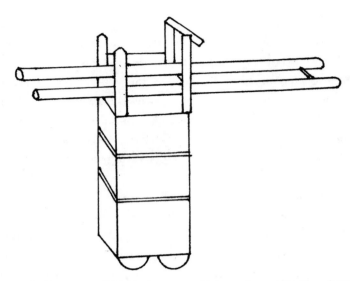

Siege tower with two parallel battering rams which can be used both against the merlons of a wall and as a boarding-bridge. Drawing from Apollodorus's book.

in a tower; soldiers could hit the defenders of the wall with arrows and javelins, being in a more advantageous position than the besieged. Finally, a tower could provide cover for operations aimed at destroying the wall (with the help of a battering ram or sap).

The assaulting bridge of a *helepolis* (Gr: *epibathra*) was built from two strong beams joined together with planking. The latter was covered with mats sewn of small shingles and woven with ropes. These mats secured a better path for the besiegers, and in case of danger could be easily drawn back. Apollodorus recommended that the bridge be 20 feet (5.9 meters) long;[213] however, the length could vary depending on the circumstances. As the *helepolis* approached a wall, the bridge was raised with the help of ropes, providing protection to the soldiers on the upper floor. An assaulting bridge could be pulled out of a tower on rollers too. Vegetius calls such a bridge an *exostra*.[214]

Siege towers were often the places where throwing machines were mounted. Heavy machines (such as stone-projectors, *ballistae*) were placed in the bottom stories, and light ones (e.g., *scorpions*) in the upper stories, as a rule. The machines fired through embrasures covered with wooden or leather shutters. In Demetrius Poliorcetes's towers, shutters were made of hides filled with wool and set in motion by a mechanical device inside the tower.

Battering rams could be placed in the bottom and in the upper stories. In the former case they were earmarked for making a breach in a wall and had the same structure as common battering rams; in the latter, their task was to destroy the parapet and merlons of the wall. According to Apollodorus, double battering rams—that is, rams joined by a crossbeam—were particularly effective against merlons and the defenders on the wall. Such a double battering ram with extra planking could also be used as an assaulting bridge to cross over to the wall (see plate 16). Also used against the defenders on the wall was a swordlike beam with a pointed front end, which was fastened, at the top of a tower, to a vertical axle so that it could revolve on the horizontal plane as well as move up and down when necessary. The front part of the beam was long and narrow, while the back end, which was in the tower, was short, heavy, and thick. As a result, even a slight motion of the back end of the beam caused its front part to move at such wide amplitude that "the beam smashed all those who stood above on the wall."[215]

Siege towers continued to be actively used in the Middle Ages (at different times they were known as *belfrey, belfriez, beffroi, berefredum,* and *belfragium*). Their construction, however, required considerable expense (both monetary and labor) and a clever architect; only the richest and greatest military commanders could afford them. Until the early 14th century, siege towers were mainly used for an assault on walls from an assaulting bridge, as well as being placed underneath a battering ram breaching a wall (see plate 17). Later, siege towers were more often employed as cover for

Assaulting a castle using a siege tower. Early 14th-century Spanish
Gran Conquista de Oltramar manuscript. (Ms. 195, Bib. Nac., Madrid)

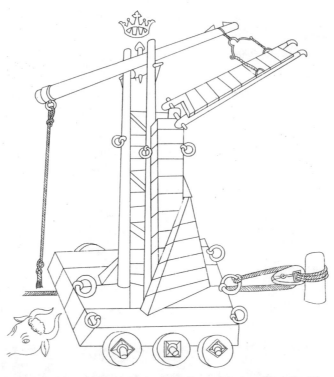

One of the constructions of siege towers according to Mariano Taccola. We can discern several basic principles of its construction, e.g. the method of raising and lowering of an assaulting bridge and of pulling a tower up to the wall with the help of a post and oxen (a ram-head is the symbol of the latter).

undermining and as bridgeheads to shoot from. Artillery was hardly ever mounted in siege towers during the Middle Ages.

Siege towers in the Middle Ages seem to have had fewer stories than in the Hellenistic Period, and were more like pragmatic Roman structures. They were usually three- to five-story towers, and their height often reached 25 to 30 meters. As to the wheels, their number varied considerably. For instance, the belfry built by the Vikings at the siege of Paris moved on sixteen wheels, while the siege tower used at the siege of Verdun sat on as few as three wheels.[216] While a three-wheeled tower (if it is possible in principle) would have been movable, it would also have been considerably less stable than towers with more wheels.

One can find an excellent description of a siege tower used by the Crusaders at the siege of Banyas in 1140 in William of Tyre:

Soon an engine of great height towered aloft, from whose top the entire city could be surveyed. From this vantage point, arrows and missiles of every sort could be sent, while stones hurled by hand would also help to keep the defenders back. As soon as the engine was ready, the ground between it and the walls was leveled off and the machine was brought up to the ramparts. There, as it looked down upon the whole city, it seemed as if a tower had suddenly been erected in the very midst of the place. Now for the first time the situation of the besieged became intolerable; they were driven to the last extremity, for it was impossible to devise any remedy against the downpour of stones and missiles which fell without intermission from the movable tower. Moreover, there was no safe passage within the city for the sick and wounded, or where those who, still strong and vigorous and sacrificing themselves in the defense of others, could withdraw for rest after their labors. In addition, they were now debarred from passing back and forth about the ramparts and could not, without peril of death, carry aid to their comrades who were falling. For the weapons and modes of assault used by those fighting below could be considered little or nothing in comparison with the manifold dangers to which they were exposed from the fighters in the tower. In fact, it seems to be rather a war with gods than with men.[217]

It was cannon that put an end to siege towers, as well as many other sorts of siege machines—but it did not do so overnight, as far as siege towers are concerned. For example, the Turks used siege towers against Constantinople in 1453, and even as late as 1565 at the siege of Malta.

A siege tower could only move on a perfectly smooth surface; otherwise, it might get stuck or turn over. Vitruvius described how, owing to the cleverness of the architect Diognetus, the Rhodians rendered Demetrius's *helepolis* harmless. The defenders made passages in the wall on the side where the tower was to approach the wall, and at night poured a great amount of water, dirt, and excrement on the ground in front of the wall. As a result, the tower became stuck in the boggy swamp, unable to move at all.[218] The besieged also resorted to other ruses. For example, they would dig a hole in front of the wall, fill it with large empty clay vessels in advance, and then cover them with turf. The vessels would break under the weight of the tower, and the tower would fall in or get stuck. The same effect could be achieved during a siege by constructing underground passageways under the path laid for the transportation of a tower.[219]

But even on a relatively smooth surface, the siege tower could only move at an extremely low speed. Plutarch says that at the siege of Thebes, Demetrius Poliorcetes's "Ruiner of Cities" moved so slowly and with such difficulty that it hardly covered the distance of two stadiums

(370 meters) in two months.[220] This must have been an exceptional case, but it is clear that speed and maneuverability were by no means typical of a *helepolis*. To facilitate the motion of a siege tower, Jaime I of Aragon (1264–1327) had a special road built, which was then covered with fat. Moreover, his engineer used rings driven into the ground by the fortress wall, as well as pulleys and ropes. As a result, the workers, who were pulling the tower up to its destination, themselves moved further and further from the area covered by enemy fire, rendering the enterprise more than successful.[221]

To be effective, a *helepolis* had to rise above the wall or a tower on which the assault was being made. Therefore, one of the methods of neutralizing a siege tower was to build a superstructure on the top of the wall, made of stone, brick, or simply planks, which prevented the besiegers from successfully firing on the defenders of the wall, or from throwing a boarding-bridge onto it. The besiegers, on their part, in order to counterbalance this effort, sometimes resorted to the following ruse: They built a tower below or on a level with the wall, positioning inside it

Laying a siege using siege towers and cannon simultaneously, from a 1475 manuscript. (see reconstruction of siege tower on plate 18)

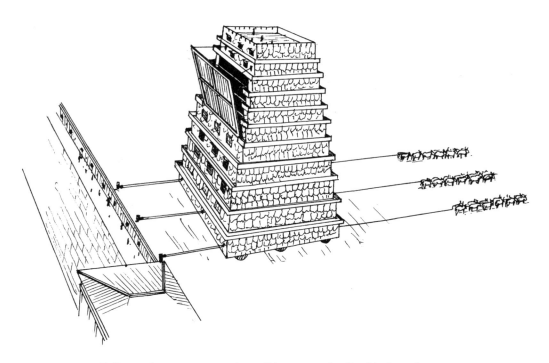

Pulling a siege tower up to the wall by means of pulley-blocks and ropes.

another smaller tower made of boards. When the *helepolis* reached the wall, they suddenly pulled the small tower out with the help of ropes and pulley-blocks, so that this combined tower rose above the wall fortifications.[222]

Other tricky devices were also invented to fight siege towers. For example, sometimes long, iron-bound beams would be extended from the wall to prevent a tower from approaching it.[223] During the defense of Tyre against the Crusaders, the defenders of the town placed a battering ram on the wall: first, the beam was swung on pulleys with the help of a windlass, and then aimed against a siege tower if it was sufficiently near the wall. Jars filled with manure would be lifted above the wall with the help of pulley-blocks and turned over on the siege towers of the Crusaders—it was not a pleasant thing to be inside the tower at such a moment.

• SIXTEEN •

SAMBUCAS

A *sambuca* (the name comes from its outward likeness to the harplike musical instrument of the same name) was a broad ladder placed in a covered tunnel bound on the outside with wet hides against fire. There were land *sambucas* and naval *sambucas*. If the former was the case, the structure sat on a wheeled cart; if the latter, on ships, which were doubled as a rule. A *sambuca* had considerable advantages in comparison with a conventional ladder: the besiegers could operate at a far distance from a wall—for example, over a ditch—and the defenders of the wall could not push it away. Structurally, *sambucas* could be of different kinds. What all of them had in common was a fairly small platform in the front (upper) part, where four to ten soldiers could be positioned. The latter were to fight off the defenders trying to prevent the installation of the *sambuca*. After the *sambuca* was fixed to the wall, the remaining soldiers climbed up the structure and onto the wall.

The only detailed description of a shipboard *sambuca* has been preserved in the writings of Polybius.[224] At the siege of Syracuse, the Romans built four *sambucas*, which they placed on eight *quinqueremes* (warships) tied in pairs (see plate 21). The *sambuca* was a long ladder about 1.2 meters wide with handrails on either side. In the initial position the ladder lay along adjoining sides of the ships and protruded far beyond the ships' bows. On approaching the walls, the ladder was lifted with the help of ropes tied to the front (upper) end of the ladder. Men standing on the stern of the ships pulled at the other ends of the ropes driven through the pulley-blocks at the top of the masts. At the same time the men on the bows of both ships saw to it that the ladder was being lifted correctly and propped it with poles. With the help of rowers placed on both outer sides of the ships, this floating structure was delivered to the walls. Above, in the front part of the ladder, there was a platform, from which four soldiers would shoot at the defenders on the walls. At the front and on the sides, the platform was enclosed with a woven fence. As soon as the ladder was adjusted to the top of the wall, the soldiers on the platform threw away the fence and assaulted the defenders of the wall; the rest of the warriors followed them closely up the *sambuca*.

There probably were various versions of naval *sambucas*. For instance, Anonymus Byzantine speaks of a roofed-ladder version of a *sambuca*, which was placed on two vertical beams, or

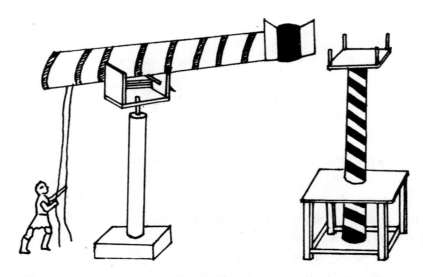

Sambuca mounted on board a ship. Drawing from Anonymus Byzantine's book.

the so-called "ship's top," and could "perform six motions like the so-called 'cranes.'" He also mentions elevating screws on which Damios placed his *sambucas*.[225] Athenaeus also asserts that these machines were commonly known, but refuses to describe them because in his opinion, ". . . it is better not to have those machines than build them badly."[226] Evidently, naval *sambucas*, as well as all siege engines mounted on ships, were extremely sensitive to weather conditions and required superior knowledge to build.

Land *sambucas* used a counterweight. This machine was a *tortoise* on wheels, fastened to which was a roofed 18-meter-long ladder.[227] A special compartment in the rear part of the *sambuca* contained 2.5 tons of stones, sand, or earth. Owing to this counterweight, as well as a windlass with a worm contrivance, it took only several men to "bring up" the *sambuca*. A *sambuca* could change its position from horizontal to an angle of 45 degrees (see plates 19 and 20). The front aperture of a *sambuca* was covered with two little doors decorated with carved, color images of a dragon or lion belching forth flames.[228] The doors protected the soldiers on the platform, and the images were designed to frighten the enemy. The use of a *sambuca* involved the following operations: ten soldiers climbed up a lowered platform in the front part of the *sambuca*; then the structure was rolled up to the wall and raised. While the ten soldiers above were engaged in fighting the defenders of the wall, the rest of the assault detachment climbed up the ladder inside the *sambuca*.

• SEVENTEEN •

AGGER (EMBANKMENTS)

An embankment (Gr: *chomata*; Lat: *agger*) was built with two purposes in mind: It might be designated for securing easy access to the fortress for the assaulting party, and then used to reach the top of the wall; or, it might be designed to secure a smooth path for bringing siege machines to the upper part of the main wall, where it was thinner and weaker than at the foot. The first earthen embankments were built in Mesopotamia as early as the third millenium BC. Later it became the favorite siege method of the Assyrians, Persians, and Romans. The manufacture of an embankment required a large labor force. That is why no earth embankments were built in the Middle Ages in Europe—the small armies of warrior noblemen neither would nor could build embankments.

It was always important for a general to know how much labor and time the building of an embankment would take. Even in ancient Babylon they knew how to calculate the amount of earth needed for the construction of an embankment, proceeding from the height of the wall. The distance from the wall to the place where the construction was to begin was always believed to be 60 meters (a distance slightly exceeding the effectiveness of the range of bows and arrows at that time). Knowing the amount of earth needed, it is not difficult to calculate the number of workers and the amount of time required. One laborer working twelve hours a day could dig out and carry about two cubic meters of earth a day. Consequently, it would take 9,500 men working for five days to build an embankment reaching the top of a 22-meter-high wall. Of course, this calculation is for idealized conditions. Things that could potentially slow the work process, like filling up the moat, or incessant fire conducted by the besieged, have not been taken into account. These impediments would certainly increase the time required for the operation. But the main conclusion is that, given the necessary amount of labor, the construction of an embankment could be carried out at relatively short notice.

As archaeological excavations on the site of the Hebrew town of Lachish show, the Assyrians' siege embankment was 55 to 60 meters wide and 16 meters high. At the bottom it had a 30-degree slope that tended to become gentler toward the top. Essentially the embankment consisted of heaps of separate stones. The upper layer of stones, however, was fastened with hard mortar, forming a hard and relatively smooth surface. The embankment had been used by the

Assyrians to bring battering rams to the upper part of the wall. Judging by surviving Assyrian reliefs, something like a track made of logs or wooden beams was built on top of the embankment to facilitate transport of siege machines.[229]

In the Hellenistic and Roman periods, in connection with the evolution of missile weapons, embankments began to be built at a distance of 120 to 150 meters from the wall. The main material used was wooden logs 6 to 9 meters long, which were piled on top of each other. The space between them was filled with earth and stones. The work was done by stages. First, logs were laid to a height of about 2 meters; then, the space between and above them was filled with earth and stones, followed by another row, and so on. The whole structure grew in length and height simultaneously. The workers were protected with stationary shields, *pluteus*, and *vineae*. At some distance from the wall the besiegers erected siege towers, from which they shot at the defenders of the wall to prevent them from hindering the construction work.

As a countermove to the construction of an embankment, the besieged could build a superstructure on top of the wall, or erect another wall beyond the first, or destroy the embankment. The demolition of an embankment could be accomplished in various ways: A secret tunnel could be driven under the wall with the excavated earth carried into the town, or the embankment could be burned down (since embankments had wooden frameworks). The latter could be done either during a sally or by driving an underground tunnel under the embankment and setting it on fire from beneath.

This last way was the most effective, because it was extremely difficult to extinguish the fire that was raging underground. Procopius provides an interesting description of this method, employed by the Persians at the siege of Edessa:

> . . . the Romans . . . began work at the bottom of the embankment, which was close to the wall. Emptying this section of the embankment from wood, stones, and earth, they got a sort of roomette, threw trunks of easily inflammable trees coated with cedar oil, sulphur and asphalt . . . the Romans immediately set fire to tree trunks stored up by them for that occasion. The fire destroyed part of the embankment, but the wood burned down before the flames had filled the embankment. The Romans, however, wasted no time, throwing fresh wood into the sap. The fire had spread under the entire embankment, and at night smoke could be seen all over the embankment. The Romans, who did not want the Persians to notice it, resorted to the following maneuver. Filling small pots with burning pieces of coal, they started throwing them in great numbers all along the embankment together with incendiary arrows. The Persians, who were on the watch here,

started running to and fro, trying to put them out. They thought that was what caused the fire . . . Sunrise saw the arrival of Khusru with the larger part of his troops. Climbing onto the embankment, he was the first to realize the source of the calamity. For he discovered that the smoke came from inside the ground and not from what the enemy threw . . . as to the barbarians, some of them put earth, others poured water on the spots where smoke would show, hoping by these means to overcome the misfortune, but all to no avail. Naturally smoke disappeared where they had put earth on it, but soon emerged in another place because fire sent it to look for an outcome wherever it could. As to water, the more of it stored in a place, the more it enhanced the effect of sulphur and tar, which caused the occasional logs to go up in flames, sending the fire further and further, because nowhere could a sufficient amount of water be stored to put out flames . . . bright fire showed above the embankment, and the Persians gave up this undertaking [the building of an embankment].[230]

• EIGHTEEN •

UNDERMINING

The term "undermining," or "sap," stands for two kinds of operations: the destruction of a wall at the foot, and underground mining operations proper.

The destruction of a wall at the foot involved making a depression in the wall with the help of such tools as crowbars, pickaxes, and axes. The hollow would be gradually enlarged, and the wall strengthened with wooden props lest it should fall in right on the sappers. Then the props would be set on fire, and the wall would fall in. This method was widely used even by the Assyrians. They also used a large woven shield sharply curving toward the top to protect the sappers (see Chapter 3, "Assyria" p.21).

The protecting function was later taken over by the so-called *digging tortoises*. These were awnings with frames made of three to five rectangular beams 3 meters long and no less than 0.3 meter thick. The ends of the beams were sometimes sharpened so that they could be driven into the ground to add stability to the structure. There were two types of *digging tortoises*: the first, with a lean-to roof, and the second, with a gable roof. Both kinds of roofs were made of boards fitted to the beams of the frame. Broad-headed 15-centimeter-long nails were driven into the wall halfway so that empty space was left between them. This space was filled up with rich, soft clay mixed with pig bristles or goat wool, lest the clay should crack when drying (see plate 22). While transported to the wall, the *tortoise* was covered with mats or hides at the front and on the sides. According to Apollodorus and Anonymus Byzantine, such a *tortoise* could successfully withstand hot sand, boiling pitch, and oil, let alone incendiary arrows and objects thrown from above.[231]

Such a *digging tortoise*, which easily moved on four wheels, was brought close to the wall. Two men standing upright inside began hollowing the wall with picks at a distance of 0.9 meters from its base, leaving a receptacle for debris. The hollow was as high as a man's height and as broad as a tortoise. It was as deep as half the way through the thickness of the wall, lest the latter should fall in. Apollodorus says that many *digging tortoises* were necessary in order to cover a considerable section of the wall, and recommended placing them at a distance of 5.9 meters from each other.

When the niches were deep enough, the *tortoises* were no longer needed, because both the sappers could stand upright back to back and go on working under the cover of the wall itself.

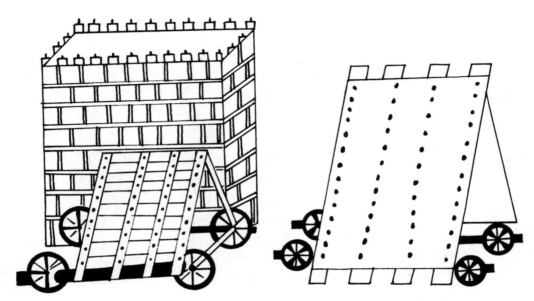

Digging tortoises with a lean-to and a gable roof. Drawing from Apollodorus's book.

To prevent the wall's falling in on the workers, it was propped with poles. (Thin poles placed closely together were preferable to thicker poles, which would have left larger spaces between them.) Boards were nailed to the poles at the top and bottom to add firmness to the props. When the niche was deemed to be sufficiently large, the space between the props was filled with brushwood, dry firewood cut in pieces, resinous splinters, and other flammable materials, and then all was set on fire. The props would burn away, causing the wall to fall in.

The underground sap, which Vegetius calls *cuniculum*, was dug with one of two goals in view: It could either serve as a passage for an assault party, which, having unexpectedly penetrated into the town, opened the gate for the entire besieging army to pass; or, it could cause a section of the wall or tower to fall in. In any case, such a sap involved the building of an underground gallery. The sappers tried to work unobserved by the besieged. Therefore, the entrance to the sap was often made a long way from the besieged town. However, the longer the gallery, the more time it took to dig an undermining. There was another way to conceal the activity of the sappers— namely, to place the entrance to the gallery inside a *tortoise* or a siege tower. Then, the gallery could be much shorter and start not far from the fortress walls. There was another problem: how to dispose of the earth dug from the undermining. Heaps of earth would have promptly attracted the attention of the defenders, and the sap would have been discovered. That is why the earth

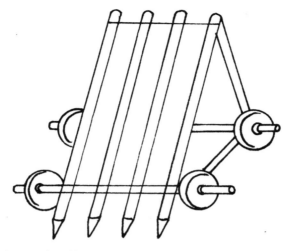

Digging tortoise with a lean-to roof, according to Anonymus Byzantine.

Warriors undermining a wall. Drawing from Anonymus Byzantine's book.

was either carried away and piled up a long way from the undermining, or spread in a thin layer and rammed smooth on the ground. This was preferably done at night or under the cover of *tortoises* or siege shields.

In order to bring down a wall or tower, the underground gallery was to be driven under the foundation of the fortification, and then, proceeding to dig on either side perpendicularly to the main gallery, a fairly large underground chamber was to be made there, under the wall. To prevent the gallery from falling in on the diggers at this stage, it was strengthened with props. In the pre-powder era, the chamber under the foundation of a wall or tower was then filled with brushwood and other flammable materials and set on fire (at the siege of Rochester, for instance, they used the fat of forty pigs for this purpose). The props would burn away, and the fortress fortifications fall in under their own weight (see plate 23).

Later on, in the 15th century, mining galleries (as they came to be called then) were stuffed with powder. To prevent the blast getting out through the entrance to the gallery, the powder-stuffed chamber was first bricked up and then set on fire. The Italians were the first to use powder mines in Europe. The first reliable reference to their use dates back to 1403.[232] The year 1449 saw the appearance of Mariano Taccola's treatise, "De Machinis," with the earliest description of the use of powder mines for the siege of a castle (see plate 9). The text includes a drawing that depicts a castle standing on a hill, two barrels of powder, and three entrances to a mine gallery. Flames are shooting out from all the entrances to the gallery, and the tower of the fortress has a crack along the middle. It is interesting that Taccola also describes the old method, too—the burning down of props.[233] An illustration found in a treatise written by another Italian, Francesco di Giorgio Martini, depicts a zigzag gallery leading to a mine. Martini was believed to have invented this gallery. The Siena manuscript of 1470–80 contains a description of such a gallery, noting that a compass was used for its design.[234]

A very vivid description of laying an underground passage is to be found in the writings of Usamah B. Munqidh. The scene is the siege of the town of Kafartab in 1115, held by the Crusaders:

> It occurred to me to enter the underground tunnel and inspect it. So I went down in the trench, while the arrows and stones were falling on us like rain, and entered the tunnel. There I was struck with the great wisdom with which the digging was executed. The tunnel was dug from the trench to the *bashurah* [outer wall]. On the sides of the tunnel were set up two pillars, across which stretched a plank to prevent the earth above it from falling down. The whole tunnel had such a framework of wood

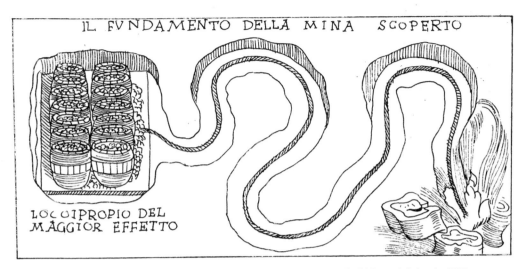

IL FVNDAMENTO DELLA MINA SCOPERTO

LOCCIPROPIO DEL MAGGIOR EFFETTO

Powder mine with a zigzag passage. According to Vanoccio Biringucio's book, 1540.

that extended as far as the foundations of the *bashurah*. Then the assailants dug under the wall of the *bashurah*, supported it in its place, and we went as far as the foundation of the tower. The tunnel was narrow; it was nothing but a means to provide access to the tower. As soon as they got to the tower, they enlarged the tunnel in the wall of the tower, supported it on timbers, and began to carry out, a little at a time, the bits of stone produced by boring. The floor of the tunnel was turned into mud because of the dust caused by the digging. Having made the inspection, I went on without the troops of Khurasan [where the miners came from] recognizing me. Had they recognized me, they would not have let me off without the payment of a heavy fine.

They then began to cut dry wood and stuff the tunnel with it. Early the next morning they set it on fire. We had just at that time put on our arms and marched under a great shower of stones and arrows to the trench in order to attack the castle as soon as its tower tumbled over. As soon as the fire began to have its effect, the layers of mortar between the stones of the wall began to fall. Then a crack was made. The crack became wider and wider and the tower fell. We had assumed that when the tower fell, we would be able to go in and reach the enemy. But only the outer face of the wall fell, while the inner wall remained intact.[235]

As we can see, the undermining had not achieved its objective. The activities of the sappers of Belek's army at the siege of Kharput (north of Edessa) in 1123 were more successful. King Baldwin II had been sent to that castle as a prisoner, but had seized the castle with the help of local Armenians. Belek, who commanded the Muslim troops, was furious:

> He immediately ordered the rock on which the castle was situated to be undermined and props to be placed along the tunnel to support the works above. Then he had wood carried in and fire introduced. When the props were burned, the excavation suddenly fell in, and the tower which was nearest to the fire collapsed with a loud noise. At first smoke rose together with the dust since the debris covered up the fire, but when the fire ate through the material underneath and the flames began to be clearly visible, a stupor caused by the unexpected event seized the king.[236]

The impression made by the undermining was so strong that the defenders soon surrendered. On the contrary, however, the Crusaders—who were holding Jaffa during the Third Crusade—proved to be prepared for such a turn of events, and, when a part of the wall "fell with a fall like the end of all things" as a result of the undermining, they did not lose their heads: "A cloud of dust and smoke arose from the fallen wall that darkened the heavens and hid the light of day, and none dared enter the breach and face the fire. But when the cloud dispersed, it disclosed the wall of halberds and lances replacing the one that had just fallen."[237]

A sap earmarked for getting inside a besieged town was made in a similar way, only the propped gallery would be preferably dug to a quiet place within the town walls or into a building as near the gate as possible. Then, at night as a rule, a small elite detachment would break into the town, murder those sleeping there, and open the gate.

An undermining could be made at very short notice. For instance, we can read in Polybius that working around the clock for three days, the men covered 65 meters.[238] However, in this case the speed was clearly above average: the men had no time to strengthen the gallery properly, and the wall fell in earlier than expected.

An underground sap had several limitations. It could not be driven in hard, rocky ground. If a moat filled with water ran along the wall, it also presented an insurmountable obstacle. Moreover, even a deep, dry ditch could considerably hinder the digging of a sap or render it quite impossible, because the sap would have had to have been dug very deep. A deep, strong foundation of fortress structures considerably hindered the work of sappers, too. At the same time, in a favorable contingency, one sap could provoke such a serious destruction of fortress structures that there would be no question of further siege. For instance, at the siege of Megalopolis, a sap "brought down the biggest three towers and a corresponding number of intratower fortifications."[239]

The primary task of the besieged in fighting an underground sap was to detect it. Quite a number of methods were contrived to do just this. As early as about 600 BC, at the siege of the town of Barca by the Persians, a blacksmith detected an undermining with the help of a bronze shield which he put on the ground in different places.[240] Hitting the ground with their tools, the sappers caused a slight vibration, and the shield began to twang in that location. Resonant copper vessels were also used for detecting a sap by the defenders of Ambracia in 189 BC.[241] In the Middle Ages, when they were no less frequent than in the Archaic Period, saps were detected with the help of bowls of water (Caen) and bells (Rhodes, 1522).[242]

Vibration provoked the heaving of water or the ringing of bells, and attack was expected at the place where the effect was the strongest. However, to confuse the enemy, the attackers would often resort to the following ruse: They would make a false sap as well as a genuine one, trying to make as much noise as possible in the former. Sometimes several saps would be driven simultaneously. For instance, no less than fourteen mines were started at the siege of Constantinople in 1453, all being driven from a considerable distance. They were very complicated saps consisting of numerous galleries. In the siege of Malta the galleries were placed one above another, apparently with the express purpose of misleading the enemy.[243]

It was possible to fight an undermining by increasing the depth of a ditch and lining its sides with big stones. It is generally believed that the citadel of Caesarea could not be demolished by means of an underground passage because antique columns had been laid horizontally through the walls.[244] This kind of structure can still be seen in the citadel of Giblet, as well as in a large number of Byzantine fortresses.

Such construction, however, could not be used everywhere because of the rarity of the material. Therefore, more often the besieged took active measures—they would dig a countergallery. When both the galleries had joined underground, hand-to-hand fighting would begin. If the besieged party succeeded in killing all the sappers, the enemy gallery was brought down. Archaeological excavations at Dura-Europos in Syria have revealed evidence of a fierce underground encounter that took place between the Persians and Romans in AD 265. The Persians had laid a tunnel beneath one of the towers. The Romans answered by laying a counter-gallery. Hand-to-hand fighting took place when both galleries met. A huge number of weapons and armor were found during the excavations, as well as skeletons, and even half-decomposed bodies. Traces of resin and sulphur, probably used to ignite thatch and bunches of brushwood, were also found.[245] All these flammable materials could have been used both for burning down the props and smoking out enemy sappers.

Mine and countermine galleries in the fortress of St. Andrews, Scotland. The galleries were built during the siege of 1546. When the galleries had reached the same spot it turned out that they had been driven on different levels—one gallery was about 1.8m above the other. Today we can walk along both these tunnels which are connected by an iron staircase.

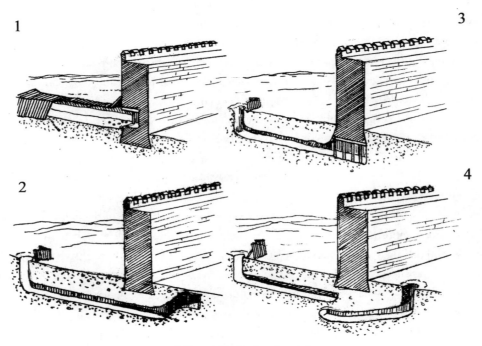

Different kinds of undermining:
1—direct destruction of a wall at the foot;
2—an underground gallery built for the purpose of getting inside a besieged town;
3—an underground sap for demolishing a wall;
4—mine and countermine galleries.

However, as a rule, it was preferable to avoid risky underground hand-to-hand fighting. An underground gallery could be flooded or filled with a suffocating gas. The former method was resorted to by the population of Massilia, who dug a long and wide reservoir outside the town wall and filled it with water from the wells and the harbor. When the undermining reached the reservoir, the water filled the gallery so swiftly that all those within were crushed by the mass of water and the resulting landslide.[246] At the siege of Apollonia, the defenders drove a counter-gallery above the gallery of the assailants, mottled the floor with holes, and poured boiling water, hot pitch, red-hot sand, and excrement down on the heads of enemy sappers.[247] Aeneas Tacticus recommended smoking the sappers out by directing the smoke coming from burning wood and straw or letting wasps and bees into a sap.[248] But the most effective method was one devised by the population of the town of Ambracia during a siege the Romans laid to it in 189 BC (see plate 24). Failing to win a victory in hand-to-hand fighting underground, the defenders brought a large jar—made of clay, probably—filled with chicken down, set fire to the down, and with the help of bellows filled the gallery with pungent, stinking smoke. To prevent the Romans approaching this hellish aggregate, holes had been made in its front lid, with *sarissa* spears driven through it. The besiegers could not bear it and left the sap.[249]

Each method of undermining had its pros and cons. A direct destruction of a wall at its base was easier to accomplish, but it was more dangerous and not always possible. Walls made of mud-brick were easy to destroy with picks and axes; however, it was not as easy to destroy walls made of blocks of stone. Besides, in this case the sappers were much more exposed to the missiles, stones, and boiling water coming from the besieged. An underground sap is less dangerous, and is concealed from the eyes of the besieged, but it requires better knowledge and experience. If the tunnel is driven too deep, the wall may never fall in. On the other hand, if the tunnel is too near the surface, there is a risk of the wall's falling in ahead of time, right on the sappers.

NINETEEN

ANCIENT AND MEDIEVAL THROWING MACHINES

Throwing machines were employed in the ancient and medieval armies over the course of 2,000 years, beginning in the early 4th century BC through the second half of the 15th century AD. Although not many variations of these machines existed during this era, they were called by many different names. The issue is complicated by the fact that the names of some machines would be changed over time, and the same name would often be passed from one machine to another. Now let us try and trace the evolution of throwing engines and their names.

ANTIQUITY

The history of throwing machines begins in 399 BC. Dionysius was preparing Syracuse for defense against the Carthaginian invasion. It was not a laughing matter, and the best engineers of Sicily, Italy, and ancient Greece were invited to come to the city. Their shops occupied all the vacant premises, including the halls of temples, gymnasiums, and even private homes. Their crowning achievement was the creation of a new weapon based on a composite bow, and given the name *gastraphetes* (Gr: "belly bow"). In modern terminology, it was just a large crossbow which had to be propped on the ground with one end and held in the belly with the other (hence the name) in order to cock it. Further evolution of the crossbow followed in two ways—creating a stationary machine, and also a hand version. We are interested in the first variation.

Gastraphetes was a powerful composite bow fixed on a stock, which fired short (40–60 centimeter) bolts with faceted metal heads. There was a slider in the upper part of the stock about the same length as the stock itself, which easily slid along it. The tension power of a *gastraphetes* was 70 to 90 kilograms, while in the case of ordinary bows, it varied from 18 to 27 kilograms. A *gastraphetes* was a very heavy weapon, so it was usually propped against a fortress wall or a hillock before firing. A low rate of fire, as compared with the ordinary bow, did not allow for its active

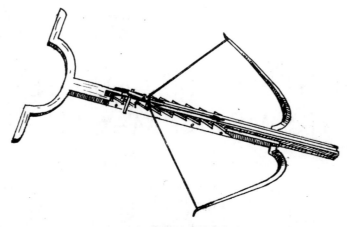

Gastraphetes. About 400 BC.

employment in field battles. *Gastraphetes* was mainly used in sieges and in defense of fortresses; therefore, it could be considered the earliest throwing engine.

To cock a *gastraphetes*, the archer would lean his belly on the breech end, which had a spe-cially made semicircular cut in it. He would bring all his weight to bear upon the breech end, while the opposite end with a jutting slider was propped against the ground (see plate 25). The slider slid backwards until it was caught by an engagement with a couple of cogs on a ratchet fas-tened to the stock.

Gastraphetes surpassed ordinary bows in the range of fire, although not considerably. Its range of fire was probably within the limits of 200–250 meters,[250] while that of an ordinary bow, even a composite one, was 150–200 meters.[251] One would think that an increase in the range of fire by as little as 50 meters would not be very essential for battle, however, apart from its high rate of fire, the *gastraphetes* also possessed a higher penetrative power. Both of these factors made a considerable impression on the enemy soldiers, who were not prepared for them.

Drawing the string of even an ordinary composite reflex bow was not an easy task; thus, it was naturally much more difficult to do so in the case of a *gastraphetes*. E. W. Marsden[252] believes that it was done with the help of an auxiliary string, and the operator acted in the following way: First, this auxiliary string was fastened at the ends of a bow. Then the slider of the *gastraphetes* was shifted with respect to the bow in such a way that the auxiliary string engaged the trigger mechanism. After that, the front end of the slider was propped against a wall or the ground, and the operator brought his whole weight to bear on the stock. The slider returned to its initial po-sition, and the bow curved, attaining the natural shape for a tightly drawn bow. Then a genuine string was put on the horns of the bow, and the fastenings and the auxiliary string were removed. The *gastraphetes* was now ready for battle.

The desire to further increase the range of fire and the striking power of the *gastraphetes* resulted in its size being augmented and the bow itself made even more powerful. The new weapon was now too heavy to carry by hand, and it had to be fixed on a support. A mechanism working on the principle of a windlass was built for drawing a string. Thus, the year 375 BC saw the emergence of the *oxybeles*.[253] There were at least two models of such arrow-firers, whose invention Biton ascribes to Zopyrus of Tarentum.[254] The first model, which the author calls "mountain *gastraphetes*," had a stock with a groove 1.5 meters long and a bow 2.2 meters long (see plate 26); the stock of the other machine was 2.2 meters long and the bow was 2.8 meters long. We know that the latter machine fired two 6-foot- (1.9-meter-) long bolts simultaneously. On Biton's evidence, there existed two versions of *oxybeles*, too, which fired moderate-sized stone balls weighing about 2.25 kilograms. The first type of such a stone-projector was invented by Charon of Magnesia, and the second by Isidorus of Abydos.[255] It was these non-torsion-powered stone-projectors that must have been first used in field battle in about 354 BC.

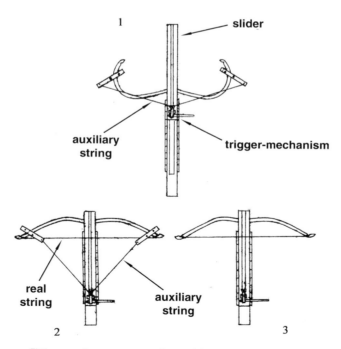

Fitting a string to a *gastraphetes*. After E. W. Marsden.

Further increased power of the weapon was limited by the possibilities of a composite bow. Therefore, engineers turned to another source of energy based on twisting thick cords of animal sinews, horse-, or human hair (women's hair was considered the best) soaked in oil. Torsion-powered machines were probably invented in Macedonia between 353 and 341 BC (see plate 27). Non-torsion-powered machines did not disappear overnight, however. Biton described them even in 240 BC, but he seems to be the last author to tell the world about these outdated engines. Thus, non-torsion-powered machines lasted for about 150 years and then disappeared, only to be revived in the Middle Ages.

The basis of a torsion-powered machine was not a bow but arms inserted into a rope bundle (torsion-spring). The torsion-springs were fastened on a wooden framework and twisted to a maximum level by special levers at the top and at the bottom. Such arrow-firing machines with torsion-springs got the common name of *catapult*, meaning "shield-breaker" (*cata*—meaning "break, penetrate"; *pelta*—meaning the shield used by the Greek light infantry). The machine is said to have been so powerful that an arrow shot from it broke through a shield and an armored warrior, standing behind it, at a distance of 400 meters.

No sooner had they appeared than torsion-powered arrow-firers were adapted for casting stones. The frame and the shape of the groove in the stock had to be changed, and the string made a bit thicker. The Greek called such a weapon *lithobolos*; the Romans named it the *ballista*. The *lithobolos* was used for the first time by Alexander the Great at the siege of Halicarnassus in 334 BC. Here they were mainly employed against live targets. However, only two years later, at the siege of Tyre, these stone-projectors were already being used for the destruction of fortifications—a task thoroughly beyond the power of an arrow-firer. The invention of a mechanism of vertical firing came as an important innovation: a projectile could now not only follow a grazing trajectory (as in the case of earlier arrow-firers) but also a plunging or ballistic one. This enabled the assailants to engage the enemy on the fortress walls and beyond them. The Romans called the small *catapults scorpions* (see plate 28).

Arrow-firers and stone-projectors had different calibers determined by the diameter of the aperture in the *peritreton*—a framework in which torsion-springs were propped. Another important factor was the correlation between the length of torsion-spring and its diameter. If the torsion-spring was too short and thick, high inner friction would develop in it. If it was too long and thin, its elasticity remained partly unclaimed and, accordingly, it would not be used at full capacity. The optimal correlation was found in about the 270s BC, possibly by a group of Greek engineers working for the Ptolemy dynasty in Egypt. As a result, two formulas were born that showed the dependence of the diameter of the torsion-spring on the size of a projectile. The

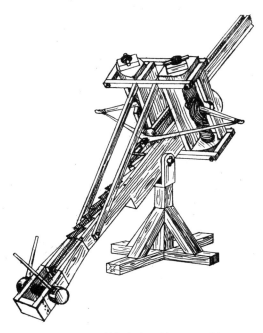

Lithobolos. About 334 BC.

diameter of a torsion-spring (d) for an arrow-firer must equal one ninth of the length of the bolt, and for a stone-projector it was expressed by the following formula:

$$d = 1{,}1\sqrt[3]{100m}$$

Where d is diameter in dactyls (1 dactyl = 1.93 cm) and m is the weight of a ball in minas (1 mina = 437g).[256]

Knowing the diameter of a torsion-spring, one could estimate all the other parameters of a machine, e.g., the full length of a stone-projector equaled approximately 30 diameters of the torsion-spring, and the width, 15. Stone-projectors were much bigger than arrow-firers (see Table 2).

Stone balls for stone-projectors were specially made and sometimes were even coated with clay to give them the spherical form which had the best ballistic characteristics. Balls for throwing machines, unlike the machines themselves, are found fairly often. For instance, 353 balls were found on Rhodes (Greece), and 961 in Pergamum (Turkey); over 200 stone balls were found in Tel Dor (ancient Dora, Israel), and about the same number in Salamis (Cyprus); and even as many as

Stone balls for throwing machines found in Carthage. There were about
5,600 balls of different calibers found here. Author's photograph.

5,600 were found in Carthage (Tunisia). These findings helped to establish the most common caliber of stone-projectors. Though all these balls differ slightly in weight, the conclusion can be reached that the main caliber of stone-projectors equaled 10, 15, 20, 30, 40, and 90 minas (4.4, 6.5, 8.7, 13.1, 17.5, and 39.3 kilograms respectively), and also 1 talent (26.2 kilograms). Most of the balls found in Carthage were about 15-mina caliber, while those found in Pergamum were mainly of a larger caliber. This might be connected with the fact that the Carthaginians were focused on the defense of the city, while the arsenal in Pergamum was meant for offensive operations.

Many balls have an inscription indicating the weight of the projectile. The balls found in Salamis have their weight indicated in tens of minas (by one or more Δ symbols, the Greek delta representing ten minas), e.g., a 35-kilogram ball is marked ΔΔT, which corresponds to 10 minas+10 minas+1 talent = 80 minas, while a ball weighing 15 minas is marked ΔΠ. Mistakes occur often, however. Thus, two balls are marked Δ and ΔΔ, even though each weighs about 15 minas, and another is marked ΔT although it really weighs only 63 minas (27.5 kilograms). The system for marking balls found in Tel Dor was different: the ordinal number of the letter in the Greek alphabet denotes the weight in minas—e.g., E (epsilon), the fifth letter of the Greek alphabet, stands for 5 minas. On one of the balls we can read KB (kappa-beta / 20+2 minas) and its weight (9.5 kilograms) practically equals 22 minas. Another ball, indicated IH (iota-eta / 10+8 minas), weighs 7.7 kilograms, which very nearly equals 18 minas (7.9 kilograms).[257]

Table 2. Approximate sizes of arrow-firers and stone-projectors depending on the length/ weight of a missile[258]

Size of a missile (length for an arrow-firer/weight for a stone-projector)		Diameter of a torsion-spring	Number of surviving artifacts*	Height of the torsion-spring	Approximate size of a machine	
					Length	Width
Arrow-firers						
31cm		3.4cm	1 (type 6)	22.1cm	Hand-held	
54cm		5.6cm	2 (type 7)	36.4cm	1.4m	0.8m
54cm		6.0cm	4 (type 4)	39.0cm	1.5m	0.9m
69cm		7.5cm	2 (type 5)	48.8cm	1.9m	1.1m
77cm		8.3cm	4 (type 2)	54.0cm	2.1m	1.2m
77cm		8.4cm	4 (type 1)	54.6cm	2.1m	1.2m
123cm		13.6cm	4 (type 3)	88.4cm	3.4m	1.9m
Stone-projectors						
10 minas	4.4kg	21.2cm	46 (13%)[1*] ___[2*] 30 (15%)[3*] 900 (16%) (from 5 to 10 minas)[4*] 2 (6%)[5*]	1.91m	6.4m	3.2m
15 minas	6.5kg	24.3cm	56 (16%)[1*] 1 (0.1%)[2*] 23 (11.5%)[3*] 3500 (62.5%) (from 12 to 18 minas)[4*] ___[5*]	2.19m	7.3m	3.6m

Size of a missile (length for an arrow-firer/weight for a stone-projector)	Diameter of a torsion-spring	Number of surviving artifacts*	Height of the torsion-spring	Approximate size of a machine	
				Length	Width
Stone-projectors					
20 minas	8.7kg	26.8cm	36 (10%)[1*] 67 (7%)[2*] 9 (4.5%)[3*] see 30 minas[4*] 11 (32%)[5*]	2.41m	8.0m	4.0m
30 minas	13.1kg	30.7cm	83 (24%)[1*] 118 (12%)[2*] 23 (11.5%)[3*] 550 (10%) (from 20 to 30 minas)[4*] 6 (18%)[5*]	2.76m	9.2m	4.6m
50 minas	21.8kg	36.3cm	7 (2%)[1*] —[2*] 12 (6%)[3*] 350 (6.3%) (from 37.5 to 60 minas)[4*] —[5*]	3.27m	10.9m	5.4m
1 talent	26.2kg	38.4cm	7 (2%)[1*] 353 (37%)[2*] 4 (2%)[3*] 300 (5%) (from 65 to 90 minas)[4*] —[5*]	3.46m	11.5m	5.8m
2 talents	52.4kg	48.6cm	—[1*] 33 (3%)[2*] —[3*] —[4*] —[5*]	4.37m	14.6m	7.3m

Size of a missile (length for an arrow-firer/weight for a stone-projector)		Diameter of a torsion-spring	Number of surviving artifacts*	Height of the torsion-spring	Approximate size of a machine	
					Length	Width
Stone-projectors						
2.5 talents	65.5kg	52.3cm	1 (0.3%)[1*] ___2* ___3* ___4* ___5*	4.71m	15.7m	7.8m

* For arrow-firers, the number (type in parentheses) of washers found in Epirus is indicated. Twenty-one washers from *catapults* were found here in all. We know that the city existed from the 4th century BC to 167 BC, when it was destroyed by the Romans. Therefore, on the strength of this finding we can trace the evolution of *catapult* washers for the indicated period. The washers have been conventionally divided into seven types depending on their size and structure. Type 1 was characterized by rachet teeth on the flange and was probably propped on a framework with the help of a couple of pawls. Later this system was given up and the flange of the washers was provided with six notches (type 2), which conformed to the holes in the framework and were fixed with a peg. However, this system of fastening apparently did not prove ideal either, and we find a more reliable system in the following five types—holes were now made in the flange, their number varying, e.g. type 3 had 8 holes, and type 7 had only 4.

Indicated for stone-projectors is the number of balls (the percent of the whole is given in parentheses) found in different places ([1*] Rhodes, [2*] Pergamum, [3*] Tel Dor, [4*] Carthage, [5*] Salamis). Many of these data are, unfortunately, not absolute. Thus, while on Rhodes, in Pergamum, and Tel Dor, all the balls were carefully weighed, the balls of Carthage were only divided into five categories: light (2.5–4.5kg), medium (5.0–7.5kg), medium-heavy (9.0–14.0kg), heavy (16.0–26.0kg), and super-heavy (28.5–40.5kg), and of those found in Salamis (over 200 pieces), only 34 have been examined. Many intermediate values are absent from the table, as well as super-light and super-heavy balls (the latter were possibly used only to throw down from a wall with a crane). That is why in most cases summing up would not give 100 percent. The object of the above column is but to show an approximate distribution of balls in accordance with their weight.

Stone balls for throwing machines found in the arsenal in Pergamum (Turkey).
Over 900 balls of different calibers were found here all in all. Author's photograph.

And what would happen if we should wittingly build a machine larger than needed? That is, suppose we build a 60-mina stone-projector and try to fire balls weighing 30 minas? Shall we achieve the same range of fire as if we were firing a 60-mina ball? Or will the range of fire be higher because the ball is lighter? Wouldn't it be better to knowingly build bigger machines and fire different balls as the circumstances require? Yes, theoretically speaking, it would be better to always build the biggest machines and use them on all occasions. The range of fire of a 60-mina stone-projector firing a 30-mina ball would certainly be higher than when firing a 60-mina ball, although not twice as high. However, if we take into account the financial aspect, the difficulties involved in building such a monster and mounting it on fortress walls or towers, or in its transportation, it will be clear why the Greeks and Romans tried to build the smallest possible machines, "sweating" them to their breaking point, and not vice versa.

The common disadvantage of all torsion-powered machines was a high sensitivity to change of climate and quick amortization of torsion-springs. Two structures suggested by Ctesibius of Alexandria as far back as the mid-3rd century BC were invented as a result of a search for ways of replacing torsion-springs, which were too sensitive to the impact of moisture and too liable to stretch. One worked on the power resulting from squeezing bronze plates with a lever,[259] and the other used a hermetic cylinder.[260] However, neither of these constructions secured power comparable to the torsion-springs, and therefore, neither method was ever developed further.

At approximately the same time, Dionysius of Alexandria invented a repeating arrow-firer, called a *polybolos*. Bolts were pushed into a vertical magazine and then entered the fighting position by means of a revolving drum controlled by a cam. The latter was fixed with string when cocked. A windlass set a chain transmission in action; the latter spanned the machine, drew the string, sent the arrow from the magazine to the groove, and released the string at the next revolution. As a result, the machine could fire automatically until the bolts ran out.[261]

Nevertheless, a *polybolos* was no substitute for a single-loading arrow-firer—its range of fire proved too low, and a close grouping of shots was too high (bolts fired from a model *polybolos*, reconstructed by General Schramm in the last century, hit each other). As a consequence, the machine did little damage to the enemy troops and led to considerable waste of bolts. (It is likely that the machine could not quickly turn aside.)

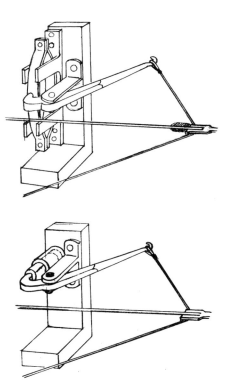

Two constructions alternative to the torsion-spring. Proposed by
Ctesibius of Alexandria in mid-3rd century BC.

143

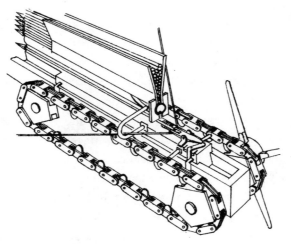

Construction of an automatic repeating arrow-firer *polybolos.*

The frame of a torsion-powered arrow-firer on the balustrade of the Sanctuary of
Athena in Pergamum (Turkey), first half of the 2nd century BC (Antikensammlung,
Staatliche Museen zu Berlin, Preussischer Kulturbesitz)

By around AD 100, the Roman army had attained the most perfect arrow-firer—*cheiroballis-tra*[262]—which replaced the *scorpion*. *Cheiroballistra* is the Greek word for "hand-ballista," and the corresponding Roman term is *manuballista*. The main innovation consisted in introducing an all-metal (iron or bronze) framework instead of the metal-bound frames of the earlier times. Metal being harder than wood, it was now possible to place the levers farther apart, which considerably increased the power of the machine. Torsion-springs were also placed in metal cylinders,[263] which isolated them from contact with moisture, and fire could now be conducted without material loss of ballistic ranges. Another innovation, produced for the first time in *cheiroballistra*, was a sighting mechanism in the form of a small arch (see plate 29). A *cheiroballistra* fired bolts of only 40 centimeters in length. Recent tests of a reconstructed *cheiroballistra* show that it possessed an extraordinary accuracy of fire.

Torsion-powered arrow-firers and stone-projectors continued in use for many centuries to come, their construction constantly being improved. E. W. Marsden suggests that these machines be divided into several categories.[264] The earliest torsion-powered arrow-firer (about 350 BC) made use of the so-called framework-type Mark I. A common framework consisted of two simple frames with torsion-springs just wound on them. However, this method of fastening torsion-springs was not conducive to their being properly wound and, consequently, the power of winding could not be fully realized. Therefore, about ten years later (~340 BC), the frames of arrow-firers were provided with holes, through which torsion-springs were pushed, and then they were fastened by being wound

Scene from Trajan's Column (Rome). We can see iron framed arrow-firers with arches (*cheiroballistra*) mounted on fortifications (top left) and on a timber platform (center). (TC 165-168. C. Cichorius, *Die Reliefs der Traianssäule*, Berlin, 1900. Plate XLVII. Courtesy of Verlag Walter de Gruyter & Co. GmbH)

around iron levers (Mark II type). This structure worked well, but after long firing, the iron levers would become so deeply enmeshed in the wooden frame that it was impossible to pull them up. So they began to place metal washers between the pintles and the frame. Besides, two separate frames were joined to have one solid framework, which rendered the entire construction more durable and much more reliable. Such frames (Mark III type) emerged sometime between 340 and 334 BC.

Further evolution of throwing machines was no longer connected with the fastening of torsion-springs but with that of arms. It is clear that the larger the angle between the extreme positions of the arms (in the initial and the drawn state), the more power that could be extracted from the same torsion-springs, given other equal conditions. Therefore, the arms were taken somewhat further apart in the initial position by making cuts of a certain form in the frame. The angle between the extreme positions was brought up to 35 degrees for arrow-firers (in the old Mark III structure, it was 23 degrees), and for the new stone-projectors, it was increased even to 45–50 degrees. As a consequence of these alterations, the frames of arrow-firers and stone-projectors proved of different construction and, in the terminology of E. W. Marsden, were called Mark IIIa and Mark IIIb respectively.

After the appearance of a calibration formula for the calculation of the size of machines in about 270 BC, arrow-firers and stone-projectors came to be built on the basis of this formula only. Such arrow-firers and stone-projectors already find themselves in Mark IVa and Mark IVb categories (see plate 31). Throwing machines of this construction were the standard artillery of Mediterranean states beginning in the late 3rd century BC to the middle of the 1st century BC. True, mid-2nd century BC saw the appearance of an improved IVa type—arrow-firers having somewhat curved, not

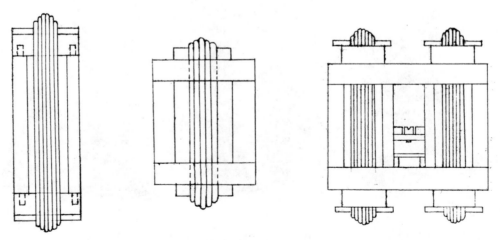

Evolution of the frames of torsion-powered machines. Left to right: Mark I, Mark II, Mark III.

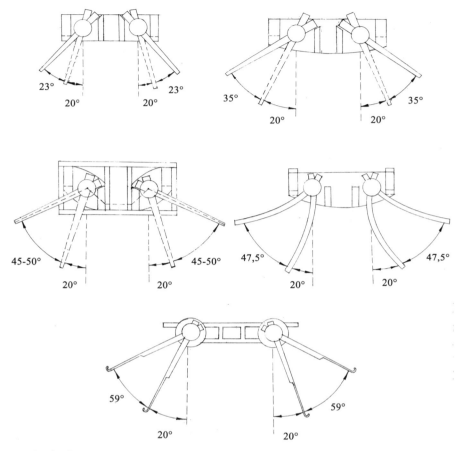

Angles between the extreme positions of an arm in the machines of Mark III type, Mark IIIa type (upper row), Mark IIIb, an improved Mark IVa type (middle row), and in *cheiroballistra* (bottom drawing).

straight, arms, which further augmented the power of the machines. But no notable changes took place until mid-1st century BC. The throwing machines described by Vitruvius[265] already have different constructive parameters from those calculated on Philon's formulas. The principal innovation was that washers were now made in an oval shape, not round. As a result, more sinews could be used in torsion-springs without materially increasing the size of the machine. This allows us to surmise that Roman *ballistae* of the time were somewhat more compact in size, even though the balls were the same weight. The arrow-firers and stone-projectors with oval washers, belonging to Mark Va and Mark Vb respectively, constituted the standard artillery of the early Roman Empire and were in use at least until AD 100, when they were replaced by the *cheiroballistra*. The latter had an all-metal framework, an arch-shaped sighting device, and arms which were placed even farther apart (up to 59 degrees). The correlation between the diameter of the torsion-spring and many constructive elements in machines with all-metal frames differed in principle from earlier ones.

Table 3. Types of torsion-powered machines and the time of their appearance (from E. W. Marsden).

Type of machine	Main improvement	Date of introduction
Mark I, arrow-firer	pair of simple spring-frames and wrapped-above torsion-springs	about 350 BC
Mark II, arrow-firer	spring-frames with holes	before 340 BC
Mark III, arrow-firer	usage of washers	after 340 BC
Mark IIIa, arrow-firer	increased angle between the extreme positions of the arms	before 334 BC
Mark IIIb, stone-projector	increased angle between the extreme positions of the arms	between 334 and 331 BC
Mark IVa, arrow-firer	built according to formula for arrow-firers	about 270 BC
Mark IVb, stone-projector	built according to formula for stone-projectors	about 270 BC
Modified Mark IVa, arrow-firer	curved arms	about 150 BC
Mark Va, arrow-firer	oval washers	about 60 BC
Mark Vb, stone-projector	oval washers	about 60 BC
cheiroballistra	all-metal frames, arch-shaped sighting device, an even larger angle between the extreme positions of the arms	about AD 100

A torsion-powered machine having been assembled, it was to be made fit for battle. The main difficulty lay in securing even twisting of torsion-springs. There were two methods of doing so: The musical method, which was considered preferable, consisted in getting both torsion-springs to issue a similar sound while vibrating. Now artillery men, lacking a musical ear, had to simply compare the thickness of torsion-springs by means of sliding calipers. Both torsion-springs having been evenly twisted, a few blank shots were fired. The elements were then reexamined and wound up. Finally, a few regular shots with a missile were fired with the string taken farther and farther away until the needed range of fire was achieved.

The *onager* had a structure that was quite different from those described above. This machine had only one arm propped vertically in a sinew-bundle. Thus, the *onager* was also a torsion-powered machine as it employed the power of twisted fiber. The machine had no vertical laying and was only used for firing along a plunging trajectory (see plate 30). So far, the exact time of the appearance of the *onager* has not been established. We find the first mention of a mono-arm machine in Philon about 200 BC.[266] It was not mentioned again by any ancient author for 300 years, until in the 2nd century AD we come across a brief description of an engine not unlike an *onager*—fastened at the end of a battering ram at that.[267] And at last, as late as the 4th century AD, an *onager* was carefully described by Ammianus Marcellinus.[268] It is also mentioned by Vegetius as a familiar engine;[269] therefore, some scholars date the invention of the *onager* back to the late 3rd century BC, while others, more skeptically minded, date it to the 4th century AD.

The *onager* was technically a very simple but at the same time very powerful machine. Large *onagers* were attended to by a team of eight men and could throw balls up to 80 kilograms, though in most cases the ball weighed 20–30 kilograms (apparently the most popular balls were those weighing one talent, 26.2 kilograms). An *onager* had a sling at the end of an arm—not a "spoon" as is customarily represented in modern films and late-medieval drawings, which were created at a time when these machines must have long been out of use. By hitting a stop beam,[270] the sling pushed the ball to the top point of an arc, giving it additional kinetic energy. The same kind of misunderstanding occurred with reference to the wheels of an *onager*. In reality, no *onager* ever sat on wheels. It could not have had them, because the downward force of recoil would have smashed a wheeled platform to pieces.

The size of the torsion-springs of the *onager*, like that of other torsion-powered machines, was calculated in accordance with the above formula proceeding from the weight of the missile. However, the *onager*, which had one torsion-spring instead of two, could only gather half the power of two-armed machines. That is, if we wanted to build an *onager* for firing a 5-mina ball, the formula should carry the figure 10 minas. In fact, however, reconstructed machines successfully threw stones whose weight considerably exceeded the data calculated in accordance with the formula. Nevertheless, the parameters, calculated according to the formula, allow the use of the machine without overload and, consequently, breakage.

In Latin the word *onager* means "wild donkey." Some authors insist that the name has been kept because of the machine's powerful recoil at the moment the arm hit the stop beam; others, because a donkey, like the *onager*, scatters stones with his hind hoofs when running away from pursuit; yet others believe that the *onager* owes its name to the long squeaking sound it issues, resembling a donkey's "eee-ya-a-a."

At some point between the 1st and the 4th centuries AD, a material alteration occurred in the terminology of throwing machines. Until at least mid-1st century AD the Romans' name for the arrow-firer was *catapulta*, and the Greeks', *oxybeles*. The smallest arrow-firers were called *scorpions*. A stone-projector was called *ballista* by the Romans and *lithobolos* by the Greeks. Now *ballistae* fired bolts only on rare occasions, when it was necessary to secure an extraordinary range of fire. By the 4th century, however, the term *ballista*, as well as its derivatives—such as *arcuballista*, *carroballista*, and *manuballista*—were already used for an arrow-firer.[271] *Ballistae* were no longer used for firing stone balls, and the *onager* became the traditional stone-projector of the period. It is especially clear from the description of a *ballista* and an *onager* by Ammianus Marcellinus; from this description, we can conclude that the *onager* was formally called *scorpion* ("the *scorpion* which is now called *onager*").[272]

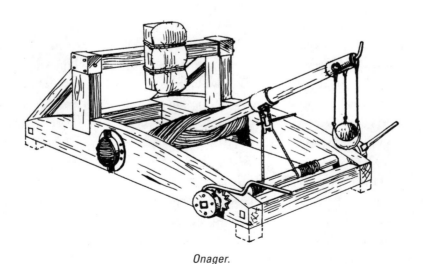

Onager.

150

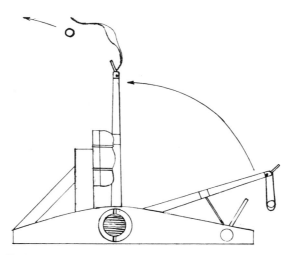

Trajectory followed by the arm when firing the *onager*.

In the opinion of E. W. Marsden, the Roman army from the 1st to the 3rd centuries AD was armed with two types of *ballistae*: arrow-firers with metal frames (*cheiroballistra*) and stone-projectors with old iron-bound frames (they had never been able to build stone-projectors with all-metal frameworks). By the 4th century, stone-projecting *ballistae* had been replaced by *onagers*.[273]

It is even more difficult to gain an understanding of the term *scorpion* and the arrow-firers of the late Empire Period. Originally the term *scorpion* was used for moderate-sized arrow-firers. Then *cheiroballistra* appeared in about AD 100, and *scorpion* was apparently given up, as *cheiroballistra* served its functions much better. Sometimes the latter must have been put on a cart, and then it was called *carroballista*. According to Vegetius, it was *carroballistae* (55 pieces) which each legion was armed with,[274] and probably it was a *carroballista* that we can see on some fragments of the Trojan Column.[275] What we see here is a cart sitting on two wheels, supposedly driven by mules. At the same time the Anonymus Reformer, who wrote his work on problems in the army in the 4th century AD, speaks of a light *ballista* sitting on a four-wheeled cart, driven by a couple of horses.[276] Undoubtedly, this "light *ballista*" and the *carroballista* of Vegetius are one and the same machine. According to the Anonymus Reformer, this "light *ballista*" could change the angle of vertical laying and turn around. The same author mentions one more type of *ballista*, which he calls *ballista fulminalis*.[277] He believes that this *ballista* was especially effective for the defense of fortress walls.

The construction of the *ballista fulminalis* leaves us with more questions than answers. From its description one may presume that it had an all-metal bow and, thus, was not a torsion-powered machine but a big stationary crossbow. E. W. Marsden, however, categorically disagrees with this point of view.[278] Besides, we can sometimes come across one more term, that of *manuballista*. Translated from the Latin, it would mean the same as *cheiroballistra* (translated from Greek)—"hand *ballista*"—and thus the two terms are synonymous. One may meet with the opinion that *manuballistas* were simply hand crossbows. According to Vegetius, however, the term "*scorpions* stood for what we now call *manuballistas*; they were called that because they could inflict death with tiny and thin arrows."[279] Proceeding from this description, *manuballistas* had better be placed in the category of light throwing machines of the *scorpion* type, which conducted fire sitting on a light tripod. The epithet "hand" must have been associated with the idea of "carrying by hand," not with that of "firing while holding in hand." The term *scorpion*, which had lost its original meaning, began to denote a new machine (according to Ammianus Marcellinus, by association with a sticking-up sting), which later was christened the *onager*.[280]

In spite of the popularity enjoyed by throwing machines in Ancient Rome, Greek masters held precedence in this respect, and for a long time provided the Romans with their military engines. Even in the days of Caesar's rule, ready-made throwing machines were often brought from Greece. They were called by the common term *tormentum* by the Romans.

If we take Josephus's word for it, it was quite easy to evade missiles sent by throwing machines. During the siege of Jerusalem, Hebrews making sorties at first managed to elude flying stone-balls,

Shown in this scene from Trajan's Column (Rome) is an arrow-firer mounted on a two-wheeled cart. Probably this is the *carroballista* mentioned by Vegetius. (TC 103-106. C. Cichorius, *Die Reliefs der Traianssäule*, Berlin, 1900. Plate XL. Courtesy of Verlag Walter de Gruyter & Co. GmbH)

which were obvious due to their white color and the singing noise they made while in flight. More-over, scouts sitting on the city towers would warn their warriors by crying out, and the latter would scatter about and drop to the ground. Then the Romans thought of dyeing their stone-balls a dark color; now, it was harder to spot them, and one stone could kill quite a number of Hebrews.[281]

Throwing machines were disassembled before being moved from place to place. Lighter machines, of the *scorpion* and *cheiroballistra* type, were taken apart into two pieces—the machine proper and the prop—so they could be carried by two men only: one would carry the machine, the other, the prop and bolts. As to heavy machines, especially stone-projectors, they had to be taken apart into at least four parts and transferred by carts or ship.

Between AD 100 and 300, every Roman legion had a park of ten *onagers* (one to each co-hort) and 55 *carroballistae*.[282] Each *carroballista* had mules attached to it for transportation and eleven men to attend to it and fire it.[283] Probably the situation in the Roman army was the same in the period of the Early Empire, only at that time, the army was armed with *catapults* and *bal-listae*. At least, even the Praetorian Guard at Claudius's time (AD 41–54) had *catapults* and *bal-listae*.[284] After AD 300, legions were no longer provided with throwing machines; detached legions of *ballistarii* were formed instead.

Throwing artillery was most effective in siege warfare. But while *scorpions* and *cheiroballis-tra* could be used in field battles as well, the *onager* should be considered solely heavy siege ar-tillery, an analogue of a mortar. Because of a plunging trajectory followed by its projectiles, the *onager* was quite useless in a field battle; however, it was indispensable and irreplaceable during a siege, when it was employed for the destruction of fortress walls and structures within them. The besieged used *onagers* to destroy siege towers, throwing machines, and other offensive means employed by the assailants. The *ballista*, too, was mainly used in siege warfare. The besiegers used the *ballista* to demolish the merlons and kill the defenders on the walls, thus neutralizing the fire of the besieged. The latter placed their *ballistae* on the walls and towers, firing at the assailants and their siege machines.

Throwing machines were, in the first place, used for conducting covering fire during an as-sault, filling in a ditch, and bringing up siege engines, as well as during sorties. On rarer occa-sions they were employed for destroying the parapet of a wall, siege and throwing machines, and finally, against individual enemy warriors. Most effective for demolishing fortifications were large-caliber stone-projectors having the caliber of 1 talent (26.2 kg) or 90 minas (39.2 kg). But 30 mina (13.1 kg) caliber stone-projectors were considered to have the broadest range of appli-cations. They could strike off merlons, destroy siege engines, and even be used as anti-personnel weapons. As to the enemy throwing machines, both the besiegers and the besieged used 10 mina (4.4 kg) caliber stone-projectors against them, as a rule.

The number of throwing machines employed during ancient times both by the besiegers and the besieged was very large indeed. For instance, when Scipio Africanus had seized New Carthage in 209 BC, he confiscated 120 very large *catapults*, 281 smaller *catapults*, 23 large and 52 smaller *ballistae*, as well as a great number of large and small *scorpions*.[285]

Practically from the very moment of their invention, efforts were made to use throwing machines in field battles. Phocian General Onomarchus was the first to effectively use them in this function in about 354 BC in a battle against the army of Philip II.[286] Moderate-sized non-torsion-powered stone-projectors called *oxybeles* were placed on the hills on either side of the battlefield. By feigned retreat the Macedonians were lured under the fire of stone-projectors, which disarranged the Macedonian phalanx, and then a counterblow was inflicted, turning Philip's army to flight. However, for a long time to come, restricted mobility and a low rate of fire precluded the possibility of positioning the machines immediately on the battlefield. Hardly having time enough to fire a few volleys, they could be easily captured by the enemy. Therefore, whenever throwing artillery figured in field battles, it was positioned either on almost inaccessible hills or on one of the riverbanks for covering or counteracting enemy attempts at ferrying across the river. This is what Alexander the Great, Philip V, Perseus, and Caesar did. Not until the Roman Empire period did light throwing machines (*scorpion, cheiroballistra*) come to be actively used in field battles.

Throwing machines were undoubtedly utilized on board a ship, too. In the first place, it was done during the siege of a coastal town. Here, throwing machines helped in blockading the enemy harbor, as well as playing a role in demolishing fortifications and supporting a general assault from the sea. The sieges of Tyre and Rhodes are two of the most striking instances of such use of throwing artillery. As to regular naval warfare, the part played by throwing machines was insignificant, due to a low carrying capacity and the relative instability of ancient ships. Large-caliber stone-projectors, which could have caused serious damage to an enemy ship (or even caused it to sink), weighed about 10 tons, which exceeded the tonnage of even the biggest warships of that time. For all that, a certain number of small arrow-firers and stone-projectors could easily be placed on board a ship. They could be very useful at a time when two ships would draw near together in an attempt to board each other.

Based on E. W. Marsden's calculations, apart from normal crew, the *quinquereme* could accommodate 120 members of the boarding team, weighing 9 tons on the average. If circumstances required, the captain could replace some of his marines with throwing machines. For instance, five 3-span *catapults* (*scorpions*, 0.5 tons), two relatively small stone-projectors (2 tons each, thus 4 tons), artillery men, and ammunition (about 1.5 tons) could be housed on the *quinquereme*, leaving room for forty warriors (3 tons).[287]

THE MIDDLE AGES

The question of whether torsion-powered machines existed in the Middle Ages is still open to debate. There is no doubt that in Byzantium, antique torsion-powered arrow-firers were in use until at least the 11th century. In many a Byzantine manuscript we regularly come across quite verisimilar representations of such arrow-firers. Torsion-powered arrow-firers continued in existence later, too. In Europe they were represented by a thoroughly new machine, the *espringal*, and in the Arab world, by the *ziyar* (see p. 158).

As to *onagers*, their existence in the Middle Ages appears extremely doubtful. We have no representation of them up to the 14th century, and then, especially from the 15th century on, we come across them fairly often, all the way up to the 18th century. In these representations most of them have a "spoon"—not a sling, as their ancestors did—which could only weaken the fighting characteristics of the machine. Some representations of the machines are absolutely fantastic—clearly the fruit of an artist's imagination—which have nothing in common with the existing engines. In this connection we might suppose that the authors of these representations reproduced engines, using the descriptions of Vegetius, Ammianus Marcellinus, and other sources, in whose late-medieval re-creations they are most frequently to be found. Not all is clear in the texts of ancient authors; consequently, the reconstructions were far from perfect. The appearance of *onagers* precisely at the time when all throwing machines were already being actively ousted by cannon, too, is indicative of the fact that their popularity was more theoretical than practical. Moreover, we can deduce from a 12th-century military treatise of al-Tarsusi that all the stone-projectors of his time were of the beam-sling type (man-powered ones, or ones with a counterweight), except the arrow-firer *ziyar*, which was torsion-powered. It may be assumed that, as late as the second half of the 6th century, *onagers* began to be actively ousted by man-powered beam-sling machines,[288] and once and for all disappeared not later than the 8th through 9th centuries as a consequence of the appearance of the more effective hybrid (man-powered and with a slight counterweight) beam-sling stone-throwers. It is precisely the representation of beam-sling machines (man-powered ones and ones with a counterweight) that we see in manuscripts until the late Middle Ages.

The only medieval torsion-powered machine, a sufficiently detailed description of which has been preserved to this day, is the *ziyar*. However, despite the fact that Murda al-Tarsusi devotes several pages to the *ziyar* in his treatise, and even includes several drawings of the machine, there is absolutely no clarity about its construction. Judging by what we know, the *ziyar* existed in a number of variations, from relatively small machines to gigantic monsters. According to al-Tarsusi, one of these monsters had a frame with sides measuring more than 5 meters, two

155

Sketches of war machines from Walter de Milemete's manuscript (1326).

torsion-springs made of horsehair and silk, two composite arms, and a huge windlass that was placed separately from the machine. The description of its construction was rather involved; information about all the necessary elements is given, however. The location of the composite arms is most difficult to understand. On carefully reading the description and examining the drawings, one gets the impression that these arms were fixed, horizontally, at their ends to a central vertical beam and, additionally, pushed through the torsion-springs. The latter were fixed at the front and at a distance of two-thirds length away from the central beam to the side ribs of the framework. However, with the arms set in this position, neither the composite construction of the arms nor the torsion power could be used in full measure. Therefore, the machine would clearly be less powerful as compared both to a purely torsion-powered and purely tension-powered one (a great crossbow).[289]

Image of a medieval *onager* in a 15th-century manuscript. Note the spoon in place of a sling.

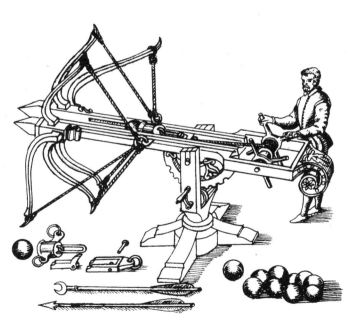

Three-bows great crossbow throwing bolts and stones. According to Ramelli, edition of 1588. This machine was obviously a fruit of the artist's fancy.

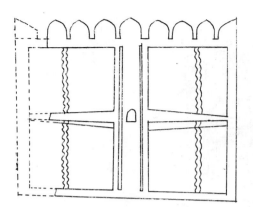
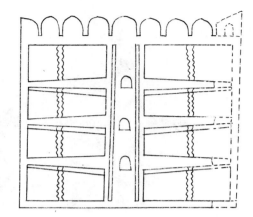

Front view of *ziyars* with one and three bows, according to Murda al-Tarsusi's treatise
(second half of the 12th century).

The throwing machine described by al-Tarsusi must have been invented not long before, and almost certainly was an experimental model, an intermediate version between a great stationary crossbow and a purely torsion-powered machine. Later on, it was undoubtedly improved, as it was used widely enough up to the 15th century. Moreover, it was probably the *ziyar* that served as the prototype of the European *espringal*. *Ziyars* were used to fire not only bolts but pots filled with an incendiary mixture, as well.

Espringal. Flemish manuscript made between 1338 and 1344.
(Ms. Bod. 264, f. 201r, Bodleian Library, Oxford)

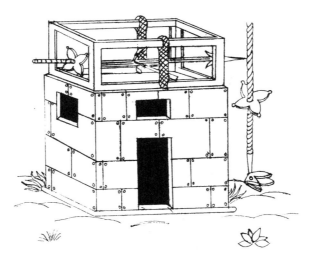

Espringal on top of a tower. According to Valturio, 1453-54.

The existence of a torsion-powered machine called *espringal*[290] (*springald*, *espringale*, etc.) in Medieval Europe has recently been proven by Jean Liebel. The term *espringal* was first found in a French source going back to 1249; it is possible, however, that *espringals* had appeared in Italy about twenty years before that date as a further evolution of Arabian *ziyars*. *Espringals* were especially popular in the first half of the 14th century, but as early as the 1380s, they began to be supplanted by cannon, and by the early 15th century, they were universally given up. The last instance of the use of *espringals* was registered in 1431.

The construction of *espringals* was based on two 70- to 80-centimeter-long arms inserted into torsion-springs. The latter were about 1.3 meters long, 16 centimeters in diameter, and weighing 7 kilograms. The torsion-springs (ropes woven of horsehair) were simply bound over a wooden framework.[291] An *espringal* was wound by means of a long screw and a windlass situated at the butt-end. The framework was about 2 meters long, 1.5 meters high, and 1.5 meters wide (see plate 33). Together with a screw pulled out to its maximum, the length was 4 meters, and the width with the arms at full swing was 3 meters. An *espringal* was usually put over a gate or on a tower, and the presumable range of fire from the tower reached 180 meters.

An *espringal* usually threw 70- to 80-centimeter-long and 4- to 5-centimeter-thick bolts. The latter were provided with 2 to 3 "feathers" made of brass or tinned iron. Such bolts weighed about 1.4 kilograms. There were, however, bigger bolts available for bigger *espringals*. The heads of the bolts had one to several spikes. A chest of bolt-heads presumably for *espringals* was found in the course of archaeological excavations at the Papal Palace in Avignon. There were also flat

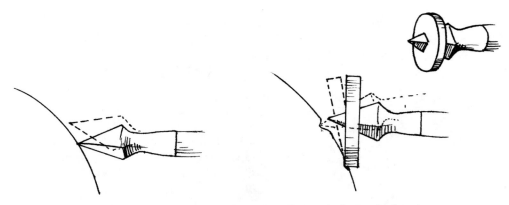

The operation of a bolt (ordinary one or one with an iron ring) when hitting plate armor.

iron rings there, which J. Liebel supposes to have been used to prevent the bolt from sliding along curved plate armor when it struck.

There were undoubtedly great crossbows in the Middle Ages, too—big stationary crossbows firing long and heavy bolts and wound by means of a windlass (see plate 34). Several big 1.2- to 2-meter-long bolts for such crossbows have been found, dating back to the 12th and 13th centuries. Some of them have a simple construction, while others feature a composite one. While *espringals* were practically used only by the defense, great crossbows were intensively used by both sides. For instance, Christine de Pisan presumes that the defense was to have two or three *espringals* and six great crossbows (*arbalète à tour*) while the assailants needed thirty great crossbows and not a single *espringal* (see Table 1). The defenders put great crossbows over a gate and on towers, as a rule. It is presumed that the wide embrasures we see in some castles were meant for these great crossbows and *espringals*. Since a bolt fired from a great crossbow or *espringal* could easily break not only any armor but any portable shield, there were not many daredevils willing to attack a gate defended by such arrow-firers. There is also evidence of great crossbows having been mounted on board the French and Venetian ships of the 13th century. At sea, great crossbows had an obvious advantage over *espringals*, as they were not as affected by dampness.

The exact origination of great crossbows has not yet been established. As was said above, non-torsion-powered machines (*gastraphetes*, *oxybeles*) disappeared about 240 BC, and the Roman army only used torsion-powered machines. Perhaps the first evidence of the use of tension-powered *ballistae* (not counting the mysterious *ballista fulminalis* of the Anonymus Reformer) was a machine described by Procopius (6th century AD). According to the author:

Belisarius put on his towers machines which are called *ballistra*. These machines look like a bow; they have a wooden, hollowed-out horn jutting at the bottom (rising up); it moves freely and lies on a straight iron bar. When they want to fire this machine at the enemy, they force the wooden parts, which are the butt-ends of the bow, to bend, by drawing them with the help of a short rope; into the hollow they put an arrow half as long as the arrows shot from ordinary bows, but four times as thick. Unlike ordinary arrows, they have no feathers but have thin wooden plates attached to them, and in appearance they are exactly like an arrow. A sharp head is added to it, a very big one, not corresponding to its thickness; men standing on either side draw a string, making great efforts and using some gadgets, and then the hollowed horn, moving forward, juts out and fires an arrow with such force that its flight is at least double as long as that of an arrow shot from an ordinary bow; hitting a tree or a piece of rock it easily breaks it through. The machine is called as it is, because it fires very well indeed. He puts other machines capable of throwing stones on top the fortifications; they resemble slings and are called *onagers*.[292]

The above description of a throwing machine does not conform to a torsion-powered construction. Procopius obviously describes a whole bow, but not two arms injected into torsion-springs. Besides, the machine has some wooden horn, which moves freely along an iron bar.[293] On the whole, the description makes one think of great crossbows with a slider, which were probably used in Medieval Russia.[294] True, in Medieval Russia, their representations are dated to a far later time; but they were possibly copied from an earlier source.

Non-torsion-powered arrow-firers were extensively used in the Arab world as well. In various sources we come across such terms as *zanburak*, *charkh*, or *jarkh* (Pers: *charkh*; Arab: *jarkh*; Turk: *carh*), *aqqar*, *qaws al-lawab*, *qaws al-rijl*, *qaws al-rikab*, and others. True, it is no easy job to understand which construction corresponds to each of these terms. *Qaws al-rijl*, first mentioned in 881, was probably a most primitive hand crossbow, but it must have been modified later on and adopted to firing "eggs" filled with an incendiary mixture. *Qaws al-rikab* was also a hand crossbow, with the additional feature of a stirrup. Meanwhile, the Fatimids' *qaws al-lawab* must have already been a big stationary crossbow, because bolts used for it weighed 5 Syrian ratles (over 9 kilograms). *Aqqar*, as compared with the torsion-powered *ziyar*, was less powerful; it, too, was spanned by means of a windlass. Its bolt weighed but one third of a kilogram; that is, it was not much heavier than a bolt shot by a *qaws al-rikab*. Therefore, *aqqar* should be considered the most powerful hand crossbow. *Charkh* was probably a stationary fortress crossbow, which could

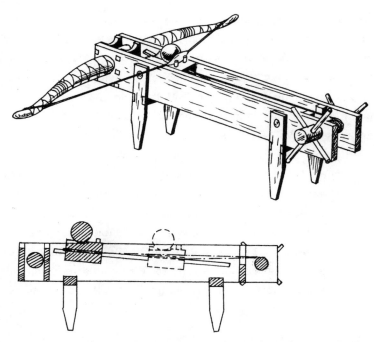

Reconstruction of a big stationary crossbow with a slide block according to representations in Russian chronicles. The principle on which the slide block worked is shown below. Drawing according to the reconstruction made by V. E. Abramov and A. N. Kirpichnikov.

shoot either bolts (up to 0.5 kilogram), stones, or incendiary "eggs." At the same time, its size was not very big. We know that following the seizure of one of the fortresses, the crossbowmen, who had attended to the *charkhs* and inflicted heavy losses to the army of Zangi (the ruler of Iran, 1084–1146), were made to hang the crossbows on their necks and their thumbs were cut off. A *zanburak* was evidently the heaviest model of a stationary crossbow, and was mainly employed in siege warfare.

It is possible that the Byzantine crossbow *tzagra*, which appeared here in the 11th century, takes its origin from the *charkh* and the *zanburak*. Prior to this time, in the 10th and 11th centuries, we hear of the existence in Byzantium of crossbows called *toxoballistra*. They must have been heavy machines propped on a strong framework and firing both bolts and stones.[295]

Seventh-century Europe saw the appearance of a machine of an entirely new construction; later on it was given the name *perrière*, by which we will refer to it in the future.[296] The motherland of these machines is China, where they had long been in use by that time. The question of how they had found their way to Europe is still open to discussion. They may have done so by means of Avar invaders descended from the Juan-Juan who came from northwestern China. In the Byzantine Empire, such machines became known some time in the second half of the 6th century; the first reliable mention of them refers to the siege of Thessaloniki by the Avar-Slavic army in 597:

> These *petraboles* were tetragonal and rested on broad bases, tapering to narrow extremities. Attached to them were thick cylinders well clad in iron at the ends, and there were nailed to them timbers like beams from a large house. These timbers had slings from the back and from the front strong ropes by which, pulling down and releasing the sling, they propel the stones up high and with a large noise . . . They also covered these tetragonal petraboles with boards on three sides so that those inside shooting them might not be wounded by arrows shot from the walls. And since one of these, with its boards, had been burned to a cinder by a flaming arrow, they carried away the machines. On the following day they again brought these *petraboles* covered with freshly skinned hides . . . [297]

We sometimes see representations of similar hybrids of great crossbows and *onagers* in late medieval treatises. It is probably the body of such a machine that stands in the Castel Sant'Angelo in Rome. However, most probably the latter is a recent attempt at reconstructing the machine, which is corroborated by the metal bow this machine has. It is extremely doubtful that such machines should have really existed. Author's photograph.

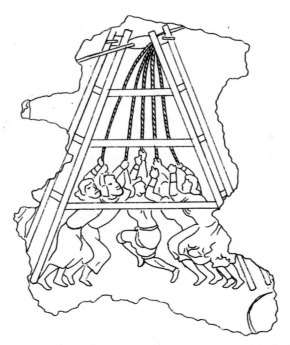

One of the earliest images of a man-powered beam-sling engine. A crew of pullers are
concealed inside a wooden structure which probably was covered with boards
and hides. Palace in Penjikent, the 7th–8th centuries.

The term *petrobolos* (*petraboles*) literally means "stone-projector," and was used in the
Byzantine Empire to describe any stone-throwing machine. Later on, these man-powered stone-
throwers would acquire the names *manganon*, *magganika*, and *manganikon*, terms which in later
times were used to describe beam-sling stone-throwers with counterweights. Various types of
man-powered stone-throwers (*manganon*) had their own names, too. For instance, *lambdarea* was
the name of a machine having a frame shaped like the letter lambda (Λ); *tetrareai*—a heavy
throwing machine having a four-sided frame; and *alakatia*—a light stone-thrower with one pillar
for a prop, which could be placed on a wheeled cart and conduct all-around fire.[298]

Based on a comparison with the Byzantine *manganikon*, the Arabs gave the name *manjaniq*
to various types of beam-sling stone-throwers. One may come across *manjaniq* being described as
"The Long Haired One," "The Bride," or "Mother's Head." All these names are associated with
the numerous ropes that were tied to one of the lever-ends and thus with man-powered stone-
throwers. *Manjaniq*, however, was a common term for all beam-sling stone-throwing machines,
and when versions with a counterweight appeared, this term was used to refer to them, as well.

Al-Tarsusi speaks of four types of man-powered *manjaniqs*: "Arabian," "Turkish," "Frankish" (European), and a small-sized *luba* (*lu'ab*). The Arabian *manjaniq* was the most accurate and reliable; the Turkish *manjaniq* was the least labor- and material-consuming in construction; and the Frankish type sits somewhere in between the Arabian and Turkish as far as its construction is concerned. Al-Tarsusi believes the *luba* to be too well known to describe it in detail; it can be gathered from his words that it was a light stone-thrower on one supporting pole which could easily turn from side to side. Man-powered *manjaniqs* continued in use in the Arab world up to the 15th century, in spite of the appearance of more powerful machines with a counterweight, and cannon.[299] Easily built, reliable, and sufficiently accurate in firing, they were the favorite weapons in siege warfare, loved equally by the assailants and the assailed.

There was also a stone-projector called *arradah* in the Arab world; this term is still debated intensely today. There are attempts at identifying it with torsion-powered machines akin to *onager* or *carroballista*. In my opinion, the *arradah* was rather a light man-powered stone-thrower on one supporting pillar, which in construction was very similar to the *luba* mentioned by al-Tarsusi.[300] We first come across mention of the use of the *arradah* in 630 at the siege of the Arabian town of Taif. In the succeeding centuries, the *arradah* becomes one of the most widely used Arab stone-throwing machines: it appears in the wars led by the Crusaders, in fighting activities in North Africa, and in the south of the Iberian Peninsula. *Arradahs* were mostly used by the defense, which put them on top of the walls or towers. We know that in 838, the throwing machines of the Abbasid Caliph al-Mutasim were mounted on carts and attended to by four men. However, I do not think we ought to deduce from this that *arradahs* were torsion-powered machines analogous to the antique *carroballista*. We should bear in mind that in China, similar small

Frames of an "Arabian," "Turkish," and "Frankish" *manjaniq* according to Murda al-Tarsusi's treatise (the second half of the 12th century). There is a beam-sling by the frame of the "Frankish" engine.

beam-sling stone-throwers were also mounted on wheeled carts, and low-powered engines could be served by four pullers, as well. Neither should we be misled by such a poetic description of *arradah* as "kicking donkey" or by the etymology of the term meaning "wild ass" in Aramaic. Undoubtedly, we can find an analogy with *onager* (Lat: "wild donkey") in both cases; however, association with a kicking ass equally fits all mono-arm throwing machines (both *onagers* and beam-sling ones), and the old term could have been simply carried over to a new machine. Numerous examples could be cited with reference to many military engines everywhere.

There are two more arguments in favor of the opinion that *arradahs* were man-powered beam-sling stone-throwing machines: First, the *arradah* is known to require a great deal of rope, which is characteristic only of man-powered stone-throwers; and second, these light engines could be easily reoriented to different targets. The latter can clearly be compared with the Chinese man-powered stone-throwers on one supporting pillar (the so-called "whirlwind stone-throwers"), whose casting arm could easily swing 360 degrees and conduct all-around fire.

There were different versions of *arradah*, as we read in Fakhr al-Din's treatises of the 13th century called *Art of War*. He mentions a simple or single *arradah* (*arradah-i yak ruy*), a rotating *arradah* (*arradah-i gardan*), a stationary *arradah* (*arradah-i khufta*), a fast-shooting *arradah* (*arradah-i rawan*) and a big *arradah* (*arradah-i giran*). In Spain the term *arradah* was transformed into *algar-rada* (from *al-arradah*).[301]

Depending on the method of fastening pulling ropes and the construction of the framework, *perrière* could be divided into several types. Pulling ropes could be fastened to the horizontal or vertical crossbeams. Each type had its advantages and disadvantages. In the case of a horizontal fastening, all the pulling ropes were fastened to the square beam at the same height so that it would be easier to exert the same effort on each rope at a given moment; this undoubtedly affected the accuracy of fire. Obviously, this construction made it easier to gather a larger team of pulling men around the machine. In case of vertical fastening, the effect on each rope was not simultaneous. Thus, common effort here took somewhat longer, and this probably allowed heavier projectiles to be cast. The framework of a *perrière* could have one supporting pillar, two props, or the shape of a truncated pyramid. The structure with a framework of the first type was lighter and more mobile, but less powerful; the third type was the most powerful one, and allowed the use of cover for the team of pullers; the second type was intermediate between the first and the third. In general, protection of a team of pullers was always of much importance for a *perrière*. The relatively low range of fire of the machine (100–150 meters) caused it to be placed near fortress walls within the range of fire from bows and crossbows. Consequently, the losses among the pullers were great. That is why in medieval representations we can often see a group of archers covering the work of pulling men. Probably, larger wooden shields called

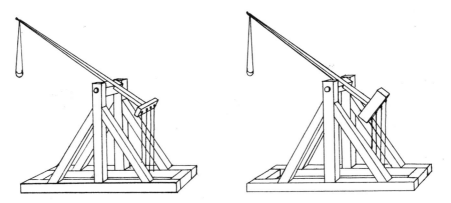

Types of *perrière* (man-powered beam-sling engine): with a horizontal and vertical fastening of ropes.

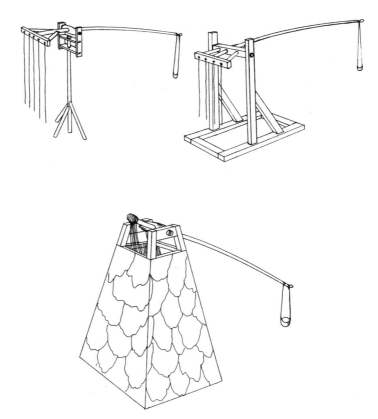

Types of *perrière*, having frames of different constructions.

mantlets were also employed for the protection of the pullers. If the framework of the machine had the shape of a truncated pyramid, it was often covered with wet hides and boards, which not only protected the team but also defended the structure from incendiary missiles. It was possible, however, to use prisoners and peasants from nearby villages in the capacity of pullers, as well, which is what the Mongols did.

At the beginning of the 8th century, in the course of Arab-Byzantine wars, further improvements were made in man-powered stone-throwers. In addition to pulling ropes, they were now provided with a slight counterweight. The resultant hybrid machine was considerably more powerful and more accurate than an ordinary man-powered engine. As distinct from a simple man-powered stone-projector, whose ball weighed from 1 to 30 kilograms as a rule (occasionally, it might weigh up to 60 kilograms), the hybrid machine could easily cast balls weighing 50 kilograms and more.

A hybrid throwing machine involving both a fixed counterweight and a team of rope-pullers.
"The Siege of Antioch" in William of Tyre's *History of Outremer*, 13th century.
(Bibliothèque municipale de Lyon, Ms. 828, f.33r)

As a result of further modification of a hybrid engine, the 12th century saw a completely new machine whose moving power was by counterweight alone, lowered by the force of gravity; the muscular strength of men was not used at all. We find the earliest description of this machine in al-Tarsusi, who wrote his work for Saladin sometime between 1169 and 1193. The machine he called the "Persian" *manjaniq* had a framework and a casting beam analogous to that of the "Turkish" *manjaniq*, only there was a network filled with stones—instead of ropes—that was fastened to the shorter end of the beam. As the framework of the "Turkish" *manjaniq* was not intended to have a dropping counterweight, a hole had to be dug near the framework so that the counterweight would keep clear of the ground.

But the most surprising thing was the presence of the crossbow called a *jarkh*, placed at the foot of the framework. None of the later constructions of Arabian or European machines of this type had a crossbow. Based on the recommendation that the crossbow should fire precisely at the moment the casting beam is released, we can suppose that the string of the crossbow was connected with the counterweight, and the shot from the crossbow made it possible to overcome the inertia of its first moment of movement. It is also possible that the string of the crossbow was connected with the trigger mechanism (which was not yet perfect enough for such a powerful machine), and the shot from the crossbow allowed a quick release of the casting beam. The opinion that they first fired a bolt at the enemy from a crossbow and then cast a stone from a sling seems extremely doubtful, as the two machines had distinct functions, and there is no sense in combining them in one structure. On the whole, one is tempted to assume that al-Tarsusi's "Persian" *manjaniq*, like the *ziyar*, was as yet an experimental model. Only its further modification gave the

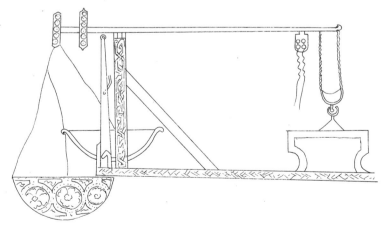

"Persian" *manjaniq* according to Murda al-Tarsusi's treatise (the second half of the 12th century).

world a really reliable and powerful machine with a counterweight. Based on al-Tarsusi's evidence, this *manjaniq* was set in motion by one single man and cast stones weighing 50 ratles (over 90 kilograms).

By the 13th century, the names of different types of *manjaniqs* were already changing. At this time in the Arab world, they distinguished the "West European" *manjaniq* (*franji*), the "Western Islamic" one (*maghribi*), the "black bull like" (*qarabugha*), and the "devilish" *manjaniq* (*shaytani*). Only the last one was man-powered; the rest were operated with counterweights.[302]

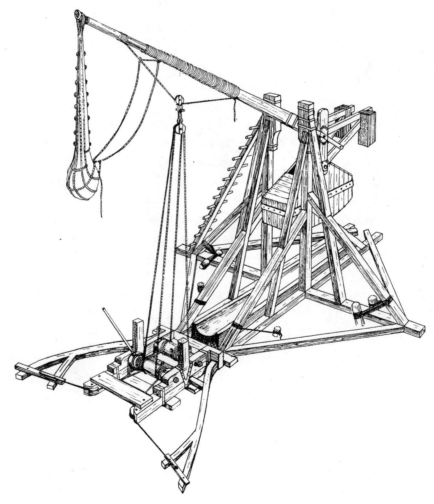

Trebuchet.

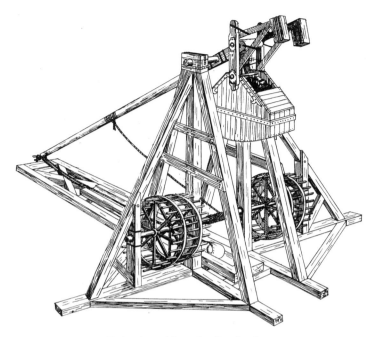

Trebuchet with squirrel's wheels.

In Europe such engines were called *trebuchet*, and they had spread over the continent by the late 12th century. The term "trabuchellus" was first registered in 1189, and then, as "trabuchus" in 1199, both times in Italy. It is more difficult to establish the actual time the weapon appeared in the Byzantine Empire. The first reliable evidence of the use of machines with counterweights refers to the sixties of the 12th century. However, even in the 11th century we can find some indirect evidence indicative of the presence of machines with a counterweight; for instance, the casting of stones weighing 100 kilograms and more, or the use of certain huge new machines capable of breaking walls. Thus, we cannot exclude the possibility of beam-sling engines with a counterweight first appearing in Byzantium in the 11th century.

The *trebuchet* consists of a supporting framework with vertical posts joined by an axle. Fixed on the axle is the casting beam. Fastened to the longer end of the beam is a sling into which a ball was pushed. A massive counterweight was fastened to the shorter end of the beam. Here, too, there sometimes were shock absorbers meant to decrease the shaking of the machine when shooting. The sling was a long rope with a leather or net pocket halfway along its length. One end of the rope was fixed fast to the end of the beam, while the other ended in a loop thrown on a metal cog at the end of the beam. (There was another system, too, which released the sling by means of a rein.)

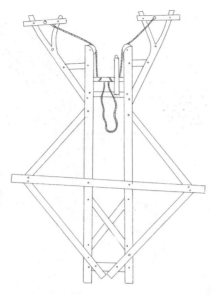

The base of the frame of a *trebuchet*. Sketch book of Villard de Honnecourt, c. 1250.

In this drawing of the early 14th century one can see a *trebuchet*
positioned behind a wall to defend the approaches to a gate. Note that the
beam-sling of this engine is made from several wooden beams tied together.
(In situ Palazzo Pubblico, Siena, David Nicolle)

To load beam-sling machines, the longer end of the beam was pulled down to the ground by means of a rope; in the case of a *trebuchet*, a windlass was used. It was fixed fast in this position by means of a trigger mechanism, and a ball was put into the sling, placed in a special directing groove.

A shot was fired in the following way: In the case of a *perrière*, specially trained people raised their hands to hold the ropes and, making long strides, tried to pull the ropes simultaneously and with equal effort. In rainy weather and with a large number of pulling ropes, it took great skill to keep hold of the ropes and prevent their tangling. The number of pullers usually amounted to dozens, or even hundreds. In some sources we even read of a thousand or more pullers, but this is hardly probable; it is hard to imagine such a large number of people gathered in a comparatively small area, pulling simultaneously, and still managing to prevent the ropes from tangling. As a result of force being applied to the pulling ropes, the casting beam curved and accumulated energy. Then the trigger mechanism was engaged, and the ball flew at the enemy. The exact construction

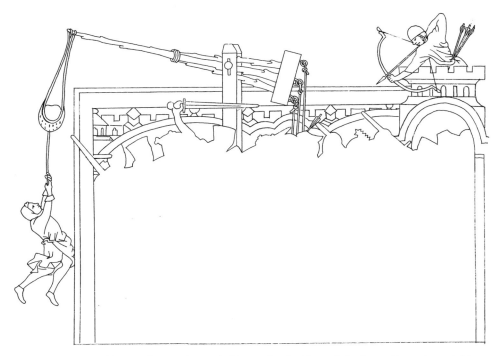

Man-powered beam-sling engine probably provided with a relatively small counterweight being used in a siege. For correcting shots and increasing the power of the engine the operator is bringing all his weight to bear on the rope joined to the sling. "Saul's army destroying Nahash," French Maciejowski Bible, about 1240.

Man-powered beam-sling engines being used in both attack and defense. Note the operators who are correcting the shots. (*Codice Griego Matritense de Skylitzes*, Bib. Nac., Madrid, f. 151b)

of the trigger mechanism is unknown. Possibly the length of the tie of the casting beam was calculated so as to cause the pulling ropes enclosing the thin curving end of the beam to slip from it on their own when the curve had reached the necessary degree. In some medieval miniatures one can often see an operator hanging down from a sling. Maybe he was trying to maintain his hold on the sling up to the last moment, supplying a resilient beam with additional energy by bringing the entire weight of his body to bear on the sling.

In the case of a *trebuchet*, the operator released the trigger mechanism and the counterweight sped downwards, propelled by the force of gravity. The longer end of the beam soared upwards respectively. The sling would tear itself off the chute in which it lay, outstripping the lifting of the beam, and would lash around the end of the beam, adding acceleration to the projectile. Depending on the construction of the sling, its end either slid off the cog on the beam or was pulled by a tie; then, the sling would unfold and release the projectile.

The counterweight of a *trebuchet* could be fixed or movable (i.e., joined to the end of the beam by means of an axle). A *trebuchet* with a movable counterweight (see plate 35) is somewhat more powerful as the trajectory of the dropping counterweight is steeper, which guarantees the largest possible vertical component of the impulse vector. In addition, these machines were more lasting and had a higher rate of fire. Therefore, beginning with the 13th century, *trebuchets* with a movable counterweight were more readily built, while ones having a fixed counterweight were only

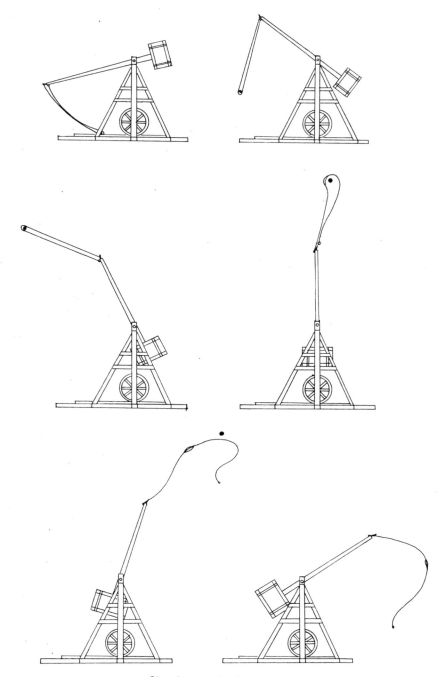

Shooting a *trebuchet*.

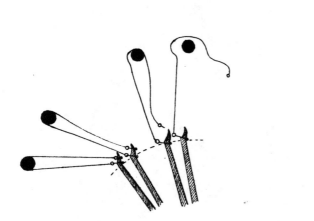 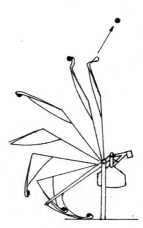

Releasing a sling, two versions.

used when it was necessary to build the simplest machine at the shortest notice. Even more progressive were *trebuchets* having two symmetrical movable counterweights, which in medieval chronicles appear under different names (*biffa*, *brigola*, *couillard*). Apart from its other advantages, these engines were the easiest to transfer and assemble.

In the late 13th century, Giles of Rome described three types of *trebuchet* which differed in the method of fixing a counterweight: *trabucium* had a firmly fixed counterweight; *biffa*, a mobile one; and *tripantium* was a hybrid model, having one part of the counterweight fixed and the other movable.

Naturally, the heavier the counterweight, the farther the projectile flies. It was calculated for an ideal *trebuchet* that a 100-kilogram projectile with a counterweight of 4 tons will fly 154

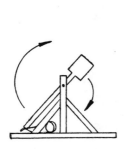 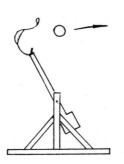 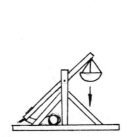 

The principles on which a *trebuchet* with a fixed (left), and one with a movable (right) counterweight worked.

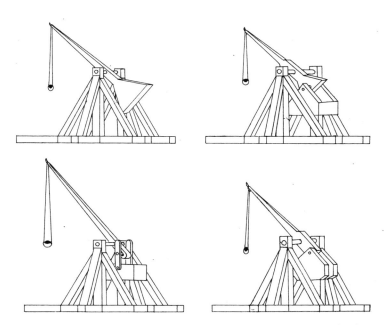

Types of *trebuchet*. The upper row: a machine with a fixed counterweight (left) and one with a fixed and a movable counterweight (right). The bottom row: a *trebuchet* with a movable counterweight (left) and with two symmetrically suspended movable counterweights (right).

meters; 6 tons—209 meters; and 8 tons—277 meters. However, the range of the flight of a projectile depended not only on the weight of the counterweight but also on the shape of the projectile, and even on the length and the curve of the cog to which the sling was fixed. The latter parameters determined the moment of the unfolding of the sling and, accordingly, the trajectory and the range of the flight of a projectile. A short sling resulted in a steeper trajectory of the flight of a projectile, while a long one resulted in a more grazing one. Modern experiments show that a *trebuchet* is capable of casting projectiles without a sling at all; however, the range and rate of the flight of a projectile are twice as low. The weight of a *trebuchet* is no less impressive: the net weight of a big machine is about 6 to 7 tons, and one with a counterweight could weigh between 17 and 21 tons.

The *trebuchet* was cocked by means of two windlasses, or a couple of squirrel's wheels. The latter method was especially convenient and effective, as the team's own weight and the inertia of the revolving wheels were both employed together. A couple of squirrel's wheels allowed a 10-ton counterweight to be lifted in five to six minutes. The team of a big *trebuchet* consisted of ten to twelve men as a rule.

Siege of the English frontier town of Carlisle by the Scotch led by Robert the Bruce in 1315. The siege lasted ten days. On the fifth day the Scotch mounted a throwing machine in order to hurl stones at the wall and gates of the town. The machine did little harm as the defenders actively fired back from stone-throwers and *espringals*. It is just this moment in the siege that we see in the picture. One of the operators is releasing the sling of a *trebuchet* working a mallet, while the other has already been fatally wounded by either a javelin or a bolt shot from an arrow-firer. On the tenth day of unavailing attempts at seizing the town, the Scotch lifted the siege and retired, leaving all their siege engines behind.

All kinds of objects were cast from a *trebuchet*. For breaching the walls of a fortress, they used stone or lead balls of a regular spherical form and equal size, necessary to ensure precision in hitting the same spot of a wall, over and over. For hitting targets and causing damage inside a fortress, crude stones of any shape could be used as well. There were peculiar explosive shells called "beehives," which were made of clay and stuffed with cobblestones. On impact with an obstacle of any sort, the beehive would break up and the cobblestones would scatter in different directions. Incendiary projectiles were also employed, including barrels of resin and pots filled with specific mixtures (see Chapter 20, "Incendiary Weapons in Siege Warfare" p. 189).

Arabs were especially fond of such projectiles, even using pots containing poisonous snakes and scorpions. The ditch in front of a fortress could be filled by throwing in barrels or sacks filled with earth. A peculiar bacteriological weapon aimed at spreading epidemic in a besieged town consisted of casting dead bodies of men and animals. In 1422 the army of Prince Coribut, in the service of the Grand Duke of Lithuania, threw a few corpses and two thousand carts of manure into the besieged town of Carolstein, which provoked an epidemic there.[303] Modern experiments have proven that casting the dead body of a cow by means of a *trebuchet* is quite possible. To weaken the morale of the enemy, they would use the decapitated heads of prisoners, intercepted messengers, and traitors. For instance, Froissart tells us that at the siege of the fortress of Auberoche in 1335, the French intercepted an English messenger and, providing him with letters, sent him back by means of a *trebuchet*. It was assumed that when the cries had died away, the messenger "had arrived."

If we compare the characteristics of *perrière* and *trebuchet*, we shall see that the former weapon undoubtedly has a higher rate of fire, while the latter is much more powerful, and capable of throwing heavier projectiles. The *perrière*'s range of fire was 100 to 150 meters, and it

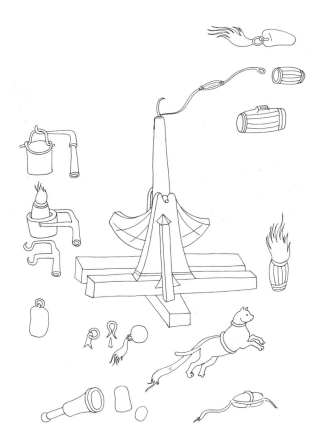

Trebuchet and various missiles for it. Drawing from Mariano Taccola's book, mid-15th century.

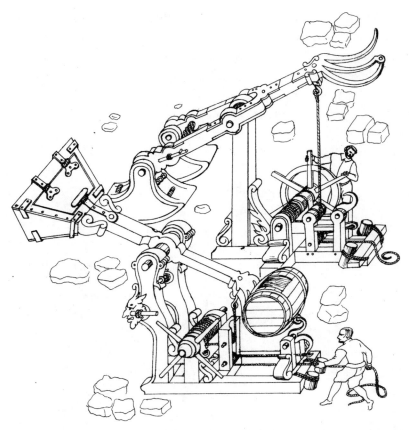

Trebuchets casting barrels of earth for filling in a ditch. From Ramelli, edition of 1588. The representation of the engines is fairly inaccurate—the details are disproportionate. Besides, one man could never have loaded such an engine. The curved forks at the turn of the beam look doubtful, too—all war *trebuchets* had a sling. Probably these machines existed only in the author's imagination.

fired at a rate of 3 to 4 shots a minute. *Trebuchets* could cast 100-kilogram balls to a distance of 200 meters at a rate of two shots an hour. Modern reconstructors have arrived at the conclusion that the *trebuchet* was considerably more accurate than the *perrière*, and its projectile was certain to hit a 5-by-5-square-meter area when shot to a maximum distance. A serious drawback in the *perrière* was that it needed a large number of pullers. Given a relatively low range of fire, the machines had to be brought close to the enemy, and the losses among the pullers who found themselves within the range of enemy bows and crossbows were colossal. Accordingly, a hybrid of *perrière* and *trebuchet* was developed—an engine having a light counterweight on which a few tension ropes were fixed. It was more powerful than an original *perrière*, and had a considerably higher rate of fire than a *trebuchet*.

A few words should be said about two throwing machines whose existence in reality is highly improbable. Both machines employed the energy of a resilient board. The first—an arrow-firer—was a vertical framework with a hole made in its central post for inserting an arrow. A system of resilient boards was fixed beyond this post, also vertically. The upper loose end was drawn off by means of a windlass. On its release the boards straightened themselves and struck hard against the tang of the arrow. Judging by its representations, the machine often had a mechanism for vertical laying. In addition, some specimens might have been capable of changing the direction of horizontal laying, as their central part revolved with regard to the stationary framework (see plate 36). Repeating models of this machine may have existed, capable of firing a volley of several bolts.

Another stone-projector was called the *Einarm* (Germ: "one arm"). The simplest model of the *Einarm* was just one resilient beam, which was curved by means of ropes tied with a windlass. At the end of the resilient beam there was a "spoon" into which they put a stone. However,

A dead horse being thrown into a besieged town with the help of a *trebuchet*.
From Leonardo da Vinci's (1452–1519) drawing.

Missiles for throwing machines, the Golden Horde, 14th–15th centuries,
Author's photograph.

the projectile in the "spoon" seems to play but a secondary part. In the pictures, the *Einarm* are also provided with a sling fastened to the end of the beam. Such a machine could fire two projectiles at a time—one in the "spoon" and one in the sling—the destructive effect of the projectile shot from the sling being more powerful. An *Einarm* of more complicated construction used not only the energy of the deformation of the beam itself, but also the energy accumulated by two springs, which were so cunningly tied with the casting beam that, when the windlass was drawn, they curved also—but in the opposite direction. The casting beam and both springs could be made of steel. Such a machine must have been more powerful than its predecessor.

The earliest images of both machines appear in editions of the second half of the 15th and the beginning of the 16th centuries. By this time, the age of throwing machines was over; they had already been replaced by cannon. Besides, the expediency of such machines is extremely

A fairly schematic drawing of an arrow-firer using the energy of a resilient board.
From Vegetius, edition of 1607.

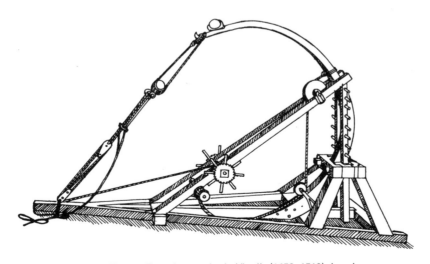

Einarm. From Leonardo da Vinci's (1452–1519) drawing.

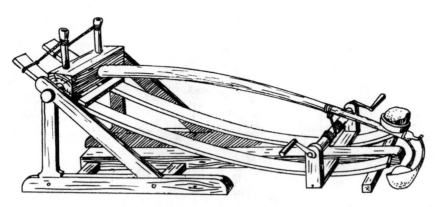

A more complex *Einarm* with two steel springs. From a drawing in a German manuscript of the second half of the 15th century. In all probability, this engine, like the one shown in the preceding drawing, was no more than a fruit of the author's fancy.

questionable: any big stationary crossbow is more powerful than the arrow-firer described above.[304] As to the *trebuchet* and *perrière*, the former is more powerful and the latter has a higher rate of fire than the *Einarm* stone-projector. Therefore, both these engines were in all probability no more than a fantasy of late-medieval authors, and were probably never actually used.

In the Middle Ages, throwing machines were used only at sieges. Field artillery as had existed in the Roman army was no more, so the rate of fire was of minor importance. The main objective was to destroy enemy fortifications, and the *trebuchet* was the best weapon for this purpose. No wonder that it was the most popular throwing machine in Europe in the Middle Ages.

From the 12th century on, the number of throwing machines used at sieges substantially increased, and they were now deployed in batteries. Thus, at the siege of Acre in 1191, the Crusaders employed about 300 machines. At the siege of Rouen in 1174, a battery of throwing machines worked around the clock, and attending personnel worked in eight-hour shifts. Like cannon, many throwing machines were given fancy nicknames in the Middle Ages, such as "Fighting Wolf," "Wild Cat," "Malvoisin," "Vicar," "Throwing Bull," "Queen," "Lady," and others. In 1480, during the defense of Rhodes against the Turks, the defenders built a *trebuchet* and called it Tribute, evidently in answer to the Turkish demand that a tribute be paid to them.

Toward the 16th century, throwing machines began to lose their military significance. Fire artillery at that time already surpassed throwing machines both in the range of fire and destructive power. However, as in case of the crossbow, the life of throwing machines had not come to an end. During World War I, after several centuries of oblivion, various countries effectively used fairly small throwing machines resembling the antique *onager* or *ballista* (true, the torsion-spring was replaced

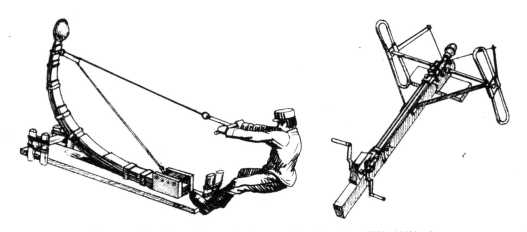

Two samples of French grenade-throwers from the time of World War I.

by powerful springs) in trench warfare; they were used for launching high explosive shells and incendiary missiles into enemy trenches. Equally interesting is the attempt, made by Britain in 1940, to arm their militia with antique throwing machines. They were designed for throwing incendiary bombs at German tanks. However, the machines that were built proved much worse than the antique ones—their range of fire was but a quarter of what was needed, and they had to be given up.

Attempts at building historical reconstructions of antique and medieval throwing machines have been made since the mid-19th century. The best known reconstructors from the second half of the 19th and early 20th centuries were Viollet-le-Duc, General E. Schramm, and

Russian grenade-thrower from the time of World War I.

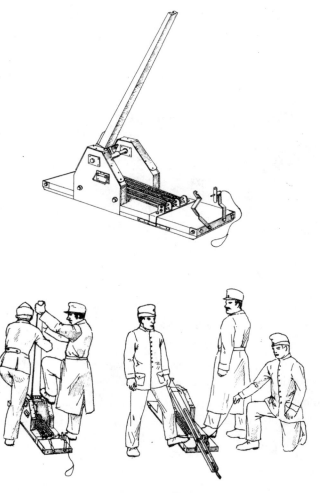

Dutch grenade-thrower, 1916.

R. Payne-Gallwey. For the past twenty years, we have observed a new wave of interest in throwing machines. Today, numerous throwing machines are reconstructed, and their characteristics are examined in France, Britain, and Denmark.

A few words should be said now about the classification of throwing machines. In the first place, they can be classified depending on the type of energy they employ. Accordingly, all the machines can be divided into two large groups (see scheme, plate section): *neuroballistic* (from Gr: neuron—"tendon, nerve") machines, which use the energy of resilient bodies or twisted ropes, and *baroballistic* (from Gr: baros—"weight, heaviness") machines, using counter-weights or the muscular force of men.

Neuroballistic machines fall into the category of torsion-powered machines that use the energy resulting from twisting ropes, and tension-powered ones, which use the energy of wood tension. *Baroballistic machines* are represented by engines with a counterweight and man-power. Both torsion- and tension-powered machines can be double-armed and mono-armed. And finally, the machines can be divided into stone-projectors and arrow-firers, depending on the type of the projectile. The Greek name for a stone-projector was *palintone*, and for an arrow-firer, *euthytone*.

Throwing machines can also be classified as engines of either grazing or plunging fire. In the machines of grazing effect, the casting of projectiles was done at point-blank range, or at an elevation angle of 20 degrees (e.g., *gastraphetes, scorpion*); and in the machines of plunging effect, at elevation angles of 20 through 45 degrees (e.g., *onager, trebuchet*). Double-armed torsion-powered arrow-firers achieved a maximum range of fire at elevation angles of 30 degrees; stone-projectors, at 45 degrees.

Table 4. European throwing machines of Antiquity and Middle Ages.

Antiquity	Middle Ages
Neuroballistic:	*Neuroballistic:*
Tension-powered:	Tension-powered:
gastraphetes	*great crossbow*
oxybeles	*Einarm*
Torsion-powered:	Torsion-powered:
oxybeles	*espringal*
lithobolos	*Baroballistic*
ballista	*trebuchet*
scorpion	*perrière*
cheiroballistra	
onager	

If we compare the destructive effect of balls launched from throwing machines and those fired from cannon, we find that in order to achieve the same effect, the balls of a throwing machine must be twice as heavy as those of a cannon. This is connected with a lower initial speed of balls launched by a throwing machine. Calculations done by P. D. L'vovskii[305] show that mono-armed throwing machines (e.g., *onager*) were better fit for firing heavy missiles at low initial speeds, while double-armed ones (e.g., *ballista*) proved more effective when firing smaller missiles, but at higher initial speeds.

A few more words should be said about the range of fire of throwing machines. The authors of ancient and medieval sources seldom cite exact data about the range of fire. In most cases, if they mention it at all, they either do it in an obscure way or with considerable exaggeration, which, on the whole, is typical of the Middle Ages. The information, imparted by Josephus, that *scorpions* (*onagers?*) and *ballistae* could cast "stones weighing talents at a distance of two stadiums [about 370 meters] and more,"[306] could be accepted as one of the fairly rare reliable pieces of intelligence. This range of fire can be deemed possible, although the weight of balls hardly exceeded one talent. Approximately the same range of fire (about 370 meters) is named by Konrad Kyeser for *espringals*, which also is quite realistic, although successful reproduction of this has not yet taken place.

Modern reconstruction shows that the maximum range of fire for an *espringal* was probably 130 to 180 meters. As a rule, we have only inconsistent data about the range of fire based on testing machines reconstructed in the 19th and 20th centuries. On the average, the reconstruction of *onagers* shows the range of fire to be about 300 meters for 2- to 3.5-kilogram balls; that of *trebuchet*—about 250 meters for 56-kilogram balls, and 175 meters for 130-kilogram balls; that of *perrière*, 100 to 150 meters; the range of fire of the aforementioned arrow-firer using the energy of a resilient board is shown as 145 meters. We should take into account, however, that some of these tests were only conducted to find out a maximum range of fire (kind of a "sport record"), while others were aimed at discovering the real fighting capacity at which they can destroy fortifications. We should also bear in mind that the range of fire depends, to a considerable extent, on the size and weight of a machine, the weight and shape of a missile, the extent of twisting of torsion-springs, the elevation angle (of vertical laying), and, finally, on weather conditions. To get an exact estimation, it would be necessary to reconstruct all machines and test them in similar conditions, using standardized missiles. No experiments of this kind have so far been made, and as to data obtained from testing individually reconstructed engines, we should be very cautious in making comparisons. To achieve effectiveness in demolishing fortifications in the course of siege operations, stone-projectors of all types were hardly placed farther than 150 to 200 meters from the wall.

TWENTY

INCENDIARY WEAPONS IN SIEGE WARFARE

Incendiary weapons have been used in siege warfare since the ancient times. The oldest evidence of the use of incendiary weapons goes back to the Middle Kingdom of Egypt (21st–18th centuries BC). Assyrian reliefs of the 8th and 7th centuries BC from Khoyundjik already show a vast assortment of incendiary weapons. One can see in them warriors setting fire to the gate of a besieged town by means of torches, archers shooting incendiary arrows to provoke fire in the town, as well as the besieged throwing burning torches down onto siege engines. In one of the reliefs of the time of Ashurbanipal, we can also discern a more advanced weapon—an incendiary spear. Incendiary weapons are mentioned in the Bible ("He has also prepared for Himself deadly weapons; He makes His arrows fiery shafts" [307]).

The Greeks and the Romans were already making use of the broadest variety of incendiary weapons. Aeneas Tacticus wrote in mid-4th century BC, recommending the kindling of fierce fire "which cannot be put out at all, doing it in the following way. If you want to set fire to something belonging to the enemy, take and set fire to pots of resin, sulphur, tow, pieces of incense, pine-tree sawdust."[308]

In general, resin, sulphur, and tow seemed to be the most common incendiary means. For instance, they were actively used at the siege of Plataea (429–427 BC), Tyre (332 BC), Ambracia (189 BC), and Jotapata (AD 68). The defenders of Durazzo in 1108 thought of a curious method of using a mixture of resin and sulphur. They blew this burning mixture into the faces of the assailants, burning quite a number of Norman beards in this way.[309]

A fairly complex incendiary machine, also using resin and sulphur, was used by the Boeotians in 424 BC against the Athenians concealed in Delium. In the evidence of Thucydides,[310] the machine was invented by the Boeotians and looked like a huge log of wood, sawed lengthwise, hollowed out inside, and restored to its original image. A copper cauldron was suspended with chains to one end of the resultant tube, and bellows were fastened to the other end. An iron tube passed from the bellows right into the cauldron. The log was bound with iron at the end. The entire structure moved on carts. The Boeotians filled the kettle with coal, sulphur, and resin, set this mixture on fire, and brought the machine up to the wooden fortifications of Delium (see plate 37). Vigorously blowing the bellows, the Boeotians kindled an enormous flame and burned down the fortifications of the Athenians.

Fire was most frequently used against siege engines and wooden fortifications. In addition, incendiary weapons were also resorted to for setting fire to a town. Aeneas Tacticus recommends fighting enemy siege *tortoises* by means of wooden chocks with sharp iron teeth. The chocks were coated with "strongly inflammatory substances" (probably resin, tow, and sulphur, as usual) and thrown down, from poles pulled off a wall, onto the engines brought up by the enemy. Owing to the spiked teeth, these firing projectiles did not roll down from the roof of a *tortoise* but lingered on it, spreading fire. Burning bunches of brushwood lowered onto enemy siege machines with the help of ropes were apparently considered an expedient—though less effective—method by Aeneas Tacticus.[311] Polyaenus says that *tortoises* were also set on fire by means of melted lead, which was poured down the wall from copper vessels.[312]

Incendiary arrows were certainly the oldest incendiary weapons. They were used from the earliest times to the late Middle Ages, until arrows eventually dropped out of use. The English army is known to have used incendiary arrows until at least 1599, and even as late as 1860 such arrows were used by the Chinese against French troops.[313] Not far from the arrowhead, the shaft was usually bound with a piece of tow soaked in oil or resin and set on fire. Such arrows, especially when there was a great number of them, spelled serious danger for any wooden structure— fortifications, dwelling houses, and siege engines alike.

More sophisticated incendiary arrows were divided by Roman historians into *malleolus* and *falarica*. A *malleolus* was an ordinary arrow to whose cane shaft a little box of iron wire was fastened, a little below the head. The box was filled with an incendiary mixture, a match was inserted into it, and it was set on fire. Ammianus Marcellinus informs us that "if we shoot the arrow carefully from a loosely drawn bow—a match goes out in case of a swift flight—and it pierces into something, it will flame up; sprays of water make the flame grow brighter, and there is no other way to put it out but by throwing sand on it."[314] A *falarica*, according to Vegetius, "resembles a spear and is provided with a hard iron head; between the tube of the head and the shaft it is coated with sulphur, asphalt, and resin, and bound with tow soaked in oil which is called inflammatory

Incendiary bolt, 15th or 16th centuries. Author's photograph.

[petroleum?]; such a spear, thrown by a *ballista*, breaks a cover, pierces into a tree, while still burning, and has more than once set this tower-like machine [siege tower] on fire."[315]

Apparently, a *falarica* was not necessarily shot from throwing machines; it could be hurled by hand, as we read in Livy:

> The head was 3 feet [about 90 centimeters] long and could go both through a shield and a man. But even apart from it, a *falarica* was a terrible weapon even when it stuck in the shield and did not touch the body: its central part had been set on fire before shooting, and the flame grew brighter by force of motion; so a soldier had to throw away the shield and face further blows with his breast unprotected.[316]

A *falarica* had a round shaft which became a tetrahedron near the head, where it was coated with a flammable substance. Incendiary spears continued to be used throughout the Middle Ages. They are mentioned (probably for the last time) at the siege of Bristol in 1643.[317]

Apart from incendiary missiles, birds were used to bring fire into a besieged town. Ignited tender was tied to the birds, which were then set free; they would fly into their nests in a town, thus setting the latter on fire. The best-known instance of such a siege is the annihilation by fire of the fortress of Iskorosten by Princess Olga in 946. The same ruse was resorted to by Harald in the mid-11th century at the seizure of a Sicilian city. These may be no more than myths, but as we know, there is often a grain of truth in every fairy tale.

It was relatively easy to burn down wooden fortifications by means of incendiary missiles or by building a campfire at the foot of a wall—but stone walls were also subject to fire at times. While it took longer and required a higher temperature, the stones would crack with heat, and the walls would eventually break down. A simple campfire at the foot of a stone wall was not effective, as the flames that touched the wall were of a lower temperature, and the fire would usually be extinguished before any real damage had been done. Therefore, they used clay pots filled with cut charcoal for the demolition of a stone wall. The pots were fastened with iron hoops, and an opening of about 2 centimeters in diameter was made in their bottom. An iron tube was inserted into the opening through which air was supplied by the bellows. Burning charcoal heated the air to a very high temperature, which could relatively quickly lead to the demolition of a wall—especially if the latter had been moistened with vinegar, urine, or some other caustic liquid.[318]

Beginning probably in the first centuries AD, incendiary mixtures began to contain petroleum. In the Middle East, close to oil fields (e.g., in Iraq and Iran), petroleum may have been used before that time.[319] The Byzantines called crude oil (and compositions based on it) "Median Fire."

Demolition of a wall by fire. Drawing from Anonymus Byzantine's book.

Ammianus Marcellinus (4th century AD) says that "Median Oil" was made in the following way: ordinary oil was placed on a certain kind of grass and then mixed with a thick oil common in Persia, called *naphtha* (meaning petroleum). According to him, as an arrow smeared with "Median Oil" pierced into something, it would "flame up," and the flame could only be put out with earth.[320]

In time, the term *naphtha* became conventional. If initially it denoted a composition that actually contained petroleum, in the 12th through 14th centuries, the words "throwing *naphtha*" came to denote compositions that didn't even smell of petroleum.

The most well-known treatise on incendiary compositions is "Liber ignium ad comburendos hostes" by a certain Marcus Graecus. It is not known when it was written; it only appeared in Europe around the end of the 13th or the beginning of the 14th century, possibly as a translation from Arabic. The recipes of incendiary compositions listed in the treatise are not marked by much variety. The principal pyrotechnic substances of the time are as follows:

- resinous tree, flax-tow (tow);
- resins, pitch, gum, rosin;

- turpentine;
- linseed oil; Ethiopian, aniseed, juniper, and "brick" oils;
- sheep fat (melted);
- sulphur ("white," "red," and "brilliant") and "sulphuric oil";
- egg yolks, "egg-oil";
- quicklime;
- petroleum;
- balsams;
- painting putty;
- wax;
- pigeon and sheep droppings.

Most recipes of the time recommended heating all the components until a homogeneous paste was formed. It was a long process because a maximum density was to be achieved—throwing a semiliquid mixture was difficult indeed.

Let us now examine the best-known incendiary weapon of the Middle Ages: *Greek Fire*. Probably no other military invention has been so shrouded in mystery or provoked such disputes as *Greek Fire*. It should be noted that the term itself only appeared during the Crusades, and then came to be used in Europe. In Byzantium—the motherland of *Greek Fire*—the term was never used, as the Byzantines called themselves Romans, and the epithet "Greek" sounded almost abusive to them. In Muslim countries, *Greek Fire*, as well as other incendiary compositions, was called *naft* (*naphtha*).

The invention of *Greek Fire* is attributed to the Greek architect, Callinicus. It took place in the 7th century, and already in the year 673 an Arab fleet was burned down with the help of *Greek Fire*. Few inventions have made such a strong impression on their contemporaries. Chroniclers note that the terrific fire turned stones and iron to dust, burned on water, and certainly annihilated all living things. For a long time *Greek Fire* remained a fearful secret weapon of Byzantium. Emperor Leo wrote in the 9th century:[321]

> We possess various weapons, both old and new, to destroy enemy ships and men fighting on board them. Such a weapon is fire prepared for siphons from which it is hurled with thunderous noise and smoke, burning down ships at which we direct it . . . Also, place, at the front on the bow [of a ship], a siphon in bronze to hurl fire at the enemies. Above the siphon, make a timber platform surrounded by an oak parapet. There place warriors to fight and shoot arrows . . .

You must also prepare pots filled with incendiary mixtures which, breaking in falling down, are to set a ship on fire. You must also make use of small hand-siphons, which we make and which warriors keep beyond iron shields: they contain fire, which is hurled into enemy's faces. You can also throw, by means of the *manganikon*, liquid burning resin and other compositions you have prepared.

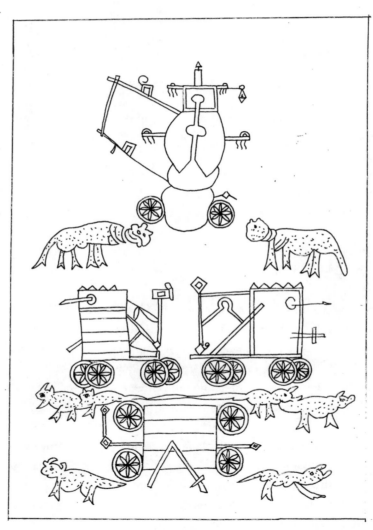

Various war machines from a Byzantine treatise of the late 10th century.
Seen above is possibly a device for throwing *Greek Fire*.

In her *Alexiad*, Anna Comnena says that, when equipping the navy for a campaign against the people of Pisa, the emperor ordered that siphons placed on the bow be mounted like heads of wild beasts, as though hurling fire. "The barbarians were horror-stricken by the fire which they did not know and which, unlike that burning by nature upwards, was thrown at objects as the thrower wished, now downward, now to different sides . . ."

A vivid depiction of the effect of *Greek Fire* is given by Liudprand, describing the destruction of the Kievan Prince Igor's fleet in 941:

> The Tsar was informed that fifteen broken *chelandrias* [Byzantine ships with *Greek Fire*], which had been left behind for their decrepitude, still remained. On hearing this, the Tsar hurriedly summoned skilled shipbuilders and said to them: "Try to repair the remaining *chelandrias* without delay, but do it so that the fire would be placed not only on the bow, where it is thrown from, but also on the stern and on both sides." *Chelandrias* having been built in conformity with the Tsar's order, the latter orders that they advance against Igor. When the ships had departed, and Igor saw them at sea, he ordered his warriors to take them prisoner but not to kill the warriors . . . At the same time stormy weather had changed to calm and the Greeks were able to throw fire. Stepping into the middle, they hurled fire all around them. Seeing this, the Russians began throwing themselves into the water, preferring drowning to being burned alive. Some of them, donned in heavy armor and carrying their shields, swam to the shore, but many sank to the bottom while swimming, and none of them had saved themselves except those who had reached the shore . . .

Several important conclusions can be drawn from the above quotations. First, *Greek Fire* came from siphons with "thunderous noise and smoke." Second, the fire could be thrown both by big stationary siphons and small hand ones. Third, a most primitive device securing horizontal and vertical firing was used for big siphons. Fourth, *Greek Fire* could only be employed in calm weather; in case of a strong wind or storm, there was probably a great danger that the men themselves would be burned.

Greek Fire, also known as "liquid," "sea," "live fire," and "Roman Fire," was first used in naval battles. However, it soon became widespread in siege warfare as well. It was used for burning down siege engines, setting fire to wooden fortifications and gates, as well as by fire-throwing weapons in close combat. This is how it is described in Emperor Leo's *Taktika*: "The other device of the small siphons discharged by hand from behind iron shields, which are called hand-siphons and have recently been manufactured in our dominions. For these can throw the prepared fire into the faces of the enemy."[322]

The image of a hand-siphon is to be found in the book of Anonymus Byzantine (10th century AD). In the picture we can see a warrior standing on a boarding-bridge, throwing fire at the defenders on the wall. The construction of hand-siphons with *Greek Fire* must have been similar to that of big siphons mounted on ships. The latter were undoubtedly breech-loading, as it was practically impossible to load a tube at the muzzle when extended beyond the side of a ship.

For a long time the Byzantines managed to keep the secret of *Greek Fire* to themselves. Their allies had often asked Byzantine emperors to help them with *Greek Fire*. For instance, in 886, Pope Stephen V asked Emperor Leo to send him fire-carrying *chelandrias* to fight the Arabs. Hugh of Provence addressed the same request to Emperor Romanus in 941. Similar requests on the part of the Khazars, Hungarians, Russians, and other northern people are mentioned by Constantine VII Porphyrogenitus.

The Muslims were the first to use *Greek Fire* after the Byzantines. Its use by the Arabs was registered in 835 and 844, but some incendiary weapons had been used by them as early as the 7th century. By the time of the Crusades they had mastered *Greek Fire* and used it against the Crusaders more than once. The Saracens resorted to *Greek Fire* at the sieges of Nicaea, Marathus,

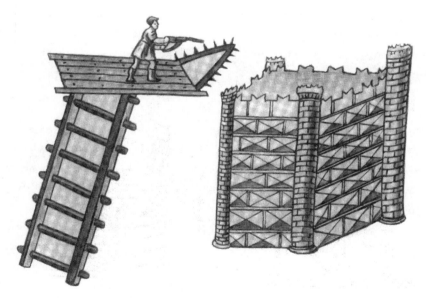

Hurling *Greek Fire* from a hand-siphon. Drawing from Anonymus Byzantine's book.

The warriors of a *naffatun* ("naphtha troops"). The horseman and both infantrymen are wearing special fireproof clothes. The armament of the first infantryman and the horseman is not quite clear. The last infantryman has a pot of *naphtha* in his right hand and a firearm called *midfa* in the left. Although the treatise is dated the second half of the 14th century, this drawing was probably added by a copyist later, in the 15th century.

and Acre, as well as at other places. At the siege of Acre in 1191, a Muslim from Damascus offered the defenders his own recipe for *Greek Fire*, which proved effective where other mixtures had been unsuccessful—that is, against the siege towers of the Crusaders. Fire born of this mixture soared with a tremendous roar through all the platforms, and the Franks, who had almost deemed themselves victorious, were panic-stricken. The above proves that the composition of *Greek Fire* was not constant; it was different at different times, and much depended on the individual circumstances.

Special units for throwing *Greek Fire* were formed in Muslim armies. They were called *naffatun* ("*naphtha* troops") and were attached to a corps of archers. Besides operating big apparatuses with incendiary mixtures, these units were armed with small pots of *naphtha*, which they cast at the enemy from a short distance. Pots for incendiary mixtures were made of burned clay, glass, tree bark, leather, paper, and metal. They were ignited by means of one or more matches. For self-protection soldiers soaked their clothes in vinegar, or fish-glue, or covered it with a layer of talc or brick dust.[323]

A hollow clay ball, the Golden Horde, 14th–15th centuries. Balls like this were stuffed
with incendiary or explosive mixture, ignited and cast from a throwing machine.
Note the hole for a match (bottom, right). Author's photograph.

Greek Fire did not reach Western Europe until after the first Crusade, early in the 12th century. Geoffrey V of Anjou was probably the first to use it in 1151. Greek Fire was also used by the Tatar-Mongols in the 13th century; on Giovanni de Plan Carpin's evidence: ". . . if they cannot take the fortification, they throw Greek Fire on it."

The composition of Greek Fire remains a subject of dispute even today. There are two main versions. According to one,[324] the base of the mixture was petroleum; sulphur, resin, and other components, which might include quicklime, were added to the former as "thickeners." This mixture was projected by means of a common pump, and was either ignited at the exit, or ignited spontaneously on its impact with water (owing to a violent reaction of quicklime to water); or, the mixture was heated in a hermetic copper vessel, from which it escaped under the pressure of the air, supercharged by bellows. The mixture was then ignited by a torch outside.

The other version[325] has saltpeter as the base of Greek Fire. The supporters of this version assume that the composition of Greek Fire invariably included saltpeter (KNO_3) and also sulphur, resin, and oil. Saltpeter was the main component, which caused a violent reaction to take place in the siphon. The burning mixture was then thrown out by itself under the pressure of burning gases.

Among other recipes, Marcus Graecus gives the recipe of Greek Fire (§ 26):

You will make *Greek Fire* in this way. Take live sulphur, tartar, sarcocolla, and pitch, sal coctum, petroleum oil, and common oil. Boil all these well together. Then immerse it in tow and set it on fire. If you like, you can pour it out through a funnel as we said above. Then kindle the fire which is not extinguished except by urine, vinegar, or sand.

It was the "sal coctum" that was the stumbling stone. The partisans of the second version believed it was saltpeter, while the supporters of the first insisted that it was common salt (NaCl) which was added so that the flame would be yellow and looked "hotter."

Marcus Graecus offers one more recipe for preparing *Greek Fire*. The recipe has only been preserved in the Munich copy of the manuscript. It contains various components (classa, galbanum, serapinum pitch, oil of bricks, alkitran, pigeon dung, distilled oil of turpentine, oil of sulphur, and liquid pitch), which were boiled and distilled. Petroleum is mentioned, but there is not a word about saltpeter.

At the same time, Marcus Graecus provides several recipes where saltpeter is successfully used. These are the so-called recipes for "flying fire":

§ 12. Note there are two compositions of fire flying in the air. This is the first. Take 1 part of colophonium and as much native sulphur, 6 parts of saltpeter. After finely powdering, dissolve in linseed oil or in laurel oil, which is better. Then put into a reed or hollow wood and light it. It flies away suddenly to whatever place you wish and burns up everything.

§ 13. The second kind of flying fire is made in this way. Take 1 lb. of native sulphur, 2 lbs. of linden or willow charcoal, 6 lbs. of saltpeter, which three things are very finely powdered on a marble slab. Then put as much powder as desired into a case to make flying fire or thunder. Note: The case for flying fire should be narrow and long and filled with well-pressed powder. The case for making thunder should be short and thick and half filled with the said powder and at each end strongly bound with iron wire.

§ 33. Another fire flying in the air is made from saltpeter and sulphur and vine or willow charcoal, which are mixed together and put into a paper container and lighted; it suddenly flies into the air. And note that for 1 part of sulphur there should be taken 3 parts of charcoal and for 1 part of charcoal 3 parts of saltpeter. [326]

As we can see, the second and third recipes are a description of powder-like mixtures containing different quantities of saltpeter, sulphur, and coal, while the first one contains oil as well. Nowhere is there any mention of throwing projectiles by means of these powder-like mixtures, so it is not yet a firearm. It is well known that powder dissolved in oil or petroleum possesses less prominent explosive properties, and the process of burning is longer. Upon ignition, this mixture may shoot from the tube, producing a long jet of flame. The partisans of the saltpeter base of *Greek Fire* believe that it is this circumstance that led to a long burning jet being thrown out. While the burning component of powder was coal, that of *Greek Fire* was oil or petroleum. The fact that the fire soared out with "thunderous noise and smoke" supports the opinion that the burning process was violent, resembling the burning of powder. Saltpeter was also included in the composition of *Greek Fire* by many medieval authors, such as Leonardo da Vinci, Baptista Porta, and Blaise de Vigenère.[327] They all lived much later, however, when *Greek Fire* had long been ousted by powder.

It could help this dispute if we knew the exact time saltpeter appeared in Europe. However, this is not so simple; some authors believe that saltpeter was described as far back as Pliny, and was known in antiquity, or at least before the Middle Ages. Others contend that refined saltpeter appeared in Europe, as well as in Muslim countries, as late as 1225, and was not used in mixtures until about 1250.[328] Two facts support the latter theory: the lack of available deposits of saltpeter in most European countries, and the high cost of saltpeter, even as late as the second half of the 14th century.

As to quicklime, it does not seem to have been a necessary component, but could have easily been contained in some mixtures. With its violent reaction to water, quicklime raises the temperature of the mixture, and on impact, can cause blindness or severe burns. In general, quicklime has been used since olden days and has often been used in siege warfare.

Summing up, we should note that the question of the composition of *Greek Fire* remains open. Full-scale investigations of different compositions in devices of varying constructions could help in answering it. For all that, it does not seem worthwhile to look for a single recipe for *Greek Fire* that was common to all mixtures. Its composition was not constant, and varied during different periods according to the objective. As we know, *Greek Fire* need not be necessarily thrown from siphons; it could be cast by hand in pots and by throwing machines as well. Pots for casting *Greek Fire* were usually made of clay. The contents were thrown out by shock and ignited. At the siege of Montreuil-en-Bellay in 1147, the incendiary mixture is known to have been prepared as follows:

[Geoffrey Plantagenet] ordered an iron jar, tied with iron bands and hanging from a strong chain, to be filled with the oil of nuts and the seeds of cannabis, and flax, and the openings of the jar to be sealed with a suitable iron strip, firmly locked. Moreover, he ordered the filled jar to be placed in a heated furnace for a long time until the whole thing glowed with over-great heat, so that the oil bubbling inside should boil. Having first cooled the chain by throwing water over it, it was taken out again, fixed to the arm of a mangonel, and with great force and care, while it was alight, was thrown by the engineers at the strong beams of the breaches. It was expelled by the impact and a fire was made by the discharged matter. Moreover, the overflowing oil joined the balls of fire, supplying food for the flames. The licking flames, belching in an extraordinary increase, burned three houses and hardly allowed men to escape the fire.[329]

This composition contained neither petroleum nor saltpeter, so it is hard to tell whether we could accurately call it *Greek Fire*. In fact, it was just hot oil igniting from any source of fire. As to the composition of an incendiary missile, which al-Tarsusi recommended launching from *manjaniq*, it contained petroleum, too, apart from various resins, pure sulphur, and dolphins' and goats' kidney fat. The recipe for its preparation was similar to the one described above: mix up

A 13th–14th-century hollow clay ball found at the excavations in Kazan (Russia). Such balls were stuffed with an incendiary or explosive mixture and ignited with the help of a match (we can see the aperture for a match on the right). Author's photograph.

all the ingredients, heat the mixture to the boiling point, then put it into a clay pot and cast it from a *manjaniq*. Al-Tarsusi promises that such a mixture would burn anything in its path and that nothing could extinguish the flames. But again, it is not clear whether or not this mixture could truly be called *Greek Fire*.

In time, the composition of *Greek Fire* came to contain coal and saltpeter (if the latter had not been part of it initially). The process of trial and error revealed the main ingredients which, if mixed in the correct proportions, later formed black powder: saltpeter, sulphur, and coal. The other ingredients were gradually given up, and the transformation from *Greek Fire* to powder-like mixtures took place. However, because of insufficient chemical purity of saltpeter and a different ratio of the components, these mixtures were not powder proper as yet; that is, they only had one property of black powder—they burned fast—but they still lacked the necessary explosive properties. It was not until the late 13th and early 14th centuries that pyrotechnics achieved a sufficient purity of components and the correct weight ratio. Black powder had arrived, with firearms following in its wake.

Mixtures were sometimes created which evolved into poisonous gases. In the 13th century at the siege of Beaucaire, during a war with the Albigenses, the defenders threw a sack full of sulphur, tow, and smoldering coals down from a wall. As the mixture burned, an asphyxiating smoke was formed, and the assailants had to discontinue the storm. In the early 15th century, Konrad Kyeser recommended using a poisonous mixture containing sulphur, tar, and horses' hoofs.[330] Thus, chemical warfare, as well as biological (throwing the bodies of dead animals and manure over into a besieged fortress), has its roots a long way back.

To complete our examination of incendiary weapons, we cannot fail to mention *fire wheels*—hoops bound with tow and soaked in pitch until they grew "as thick as a leg." The wheels were then set on fire and rolled along, sowing fire and creating a smoke screen. The time of their first appearance is unknown. They were used during the Crusade to the Baltic lands in the 13th century, and also used much later at the siege of Malta in 1565, when many a Turk was burned with their help.

With the invention of powder, wheels came to be used in another way, too. An explosive wheel was used to make a breach in a stockade or a wattle-fence, which was difficult to fire at with cannon. A powder charge was fastened to a common wheel, which was then tied to a stockade and a match was ignited. The force of a shock wave caused the wheel to make a wide breach in the stockade.

Fire is a terrible and effective weapon, always capable of inspiring awe in battle. Pouring water on it was, naturally, the most frequent way of putting out fire. The besieged often put barrels of water on the walls, using the water to put out fires, or diving into the barrels to save them-

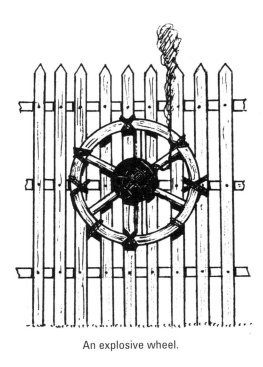

An explosive wheel.

selves if their clothing caught on fire during battle. However, not every fire could be put out with water. For example, it was impossible to extinguish a fire caused by incendiary mixtures made of oil or petroleum; instead, sand or earth was used for that purpose. Aeneas Tacticus also recommended using vinegar for putting out fire caused by strong incendiary weapons, because "it is not so easy to kindle it anew in that case. And it is even better to moisten these spots with vinegar in advance because then fire could not hurt them."[331]

Marcus Graecus (§ 11) says that inextinguishable fire could be put out with four substances: strong vinegar, stale urine, sand, or thick felt thrice soaked in vinegar and dried up. We know that in the 14th century the Venetians used wool soaked in vinegar for protecting their ships from *Greek Fire*.[332] Vinegar was only slightly more effective than water, and it's not clear why such strong faith was placed in its powers during antiquity and the Middle Ages. Maybe at that time vinegar contained some salts which, as the vinegar evaporated, formed a film on the surface, preventing further burning. This view is substantiated by Aeneas Tacticus, who recommends moistening surfaces with vinegar in advance. Alum was also often used to protect siege machines; wooden structures saturated with alum were harder to set on fire.[333]

• TWENTY-ONE •

GUNPOWDER AND SIEGE CANNON

In 15th-century manuscripts and later, the honor of inventing powder and firearms is usually ascribed to the mysterious alchemist, wizard, or monk, Berthold Schwartz, who allegedly lived in the 13th or 14th centuries and was of German, Danish, or Greek descent. However, this has long been proven to be no more than a legend.

The invention of the first recipe of powder in Europe is credited to Roger Bacon. While this took place around the middle of the 13th century, it is remarkable that the recipe had been codified and was not unraveled until the early 20th century. The composition of Roger Bacon's powder was still fairly different from the ideal (see Table 5), and was designed for incendiary mixtures rather than for throwing projectiles. Better adapted for using in firearms was the powder proposed by Albertus Magnus twenty-five years after Roger Bacon's discovery. The quantity of saltpeter used, as in Marcus Graecus's recipe, was still too low as compared with the ideal composition. As one can see in the table, however, powder of this composition (containing 50 to 70 percent saltpeter) was widespread even in the 16th and 17th centuries; it was only toward the end of the 17th century that its composition was firmly established as 75:10:15 (saltpeter, sulphur, coal). In general, a lowered quantity of saltpeter was characteristic of large cannon. Until about the end of the 15th century, it was sometimes recommended that some useless—but necessary, in the view of alchemists—substances, such as mercury, arsenic, camphor, and amber, be added to the powder.

The first reliable[334] mention of cannon in Christian Europe goes back to 1326, when the decision was made in Florence to prepare "iron bullets and cannon made of metal" (*palloctas ferreas et cannones de metallo*) for the defense of castles and villages.[335] That year saw the first representation of cannon, which we find in Walter de Milemete's treatise (see plate 32). In the drawing we see a warrior firing an arrow (bolt) from a strange-looking cannon resembling a vase. Strange though it may seem, nothing is said about the cannon in the treatise.

Table 5. Composition of gunpowder at different times.[336]

Source	% of Saltpeter	% of Sulphur	% of Coal
Roger Bacon, c. 1260	41.2	29.4	29.4
Albertus Magnus, c. 1275	66.7	11.1	22.2
Marcus Graecus, c. 1300	66.7	11.1	22.2
English (Arderne), c. 1350	66.7	11.1	22.2
Nürnberg, 1382	66.6	16.7	16.7
Montauban, c. 1400	71.0	12.9	16.1
German, 1400	71.0	12.9	16.1
Konrad Kyeser, c. 1400	75.0	12.5	12.5
Burgundy, c. 1413	71.5	21.4	7.1
German, 1546 Large guns Medium guns Mortars	 50.0 66.7 83.4	 33.3 20.0 8.3	 16.7 13.3 8.3
German, 1555	66.7	22.2	11.1
Swedish, 1560	66.6	16.7	16.7
French, 1598	75.0	12.5	12.5
English, 1647	66.6	16.7	16.7
German, 1649 Large guns Muskets Pistols	 66.8–70.0 72.5–75.5 78.7–85.6	 16.6–14.0 13.0–11.2 9.4–8.5	 16.6–16.0 14.5–13.3 11.9–5.9
Prussian, 1800	75.0	10.0	15.0

Source	% of Saltpeter	% of Sulphur	% of Coal
Most countries of Europe, America, and China, 1895 (cannon and hand firearms)	75.0	10.0	15.0
The ideal composition calculated according to a chemical equation	74.6	11.9	13.5

For a long time many questions arose in connection with the vaselike shape of Walter de Milemete's weapon, as well as whether an arrow could even function as a projectile. What if the weapon should blow up while shooting? Was it possible to charge a gun with an arrow without powder gases escaping? Questions gave rise to doubts: Did the weapon ever exist? And *could* it even exist in reality, or was it merely the fruit of an artist's imagination?

To find the answers to these questions, British researchers at the Royal Armories reconstructed Walter de Milemete's weapon in 1999 and conducted test shootings.[337] The results showed that the bore of the barrel did not conform to the outer appearance of the weapon, but instead, was cylindrical in shape. Thus, there was no threat of the cannon blowing up, as the loading chamber had very thick walls.

In theory the arrow could be put into the gun in two ways: either together with the feathering, or only with the end of a shaft. In the latter case, the feathering was to be placed rather far from the end of the shaft; otherwise, the arrow could not be pushed in to the necessary depth.

The earliest representation of a cannon, Walter de Milemete's treatise, around 1326.
(The Governing Body of Christ Church, Oxford)

In this connection the question arose as to what is actually pictured: the moment of shooting, or merely the preparation for it? According to later treatises of the 14th and 15th centuries, as well as some archaeological findings, it was established that the shaft of the arrow was made of wood, and the feathering consisted of two bronze "feathers," the latter being about half the length of the arrow and narrowing toward the head. So, the reconstructors decided that the caliber of the barrel must have corresponded to the diameter of the shaft.

The size of the cannon and the arrow was estimated based on the size of a man standing nearby. As a result, they got the following parameters: length—90 centimeters; the largest diameter—46 centimeters (later it was brought down to 40 centimeters); the smallest diameter—15 centimeters; and the diameter by the muzzle—28 centimeters. The total weight of a cannon cast in bronze was about 410 kilograms. The arrow together with the arrowhead was approximated at 135 centimeters, the center of gravity finding itself slightly ahead of the feathering.

In the course of the first test shooting, the cannon did not show itself to be very powerful. The longest range (about 180 meters) was only achieved by considerably reducing the quantity of powder as compared with what was calculated. Otherwise, the shaft of the arrow was torn asunder by the shot. The scholars had achieved their main goal, however, by proving that such a cannon could have existed (see plate 38).

The question of when the cannon appeared in Muslim countries remains disputable, as all evidence of their early use is extremely unreliable. Doubtless, saltpeter (*barud*, as the Arabs called it) and mixtures based on it were known to the Arabs as far back as the 13th century. Ibn Khaldun (1332–1406), describing the siege of Sijilmasa in 1274, mentions certain devices firing pieces of iron by means of powder. However, they were probably not cannon, but rather some

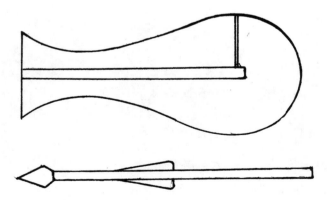

Walter de Milemete's cannon and arrow in cross section.

sort of hand firearm resembling bamboo tubes stuffed with powder, which were recorded in China in 1232 and 1259.[338] Besides, the author lived much later than the events he described—already in the age of cannon—and he could have easily transferred contemporary cannon into an earlier time. It is sometimes extremely difficult to distinguish incendiary weapons based on *naphtha* thrown by a *manjaniq* from cannon. For instance, James Partington believes that the powder bombs mentioned in Spain in 1324–25 were cast by throwing machines and not cannon. He also maintains that *makahil al-barud* was a throwing machine. We know that both fire and solid missiles were thrown with the help of this machine.[339]

Cannon may have first been used by the Muslims in 1331 (at the siege of Alicante), or in 1343 (at the siege of Algeciras). There is no doubt that no one was more experienced in using powder in the early 14th century than the emirs of Granada. Most probably this is because Spain is the only European country which has natural deposits of potassium saltpeter. Of several Arabian treatises that have survived from that time, the one that is particularly well known to us is called "Collection combining the various branches of the [military] art," now kept in St. Petersburg. Contained in it is an almost ideal composition of powder (saltpeter, sulphur, coal = 74:11:15) and a description of a shot fired by means of this composition from the firearm called a *midfa*. It could fire an arrow as well as a ball. It is not quite clear what a *midfa* was—a hand firearm or a cannon. The picture in the manuscript clearly shows a short-barreled hand firearm on a long stick. If this is so, we have to conclude that hand firearms appeared in Muslim countries earlier than cannon (in Europe, the reverse has been found). On the other hand, it is known that later, the term *midfa* clearly stood to describe cannon. The manuscript is dated from the first half of the 14th century; however, the copy that has reached us was made in the 15th century, when it was possibly supplemented with illustrations and even certain fragments of the text.

The spread of firearms throughout Europe was rapid: in 1326–27, the use of firearms was recorded in England and Italy; in 1338 and 1339, in France; in 1342, in Spain; and in 1346, in North Germany. However, the effectiveness of firearms was extremely low at first. Their impact was mainly psychological at this time, as the terrific roar accompanying the shot frightened both men and horses.

The earlier cannon had rather short barrels and resembled beer mugs or barrels in shape. So in Germany, they were called *bückse*, which means "jar or mug," and the English word "barrel" still has the other meaning as well, namely "keg." In France the early guns were called "iron pots" (*pot de fer*), and in Italy—"vases" (*vasi e scioppi*), which is not surprising if we remember the shape of Walter de Milemete's cannon.

From about 1360 and up to the late 15th century, large-sized cannon in France, Spain, Italy, and the Netherlands were called *bombards* (from Gr: *bombos*—"rumbler, hooter"; hence, "bombing, bombardment"). Beginning in the mid-14th century, large cannon began to receive individual names.

The term "artillery" (from the old French: *atillier*) appeared in France and Burgundy in the 13th century, and initially meant armaments in general. Later on it began to denote throwing machines. In the 14th century, with the appearance of cannon, the term spread to include them, too. Later, with the disappearance of throwing machines, the term began to be applied to cannon alone.

Cannon of immense size began to be made toward the end of the 14th century (see Table 6). Every sovereign and even some independent cities competed with each other in the size and caliber of their cannon. It was believed that the larger the cannon, the more destructive a psychological effect it produced. Giant cannon made their appearance, having between 3- to over 5-meter-long barrels and weighing dozens of tons. They were capable of firing balls weighing several hundred kilograms. Although they were exclusively designed for the demolition of fortifications, even here they sometimes proved useless. The Turkish cannon used by Mehmed II against the walls of Constantinople in 1453 played a decisive part during that siege. As to the Moscow "Tsar Cannon" cast in 1586, but made using the pattern of 15th-century cannon, it never

Shooting from a *midfa*. The shot is apparently concealed behind a stationary shield. Drawing based on a miniature in the Arab treatise "Collection combining the various branches of the [military] art" (St. Petersburg). The treatise was written in the first half of the 14th century, but the illustrations were probably supplied by the copyist in the 15th century.

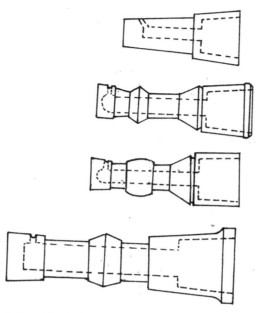

Italian *bombardelles* of the 14th century. The bore of the barrel is shown by a dotted line.

The Tsar Cannon, Moscow. It was cast in 1586, but made on the pattern of 15th century cannon. Its barrel is 5.34m long and weighs 40 tons. The decorative gun-carriage was made in the 19th century and the cannon has, certainly, never shot from a such wheeled carriage. Author's photograph.

Turkish bronze cannon of the time of the rule of Mehmed II the Conqueror (1451–1481). The length of the barrel is 3.46m, the weight is 11 tons, the caliber is 37cm. The walls of the barrel are 10.5cm thick. Projectile chamber length is 1.65m, gunpowder chamber length 1.70m, gunpowder chamber diameter 18.0cm. The weight of the ball is 218kg. These or similar cannon were used at the siege of Constantinople in 1453. Author's photograph.

Another Turkish bronze cannon of the period of the rule of Mehmed II (1451–1581). The length of the barrel is 4.24m, the weight is 15 tons, the caliber is 63cm. The thickness of the walls of the barrel is 14cm. Projectile chamber length is 1.86m, gunpowder chamber length—1.67m, gunpowder chamber diameter—23.0cm. The weight of the ball is 285kg. Author's photograph.

participated in real battle, having been cast simply to demonstrate the might of the country. The "Faule Mette," remelted in 1728, made only nine shots in the course of the 317 years of its life, none of them hitting the target.

Table 6. Parameters of cannon and balls for some gigantic *bombards* of the 14th through 16th centuries.

	Barrel				Ball	
	construction	length, m	weight, kg	caliber, cm	diameter, cm	weight, kg
"Faule Magd," 1430			1,383		34.5	
"Dulle Griete," Ghent, 1450–52	forged of iron strips	4.96	16,400		64	325
"Faule Mette," 1411	cast of bronze	3	8,700		64	325
"Mons Meg," 1449 (Edinburgh)	forged of iron strips	3.9	6,040	48		
Luxembourg, 1447		5.4	23,600		75.6	465
Turkey, 1453 (siege of Constantinople)	cast of bronze		32,000		91	590
Turkey, 1464 (now in Tower of London)	cast of bronze	5.25	17,000	63.5		306
"Tsar Cannon," 1586, Moscow	cast of bronze	5.34	40,000	89		750–1,000

The maximum range of fire for such cannon was 1,000 meters and more. However, unpredictable behavior of the cannon's barrels and poor quality powder considerably reduced the range. To prevent the explosion of the cannon, cannoniers often used a smaller quantity of powder, playing for safety. That is why giant *bombards* were quite often surprisingly low-powered. In fact, they were probably positioned at a distance of no more than 200 to 250 meters from a fortress wall. Frequent employment of large protective shields testifies to the fact that they were positioned at a distance from a fortress of one shot from crossbows or hand firearms. The shield protected the gun detachment during reloading, and was only lifted immediately before firing. For making a breach in a wall, it was recommended that balls be fired so that they would find themselves within the figure of a triangle. That is, after the first ball hit the target, the second ball was to be shot, moving about 10 to 13 meters aside from the spot hit by the first, and the third—so that the spot hit by the three balls would form the figure of a triangle.

These enormous *bombards* were only used at sieges and, of course, never from wheeled carriages. They were driven into the ground or mounted on timbered platforms assembled on the spot. There was a whole system of transversal and longitudinal beams driven into the ground behind the barrel, but even this structure had to be restored every three or four days. Owing to the problems of recoil, large-caliber *bombards* (the so-called main-caliber cannon) could not fire more than seven shots a day.

The process of loading and shooting them proceeded as follows: Assistant gunsmiths pushed several sacks of powder (large *bombards* needed 20 to 50 kilograms of powder) into the barrel and packed the loading chamber full of them. Then, they drove a wooden plug into the opening to prevent powder gases from breaking through between the ball and the walls of

Wooden model of a siege cannon on a wheeled platform. The barrel of the cannon was fixed on the platform with the help of chains driven through special rings on the sides of the barrel. One can see such rings on many a Turkish barrel of the 15ᵗʰ Century. Carts like that were used for transferring cannon, but it was impossible to shoot heavy cannon from such a wheeled platform. Author's photograph.

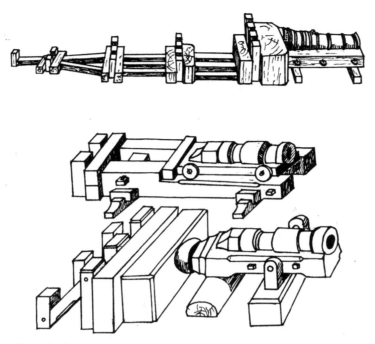

Methods of strengthening heavy siege cannon of the 14th–15th centuries.

the barrel. The ball, too heavy to lift, had to be rolled along specially built embankments and pushed into the barrel with the help of levers. Then the bombardier, through a touchhole in the barrel, pierced a sack of powder with a thin, pointed rod, put fine powder inside, and made a powder path on the surface of the barrel. The crew sought shelter in a trench and the bombardier set fire to the powder path with a red-hot iron rod, and swiftly made for the trench (see plate 39). A horrific crash was heard and everything around it was enveloped in a cloud of smoke. With luck, the ball would fly toward its target; otherwise, the *bombard* would be blown to pieces. If the cannon were not damaged, some of the crew started collecting the beams broken by the recoil, while others would wash the bore of the barrel, clearing out the smoldering remains of the sacks and particles of powder.

Small and medium cannon were placed in wooden bracing or laid on a bed (prototype of a gun carriage). In the 15th century, builders began to construct the bed with an inclined tang in order to direct the recoil downwards. To protect the crew during the reloading, a gun was often screened by a wooden shield, which was raised immediately before firing. By the mid-15th century, the first sighting devices on the barrel had made their appearance.

Ribaudequins or *ribaulds* were a curious type of gun. They consisted of small barrels joined together so that they could fire simultaneously with a volley. The barrels were placed on two-wheeled carts, sometimes described as "carts of war." To protect the crew, the cart was often screened with a shield at the front, which was only lifted right before firing. Sometimes sharp spears jutted out in front of the cart, which prevented anybody from approaching the gun (see plate 40).

Ribaudequins were the earliest samples of mobile fire artillery. Because of the small caliber of the barrels, they could not be used for destroying fortifications and were only employed against enemy manpower. At the same time, owing to concentrated fire, they proved very effective in defending a gate or a breach in the wall.

Ribaudequins were first mentioned as early as 1339; that is, only some fifteen years after the appearance of the first cannon. In the mid-14th century they were perhaps the most common type of gun. For instance, in 1345 Edward III is known to have taken 100 *ribaudequins* from the Tower—a huge number for those times. In 1387 the largest *ribaudequin* was made in Verona at the order of Antonio della Scala, where 144 barrels were placed one above the other in three tiers. Each tier had four sections, and there were twelve barrels in each section that could fire a volley. There was one gunner in each tier. The whole affair, which was about 6 meters high, sat on a cart driven by four horses.[340]

In the 15th century, the popularity of these guns dropped somewhat; at least, their number is dramatically reduced as compared to other types of cannon. At the same time the idea of creating a multibarreled gun capable of firing volleys, or one after another without interval, gave inventors no rest until a machine gun was invented. A great number of multibarreled constructions appeared in the period between the 15th and 18th centuries. For example, they tried to put the barrels not only in a line but also on one large wheel; after each shot, the wheel turned and another shot could be fired from another barrel. The 19th century also saw the appearance of multibarreled constructions, e.g. *mitrailleuse*.

The loading chamber of the cannon of 14th and 15th centuries was narrower than the rest of the barrel. It was made to allow powder gases to hit the center of the ball precisely. Later on, an increase in the initial speed was achieved by enlarging the charge, which involved certain difficulties in using loading chambers of smaller diameter. They had to be given up, and new, chamberless cannon emerged. Chambers were only retained in *mortars* (the name comes from their resemblance to kitchen mortars), which appeared in the mid-15th century. These were short-barreled, large-caliber cannon that threw balls along a steep, plunging trajectory.

During the 14th and 15th centuries, cannon fell into two categories: breech-loading and muzzle-loading. The former, called *veuglaire* (from Lat: *fulgurare*—"casting lightning"), consisted of a barrel and a separate loading chamber. The barrel was fixed in a wooden block and a cham-

Muzzle section of a Turkish cast bronze cannon. We can see how much narrower than the projectile chamber of the barrel the powder chamber is. Author's photograph.

ber was put into it and fixed with a transverse wedge. The chamber contained powder, and a ball was pushed into the barrel. Cannon loaded at the muzzle were made of one piece. Either construction had its advantages and disadvantages: breech-loading cannon had a higher rate of fire, as a large number of loaded chambers could be prepared beforehand; muzzle-loading ones were stronger, more reliable, and had a longer range of fire. The muzzle-loading guns won the competition, mainly due to the fact that it was impossible to achieve a complete isolation (obturation) of the breech end from the exhaust of gases at the moment of the shot. By the 16th century, breech-loading cannon only remained in the navy, but even those were later replaced by the muzzle-loading variety. All the cannon of the period in question were smooth-bored.

The barrels of the 14th- and 15th-century cannon could be forged or cast. Forged barrels consisted of several layers. The first layer was made of a thick iron plate, which was bent around the mandrel and then forged into the tube. Several layers were put around it, which were grabbed with several rings. It is because of these rings that the barrels of forged cannon looked "ribbed." Cast barrels were made of so-called gunmetal, composed of 90 percent copper and 10 percent tin. Up to the 16th century the bore of a barrel was not drilled, but was finished during the casting. In the 15th century iron was six times cheaper than bronze, making forged-iron cannon about three times cheaper than those cast of bronze. The latter, however, won the battle in the long run.

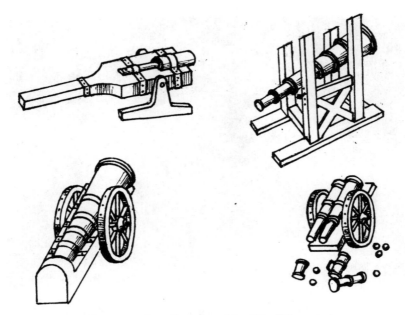

Medium and small cannon of the 14th–15th centuries.

The fact is, cast cannon had walls of equal thickness and solidity, while the numerous welded joints of forged cannon could slacken at any moment and cause the cannon to explode. Therefore, they had to use low powder charges in forged cannon as compared with cast bronze ones of the same caliber, which negatively impacted their power and range of fire.

The progress of artillery was badly hampered by cannon being produced domestically. Each gunsmith made the barrel as he deemed best, keeping his own secrets and only handing them down to his sons or apprentices when on his deathbed. As a result, each cannon was unique as to its length and caliber. This often led to curious situations: there were plenty of balls that could not be used because the cannon that could fire them had been put out of action. Besides, artillerymen did

Breech-loading cannon (*veuglaire*), the 15th century. Author's photograph.

Cannon of late-14th–early-15th centuries. The gun carriage was reconstructed in the 19th century. Author's photograph.

Forged barrel of a 15th century cannon. Author's photograph.

The muzzle of a forged cannon, the 15th century. Author's photograph.

not exist as a branch in their own right—the gunsmith who had made the cannon was the man who loaded and fired it. These civilians were not noted for their courage, and would abandon their cannon and scatter about the place at the slightest sign of danger.

Early powder was a powder-like paste, which burned very slowly. Accordingly, powder gases exhausted slowly; it took a fairly long time to speed up a ball, and its initial speed was low. In addition, such powder separated from jolting during transportation, and it soon became damp as it absorbed moisture from the atmosphere. Therefore, the armies did not carry ready-made powder along with them, but had saltpeter, sulphur, and coal transported separately, as a rule. The components were mixed up on the spot immediately before using them, knowing that a few hours later the powder might become unreliable.

In the first half of the 15th century they had learned how to make corned powder: a wet powder paste was pushed through a sieve and the resultant grains were dried. Probably the first mention of corned powder was registered in Nürnberg in 1449–50.[341] Corned powder burned much more intensely and released more gases. It was also less hygroscopic and could keep longer without loss of quality. At first, however, corned powder was only used in moderate caliber cannon. Large-caliber *bombards* would not bear the power of corned powder and continued using the more common powder-like mixture.

Stone balls stuck in the walls of the Rhodes Fortress (Italian sector),
dumb witnesses of a six-months' siege laid by the
Turks in 1522. Author's photograph.

14th–15th century balls:
1—stone balls;
2—a stone ball coated with lead;
3—an iron forged ball. Author's photograph.

It is curious that even in the 16th century, the composition of powder or the degree of purity of the components was somewhat different in the East and the West. Thus, an eyewitness of the siege of Malta by the Turks (1565) remarked that it was always possible to determine who was firing, the Turks or the Christians, as the smoke from a Christian shot was different from that of "theirs"—it was thick and black.[342]

The projectiles used for *bombards* and *mortars* were stone balls. They were rounded by hand from limestone, in an effort to give them a spherical shape. Forged-iron balls were used for smaller-caliber cannon; however, here it was difficult to achieve a regular spherical form, so they were often coated with lead to make them smooth. A radical turn in the quality of ammunition came in the last quarter of the 15th century, when the manufacture of cast-iron balls was mastered. Cast-iron balls were considerably more solid than stone ones and caused more destruction. Besides, while being the same weight as stone balls, cast-iron balls were considerably smaller in diameter (as the density of cast iron is about 2.5 times that of stone). For instance, 15 to 20 centimeters (in diameter) cast-iron balls could be successfully used instead of 30 to 60 centimeters (in diameter) stone balls. This led to the caliber of cannon becoming smaller and the barrels longer, which was necessary for maintaining the mass of barrels and increasing the range of cannon.

• TWENTY-TWO •

OTHER SIEGE DEVICES

Watchtowers were built by the besiegers in order to assess the size of defense works of the besieged, and to keep an eye on their movements inside a town. A watchtower often resembles a common siege tower. If it was at a considerable distance from town defenses, out of reach of missiles, it was just a frame made of beams. However, more often it was necessary to bring the tower closer to the walls; it was then bound with boards and leather, like a siege tower. In many cases mobile siege towers themselves played the part of watchtowers.

Of more complex structure were watchtowers that could be raised and lowered. Platforms for these towers were usually made of rectangular beams in the shape of the letter H. Fixed to it were two vertical square beams fortified with four inclined poles used as props, as well as stretched ropes tied to pegs driven into the ground. Then, with the help of a pivot, the vertical beams were straddled with a "rocker" of two parallel beams. The shorter end of the "rocker" ended with a crosswise beam and the longer with a pivot, to which a light ladder was attached. A shed of thick leather like a curved shield, or even one with a rib along the middle, was arranged on the very top of the ladder. An observer was placed under the shed, the leather meant to guard him from enemy missiles. When the shorter end of the "rocker" was lowered, the longer end, together with the ladder and the observer, would go up. In the raised position the ladder and "rocker" were fixed with spikes (see plate 41). The calculation of the size of every detail of the tower was made based on the height of the fortress wall. The height of vertical beams was one third that of the wall; the length of the longer end of a "rocker," as well as that of a ladder, were each one half the height of the wall. Thus, the observer was raised one third of its height above the wall.[343]

Firing on the defenders from above, or the transfer of a small party of soldiers onto the wall, was done with the help of a fairly simple device called a *tolleno*. The latter consisted of a tall vertical pole with a long beam fixed crosswise to it at the top. A large wooden box with several soldiers in it was suspended from one end of the beam, and ropes were tied to the other end. When one end was pulled down with the help of the ropes, the other end with the box would go up (see plate 42).[344]

There was also a hook for the destruction of walls which Vegetius calls *falce* and Vitruvius, a "demolishing raven" or a "crane."[345] It was a beam suspended like a battering ram, having a

223

powerful iron head shaped like a hook (see plate 43). With that hook they caught the parapet and pulled out stones from it, one after another. The Athenian general Timotheos successfully employed a raven with sickles and pikes against obstacles of sand baskets built by the defenders of Torone.[346] It seems, however, that this siege device was never very popular, as according to Vitruvius, Diades did not think it worthwhile, and described it as decidedly useless.[347] The raven was sometimes used by the besieged, too, who used it to catch the assailant soldiers, or the protective covers of the besiegers (see plate 44). For instance, a raven was used by the defenders of Ludlow in 1139. At the siege of Vatteville, a knight is known to have been caught by an "artificial hand" with iron hooks.[348]

Lassos were also used for catching soldiers. Aeneas Tacticus gives the following description of their construction:

> The loop itself should be made from the strongest possible rope; the lifter, from two cubits [about 93 centimeters] of chain, so that it could not be cut; and the remaining part, the one that is pulled at, from rope made of reed. All this is suspended on the outside and pulled in with the help of ropes or a lifting pole.[349]

The simplest siege weapon—but a very effective one, nonetheless—proved to be the *tortoise* (Lat: *testudo*). This was a battle formation of Roman legionaries that covered themselves with shields at the front, on the sides, and above. The *testudo* is first mentioned at the siege of Aquilonia in 293 BC. Livy gives a detailed description of how young soldiers formed a *testudo* on the arena to show their skill:

> Amongst other exhibitions, bodies of youths, numbering generally about sixty, but larger in the more elaborate games, were introduced fully armed. To some extent they represented the maneuvers of an army, but their movements were more skillful and resembled more nearly the combat of gladiators. After going through various evolutions, they formed a solid square with their shields held over their heads, touching one another; those in the front rank standing erect; those in the second, slightly stooping; those in the third and fourth, bending lower and lower; whilst those in the rear rank rested on their knees. In this way they formed a *testudo*, which sloped like the roof of a house. From a distance of fifty feet two fully armed men ran forward and, pretending to threaten one another, went from the lowest to the highest part of the *testudo* over the closely locked shields; at one moment assuming an attitude of defiance on the very edge, and then rushing at

one another in the middle of it just as though they were jumping about on solid ground.[350]

The only difference [between entertainment and battle *testudo*] was that the front rank and the files did not raise their shields above their heads for fear of exposing themselves; they held them in front as in battle. Thus, they were not hit by the missiles from the walls, and those which were hurled on the testudo rolled off harmlessly to the ground like a shower of rain from the roof of a house.[351]

In the front rank of a *testudo*, there was one fewer man than in the others. For instance, if a *tortoise* was formed by twenty-seven men, the front rank consisted of six soldiers, four of which were in the center holding shields before them, and the remaining two, one at either end, would cover the right and left sides. The second, third, and fourth ranks had seven men each, five holding the shields over their heads and those at the ends protecting themselves on the sides. A party any number strong could draw up in this way.

A *testudo* enabled an army to assault walls of medium height without a ladder, let alone approach fortress walls. In the former instance a sloping *tortoise*, like the one described by Livy, was employed. The front rank of soldiers stood up straight; the next ranks would bend lower and lower; and the soldiers of the back rank would be kneeling down. Advancing on such a rostrum, the detachment that followed the *testudo* could easily climb up the wall (see plate 45).

Testudo formation. For the clarity of the formation the warriors of different rows have different drawings on their shields.

Sometimes the *testudo* formation was used for an attack from the sea. For this purpose, three ships were tied together. On the rowers' benches the front rank of soldiers stood upright followed by two ranks of bending soldiers, and finally, the squatting soldiers of the back rank. All of them were holding shields over their heads. Such a construction guarded the soldiers against missiles and stones, as all of these would slide down "like rain."[352]

The *testudo* formation was apparently used in the Middle Ages, too, although it is sometimes difficult to discern what the medieval authors meant by *testudo*—a formation made of soldiers with shields, or some type of mobile shed. We find mention of *testudo* in the descriptions of the siege of Barcelona in the time of Charlemagne, and the siege of Paris by the Vikings. There is no doubt it was this formation that we see at the siege of Bergamo in 894, where the assailants made an assault "holding their shields above their heads like a roof." "A roof of shields" was employed during the first Crusade, and Count of Raymond used a *testudo* at the siege of Nicaea.[353]

If a besieged fortification stood on a hill with steep slopes, the defenders would let heavy objects, like round stones, columns, wheels, stone rollers, logs of wood, heavy loaded carts, bas-

Defense against rolling objects with the help of *tridents.*

Defense against rolling objects with the help of a ditch and a wall.

kets, or barrels filled with cobbles, shells, or earth, roll down the slope. Such objects, when they had gathered speed, could not only be injurious to the assailants' legs but also do considerable harm to siege engines as well. Athenaeus says that "while dashing down, they make everything tremble and are an insurmountable force."[354]

To protect themselves from these objects, the besiegers employed *tridents*. Each *trident* was 2.2 meters long and as thick "as a man's waist." The *tridents* formed three or four rows and barred the progress of all the rolling objects.[355]

A ditch driven diagonally from the assailants' position to the intended section of the fortress wall could furnish protection against rolling objects. Such a ditch would be up to 1.5 meters deep. A plumb wall was erected beyond the ditch closer to the besiegers, and stakes about 2.7 meters long were driven obliquely between the wall and the ditch. They piled boards, bunches of trees, and the dirt removed from digging the ditch onto the stakes.[356] This triple row of fortifications offered good protection from rolling objects, and allowed the besiegers to safely bring the siege machines to the wall.

Cranes—by means of which heavy objects (stones and logs as a rule) were thrown or burning pitch was poured on siege machines—enjoyed great popularity with the defenders in all times and in all countries. During the defense of Syracuse in 213–211 BC, Archimedes built cranes, which allowed heaps of lead and 10-talent (about 260 kilograms) pieces of rock to be thrown down onto Roman ships. Moreover, these cranes had special claws with which they could catch the bows of ships, raise them, and then overturn them.[357] By means of these cranes it was possible to pour excrement down onto the besiegers, which was done on the suggestion of an Arab naval officer at the defense of Tyre against the Crusaders in 1112. In general, sailors, owing to their skill in handling ropes and pulley-blocks, were especially valued in building various siege machines, and particularly cranes. As a rule, cranes apparently consisted of a square, wheeled

The most detailed drawing of a war crane from Maciejowski Bible (about 1240). Such war cranes were widely used in the ancient and medieval times for throwing various heavy objects down onto the siege engines of the besiegers. In this case the artist depicted the body of the Israelite King Saul (ruled 1021–1000 BC) suspended on a crane. The equipment of the warriors, and other details, are characteristic of the Middle Ages, though.

platform with a powerful beam fixed to it vertically. Fastened to this beam was a lever with the longer side ending in a T-shaped crossbeam, and the shorter side ending in a medium counterweight, which facilitated the lifting of loads. The raising and lowering of the lever was done with the help of ropes fastened to the shorter end.

Finally, there was a device whose construction remains not quite clear. It was only described by Procopius,[358] who calls it a "wolf." The description is vague, and no other source mentions a similar device. Judging by its description, the "wolf" consisted of two gratings, which could be raised or lowered. When extended, they covered the space from the ground to the top of the fortification. Each grating was dotted with spikes. The "wolf" was positioned on the outside of a gate. When the besiegers approached the gate, the besieged pushed the upper grating, and the latter, turning on hinges, shut down like a wolf's jaws, killing those who had been caught between the two gratings (see plates 46-1 and 46-2).

PART III
METHODS OF ATTACK AND DEFENSE

TWENTY-THREE

METHODS OF ATTACK

A siege was usually laid in spring or summer when it was easier to do earthwork and when hot dry weather contributed to a rapid spread of fire in the fortress. A winter siege was a rare event, as ice-coated approaches to the fortress were hard to storm across, and the frozen ground bedeviled earthwork, particularly building an embankment and driving underground tunnels. In addition, elements of throwing machines that were sensitive to moisture could be put out of action if it rained or snowed. The moment for an assault was sometimes chosen so that the besieged had already run out of the previous year's harvest and had not yet gathered the new one.

Generally speaking, there were two methods of capturing a fortress—an assault (Lat: *oppugnatio*) and a passive blockade (Lat: *obsidio*). Each had its advantages and disadvantages. Carrying fortifications by escalade without any complex siege engines was only possible provided the fortifications were rather weak and the attackers were considerably superior in numbers. The use of siege engines required the presence of specialists within the army who were experienced in building and using such machines, as well as strict discipline. In any case, a direct attack was a costly measure.

A passive siege could ideally lead to the surrender of a fortress with no loss at all. It had, however, serious disadvantages. A long-term siege could allow the enemy to gather sufficient force and come to the rescue of the besieged town. Then the besiegers found themselves in an extremely vulnerable position between two armies—the one that had come to the rescue and the fortress garrison. Moreover, the longer the siege went on, the more expensive it became; for example, it is documented that Athenian hoplites were paid two drachmas a day. With 3,000 hoplites brought into the siege of Potidaea, each day of the siege cost Athens 6,000 drachmas (one talent)—for the hoplites alone. The siege, which lasted over two years, was worth 2,000 talents. Compare this figure to Athens' annual income, which was about 6,000 talents.[359]

Keeping the men in the camp during a long time required a professional army with strict discipline, as well as a regular supply of food and sufficient money for the soldiers' wages. When an offending army found itself deep in the enemy's territory, it often suffered from lack of food supplies more than the besieged town did. This was especially true if the townsfolk were well prepared for the defense, having stored plenty of provisions for themselves while simultaneously depleting any extra supplies that might otherwise have been available for the offending army. Wages had to be paid on time or the soldiers might revolt—particularly if there was no other source of income. If an army was not made up of mercenaries but based instead on feudal relationship, desertion was the main factor that contributed to the breakdown of the army during a long siege. Vassals could leave their lord after campaigning for about forty days a year.

Disease and boredom, too, undermined discipline and lessened vigilance. To entertain themselves in camp, the besiegers invited tradesmen and actors to come and arrange fairs. Such diversions reached their widest range in the Middle Ages, when splendid tournaments were sometimes arranged by the attacking army right under the town walls, with not only the besiegers but also the besieged taking part in them. It could, however, lead to serious troubles. For instance, in 1113 a group of knights cantered out of a besieged castle to take part in a tournament and was attacked by an enemy force, who had not yet received the news of a temporary armistice. The knights of the garrison rushed back into the castle, but they were not quick enough to close the gate, and the castle was seized by the enemy. That is why tournaments between the besieged and besiegers were thereafter held across a wooden barrier; this, by the way, happened long before a barrier ever appeared at an ordinary tournament.[360] A wooden barrier built at a castle's gate allowed the knights to fight unmounted without fear of a sudden attack of the besiegers, or a surprise sortie of the besieged.

"REGULAR" ACTIONS OF THOSE IN OFFENSE :

1. SUGGEST A CAPITULATION.

First of all, the besieged town or fortress was invited to capitulate on fairly favorable conditions. For instance, during his campaign in Chalcidice in 424 BC, the Spartan general Brasidas offered complete freedom to the towns willing to renounce Athens and surrender; however, he fully destroyed those that put up resistance. Julius Caesar would accept the capitulation of a town prepared to give up the arms and hostages. If the defense agreed to the terms before a ram touched the walls, the town and townsfolk were safe. Gaulish towns Noviodunum, Bratuspantium, and Vellaunodunum surrendered to Caesar on these conditions.[361] A similar method was often used in the Middle Ages. A code of honor demanded that, before laying a siege, terms of capitulation should be proposed to those in defense. If the terms were accepted before the first shot was fired from a cannon or a throwing machine, the garrison was, as a rule, allowed to leave the castle, often carrying arms and armor.

PLATE SECTION

◄ **PLATE 1**

Complex structure of three ladders with a boarding-bridge (according to Apollodorus). Each ladder was 3.5m long. At junction points the ladders were bound with iron. The bottom, central and upper steps of each ladder were also bound with iron for the sake of solidity.

PLATE 2

Structure of several ladders for pouring boiling water or hot oil down onto the defenders (according to Apollodorus). Hot liquids were delivered upwards in buckets by means of rope driven through a wheel. A man standing on the upper platform poured them out through a funnel into the groove of the central beam. A copper net dispersing liquids over a larger part of the surface of a wall was suspended at the front end of the beam. Although Apollodorus does not say anything about protective sheds for those working at the bottom and at the top of this structure, there must have been some cover, or the workers would have been an excellent target for shots. ►

◄ **PLATE 3**

Antique *pluteus*. These light sheds for archers and slingers were made of brushwood and were covered with Cilician goat coverlets or hides at the front. A *pluteus* moved on three small-sized wheels, one of them at the center, the other two at the sides.

PLATE 4

Medieval siege shields (*mantlets*) and large individual shields (*pavises*), 15th century. Concealed behind them, crossbowmen, archers and hand-firearm shooters conducted fire during an assault. On the left is a woven basket: hiding himself in the latter, a warrior could approach a besieged castle. The basket could hardly have provided adequate cover from crossbows or hand firearms. We have only one representation of it, so such baskets hardly were very popular. ▶

◀ **PLATE 5**

Reconstruction of siege shields after the drawings in Mariano Taccola's treatise "De Machinis" (1449). Concealed behind ordinary shields were crossbowmen and shooters from hand firearms. More sophisticated models of shields had hooks at the front with pots or barrels of burning mixture fastened to them; they were mostly used for setting fire to gates.

▲ PLATE 6

Protective passage made up from *vineae*. A *vinea* was a shed, about 4.8m long, carried by hand. The body of a *vinea* consisted of stakes covered with grape-vine and a double layer of loosely hanging hides.

▲ PLATE 7

Ditch-filling *tortoise*. The structure was a square whose sides were 6.2m long. At the front the roof jutted out about 3.5m beyond the body. The *tortoise* sat on four or eight wheels, which were 1.3m in diameter and 0.3m thick each. The roof and sides of the *tortoise* were covered with boards, then mats of new twigs, and finally with raw hides, sown in two and stuffed with seaweed or chaff steeped in vinegar.

PLATE 8

Ship's prow (beaked) *tortoise*. These structures had a triangular (as in the picture) or pentagonal frame directed at the enemy with its acute angle. It was recommended that ship's prow *tortoises* be used in assaulting fortresses on steep slopes as, owing to their beak, they could easily deflect the objects rolled down onto them. They were fairly light and therefore were not provided with wheels but carried by hand; they were also provided with iron nails on the bottom, which were driven into the ground to keep the structure in place. ▶

◀ PLATE 9

Reconstructions of tortoises after Mariano Taccola's treatise "De Machinis" (1449). In the original drawings the tortoises are only covered with boards; however Taccola, in describing them, repeatedly mentions the necessity of covering these structures with hides of cows, oxen and donkeys. Like siege shields, tortoises were often used for setting fire to gates.

Assyrian battering rams of the 9th – 7th centuries BC. On the right we can see a big battering ram used at the time of Ashurnasirpal II (884 – 859 BC). This complex and heavy structure moved on 6 wheels and had a 5m long by 2 to 3m high body. A 3m high turret provided with loopholes for archers was put in the front part of it. A flattened head allowed the battering ram to easily demolish the laying of mud-brick and attack the joints between stone slabs. On the left, we can see the Assyrian battering ram of the 8th–7th centuries BC. At that time battering rams were already smaller and more mobile accordingly. The elevation at the front part is open at the rear. A starting fire could be put out through it. The Assyrians covered their battering rams with wet hides against fire.

PLATE 11

Large ram-*tortoise* according to Vitruvius and Athenaeus Mechanicus. Such ram-*tortoises* were built by Diades and Charias, engineers in the army of Alexander the Great. The *tortoise* was 17.7m long, 13.3m wide and 7.1m high. A turret rose on the roof of it, on the upper story of which there were moderate-sized arrow-firing machines while the lower stories had a store of cisterns of water in case of fire. The head of the battering ram had the shape of a ram-head. ▶

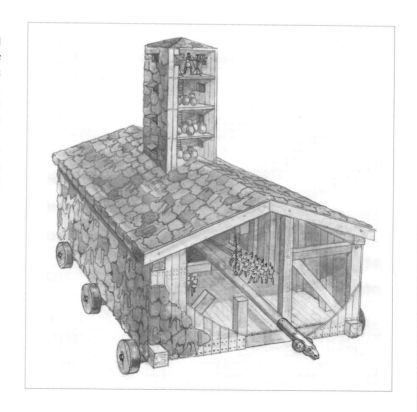

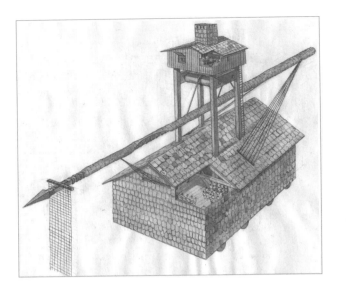

◀ **PLATE 12**

Hegetor of Byzantium's ram-*tortoise* used by Demetrius Poliorcetes at the siege of Rhodes in 305-4 BC. The tortoise was 18.6m long, 12.4m wide and 10.6m high; it moved on 8 wheels. There was a two-story turret at the top; the bottom story housed throwing machines while the upper story was an unroofed platform enclosed with a parapet for two scouts. The battering ram was a rectangular beam about 53m long bound with four ropes and sown round with raw hides. A wedge-shaped iron head was put on the beam at the front; behind it, at a distance of 4.5m, the beam was bound with four iron hoops preventing the splitting of wood. A board with a rope net, climbing which the warrior could easily reach the wall, was fastened to the front end of the battering ram near the head.

PLATE 13

The borer contrived by Diades, engineer of Alexander the Great. A 25m long sharpened beam bound with iron at the end traveled in a groove on numerous rollers which decreased friction. The tortoise consisted of arch-shaped wooden beams covered with rawhides to protect against fire. ▶

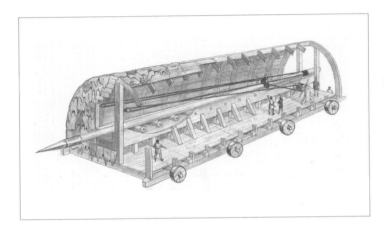

◀ **PLATE 14**

Reconstruction of a borer as described by Apollodorus and Anonymus Byzantine. A 1.5m long drill was inserted into a wooden cylinder, which revolved by means of a rope or a crosspiece (like that of a windlass). The cylinder came up against a wooden restricting device which, as the drilling proceeded, was brought nearer the wall with stakes being driven following it step by step. A borer was especially effective against brick walls; it was recommended that the drilling be done at an angle upwards so that the borer had a firm support and the debris came out of the hole by itself.

◀ **PLATE 15**

Ten-story siege tower of Diades and Charias, engineers in the army of Alexander the Great. The picture shows the smallest of the towers submitted by the engineers. Other towers had 15 and 20 stories. The 10-story tower was 26.6m high and like other towers narrowed upwards — the size of the upper story was 1/5 less than the size of the base. Each story had a passage way around the tower from which it was easy to put out fire. Additionally, each story was provided with window loopholes, from which fire could be brought to bear upon the enemy from throwing machines or bows. Javelin-throwers and slingers were usually placed at the top.

PLATE 16

Reconstruction of siege tower having a double battering ram, after Apollodorus. A battering ram, in siege towers, could be placed not only downstairs but upstairs as well, where it was used to demolish the parapet of a wall. Two battering ram beams, joined by flooring made of boards, enabled the assailants to first demolish the parapet and then quickly get over onto the wall. ▼

◀ **PLATE 17**
Medieval siege tower having a battering ram. A battering ram and an assaulting bridge are often to be found in siege towers in the Middle Ages. But on the whole, the towers had fewer stories than in the Hellenistic period.

PLATE 18
Reconstruction of a siege tower of the late Middle Ages. Made after a 1475 miniature. At this time towers were mostly used as bridge-heads for shooters. ▶

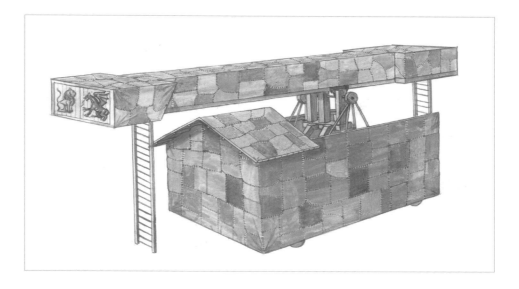

▲ PLATE 19

Land *sambuca* in a lowered position. A land *sambuca* was a *tortoise* sitting on wheels and having an 18m long roofed ladder-gallery attached to it. At the front, a *sambuca* was closed with two small doors often carrying the image of a lion or dragon belching fire. At the back of a *sambuca* there was a load of about 2.5 tons, owing to which a *sambuca* could be raised by a few men only.

◀ PLATE 20

Land *sambuca* in a raised position. 10 men had climbed up a ladder in the front part of a *sambuca*; then the machine was rolled up to a wall and raised. While these 10 men were engaged in fighting the defenders of the wall, the remaining warriors climbed up the ladder inside the *sambuca*.

PLATE 21 ▲

The storm of Syracuse from the sea, 213 – 211 BC. The Romans had built 4 *sambucas* to assault the town from the sea. Each of these machines was placed on two quinqueremes joined together. The *sambuca* proper was a long 1.2m wide ladder with handrails on either side. In the initial position the *sambuca* lay horizontally along the adjoining sides of the ships. On approaching the wall, its front end was raised by means of ropes driven through pulley-blocks at the top of the masts. It was propped with poles from beneath for added stability. In its front part a *sambuca* had a platform where 4 warriors were engaged in fighting with the defenders while an assaulting party was climbing up the ladder. In the same picture one can also see cranes built by Archimedes. With the help of these cranes the defenders threw heaps of lead and stones weighing 10 talents (about 260kg) down onto the Roman ships. Additionally, these cranes caught the bows of ships with special paws, raised them and then turned them over.

▲ **PLATE 22**

Digging *tortoise* with a lean-to roof. We find the description of such *tortoises* in Apollodorus and Anonymus Byzantine. The body of the *tortoise* consisted of beams no less than 3m long, sometimes sharpened at the end so that they could be driven into the ground for stability. The roof was made from boards and dotted with broad-headed nails; the space between the heads of the nails and the boards was filled with clay mixed with wool. Owing to this construction and such a covering, a *tortoise* was well defended from incendiary missiles, hot resin and oil while heavy objects simply rolled down its surface. On approaching a wall, the *tortoise* was covered with coarse canvas, mats or hides at the front and on the sides. Two men worked inside one such *tortoise*.

1

2

3

4

▲ PLATE 23

The driving of an underground sap:

1—The digging of the underground gallery and propping it with supports;

2—The building of an underground chamber under the wall;

3—The filling of the chamber with brushwood and other inflammatory materials;

4—The burning down of the supports resulting in the falling in of the wall.

1

2

3

4

▲ PLATE 24

Roman siege of the Greek town of Ambracia, 189 BC. First the Romans tried to take the town by storm using battering rams and poles with hooks. The defenders, however, fought staunchly, and all the attacks were repulsed. Then the Romans set about to dig an undermining (1). The defenders answered with digging a ditch on the inner side and began listening to know where the digging was being done (2). Having detected the Roman underground gallery, the besieged drove a counter-gallery and hand-to-hand fighting began (3). Failing to gain an advantage in the hand-to-hand fighting, the defenders resorted to a stratagem. They put a large clay vessel (or a barrel) across the underground passage, filled it with chicken down, set fire to the down and directed a poignant stinking smoke against the Romans by means of bellows. To prevent the Romans from approaching this hellish aggregate, the Greeks had made holes in the vessel driving *sarissa* spears through them (4). The besiegers gave in and quitted the gallery. The Romans never took the city and a peace treaty was signed in the end.

◀ **PLATE** 25
Spanning a *gastraphetes*. *Gastraphetes* means "belly-bow"; it owes its name to the manner of spanning the string — propping one end in the ground and the other in one's belly.

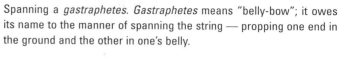

PLATE 26
Non-torsion-powered arrow-firer *oxybeles*, a mountain *gastraphetes* according to Biton. About 375 – 350 BC. A reconstruction after E. W. Marsden. ▶

◀ **PLATE** 27
Torsion-powered arrow-firer *oxybeles*. About 340 BC.

▲ PLATE 28
Fairly small Roman arrow-firer — *scorpion*. About 50 BC.

▲ PLATE 29
Cheiroballistra. About AD 100. The *cheiroballistra* ("hand ballista" or *manuballista*) took over from the scorpion. Unlike the latter, it had an all-metal frame-work (not a wooden one bound with metal), a sighting mechanism and an even larger angle between the two extreme positions of the arms. Additionally, the torsion-springs had been placed in cylinders, which is why they were less subject to moisture. According to Heron's de-scription and E. W. Marsden's reconstruction.

▲ PLATE 30
Onager, 4th century AD.

PLATE 31

Ballista, Mark Vb type, about 60 BC. ▶

◀ PLATE 32

Reconstruction of a throwing machine for casting incendiary missiles, after a drawing in Walter de Milemete's treatise (1326). It is highly improbable that such a machine should have existed in reality. Although a counterweight will allow a wheel with spoons to make one or several revolutions, the range of fire would be far from high with such a construction. In Walter de Milemete's picture the fire shoots up right from the spoons of the engine, but probably the engine hurled pots with incendiary mixture. Another drawing in this treatise shows a similar engine, but designed for casting beehives.

PLATE 33
Reconstruction of an *espringal*, the principal if not the only torsion-powered arrow-firer in medieval Europe. Debuted in the 13th century, these arrow-firers remained very popular up to the early 15th century. ▶

PLATE 34
Medieval great crossbow. ▶

◀ **PLATE** 35

Trebuchet, 13th century. This picture shows a *trebuchet* with a movable counterweight. Such engines were somewhat more powerful, more rapid-firing and more lasting than the machines having a fixed counterweight.

◀ **PLATE** 36

Arrow-firer using the energy of a resilient board. What you see here is a machine, which can change the angle of both the vertical and horizontal layings. It is highly improbable that these machines should have existed in reality: any stationary great crossbow is more powerful and more compact than this arrow-firer. We can only see images of such arrow-firers in later sources (the second half of the 15th – the beginning of the 16th centuries) when throwing machines had already been replaced by cannon. From a reconstruction by Viollet-le-Duc.

PLATE 37

Fire engine used in 424 BC by the Boeotians against the Athenians fortified at Delium. The machine was contrived by the Boeotians themselves and was a huge hollowed log transferred on carts. There was an iron tube driven inside the log, going from the bellows right into the copper head filled with coal, sulphur and resin. Pumping air into the copper by means of bellows, the Boeotians created great flames and burned down the fortifications of the Athenians. ▶

◀ **PLATE 38**

Reconstruction of a cannon after a drawing in Walter de Milemete's treatise (1326). The treatise contains the first image of a cannon which had the shape of a vase and fired arrows. Recent tests of a reconstructed model of such a cannon by British researchers from the Royal Armouries have proved a practical possibility of the existence of such cannon.

PLATE 39

Bombard, late-14th century. Heavy siege *bombards* of the second half of the 14th – the first half of the 15th centuries never shot from wheeled gun-carriages. They were dug into the ground or mounted on special wooden platforms. A whole system of transverse and longitudinal beams designed for lessening the recoil was dug into the ground beyond the cannon. Destruction was achieved at a distance of no more than 200 – 250m from a fortress wall. Therefore, during reloading, the cannon was covered with a large shield to protect the gun crew from the arrows and bullets of the defenders. In the picture we see the cannon just before firing. The gunsmith is igniting the primer powder. Immediately after he will jump down into a trench where the rest of the crew are hiding — the explosion of a cannon was a common thing at that time. On the right-hand side of the picture we can see a *trebuchet* coexisting with cannon. ▶

▲ PLATE 40

Ribaudequin, 15th century. In siege warfare such multi-barreled guns on two-wheeled carts were especially effective in defending a gate or a breach in the wall. Spears preventing the enemy from approaching the gun were sometimes placed in front of it.

PLATE 41

Watchtower in a raised and lowered positions, according to Apollodorus and Anonymus Byzantine. The calculation of all the dimensions of the watchtower was done proceeding from the height of the wall: the length of the ladder equaled half the wall's height; as was the length of the longer end of the "rocker" arm, and the height of the vertical beams was 1/3 of the height of the wall. Thus an observer would have found himself rising 1/3 of the wall's height above it. ▶

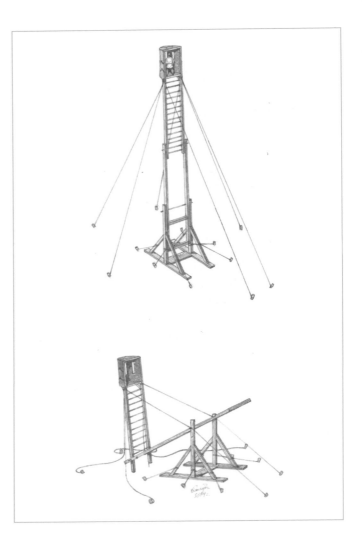

◀ **PLATE 42**

Tolleno. This simple siege contrivance allowed several men to be lifted quickly onto the wall or gain a height advantage for attacking.

◄ **PLATE 43**

Pole with a hook (*falce*) for demolishing walls.

◄ **PLATE 44**

The use of the *demolishing raven* by the defenders of a fortress.

▲ **PLATE 45**

Testudo formation employed for the assault of a wall.

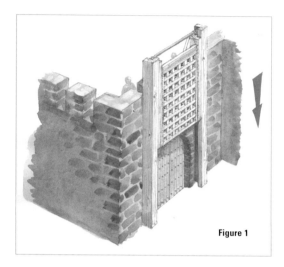

Figure 1

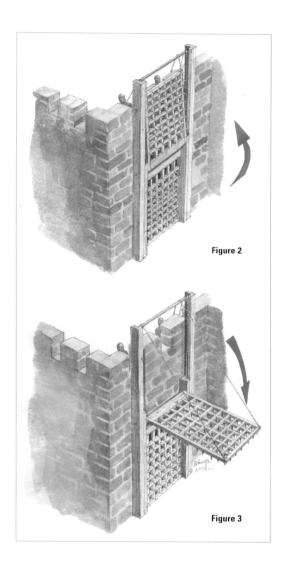

Figure 2

Figure 3

▲ PLATE 46-1   PLATE 46-2 ▶

A possible reconstruction of a "wolf." The structure was only described by Procopius and fairly vaguely at that. Judging by his description, two gratings from the top to the bottom of the fortifications were placed on the external side of a gate. Each grating was dotted with tenons. When an enemy approached the gate, the defenders pushed the upper grating and it fell down, killing everyone caught between the two gratings. In this reconstruction we can see both the gratings in a raised position (1); one of the gratings has been lowered and the "wolf" is ready for action (2); and finally, the "action" itself — the upper grating drops and shuts like a wolf's jaw (3).

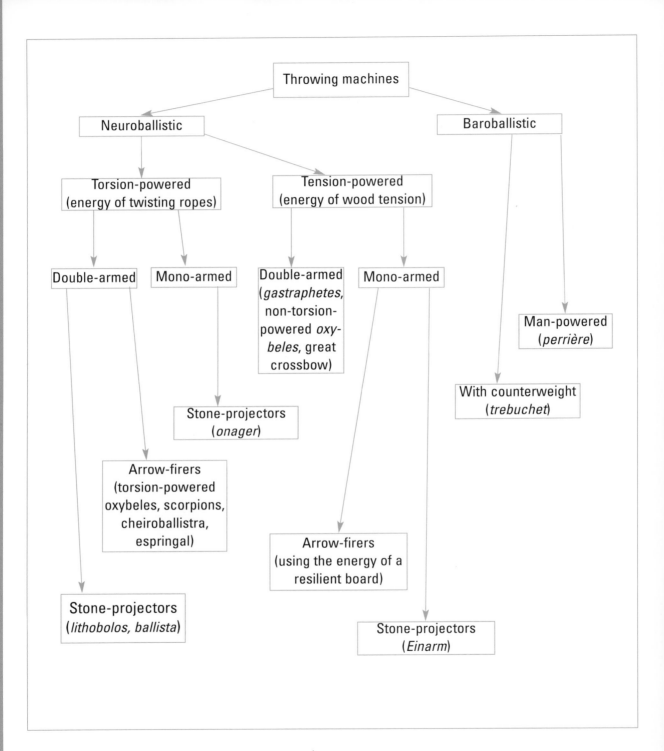

▲ SCHEME

It often happened that the commander of a garrison found himself in a difficult situation, being faced with a numerous army and having no clear instructions from his superior. Should he hold the castle with all his force, risking people's lives, or surrender without firing a shot? In this situation he usually tried to communicate with his superior and take directions from him. The offense sometimes granted him a few days' grace for that purpose. In 1102, after a three months' siege, the garrison of Arundel sent an envoy to their lord Robert of Bellême asking him to send reinforcements or to allow them to surrender. Robert could not help them with reinforcements and gave permission for capitulation.[362]

If all proposals for a capitulation were turned down and the defense was going to offer resistance, the offense set about laying a siege.

2. LAUNCH A SURPRISE ATTACK WHILE THE DEFENSE IS NOT READY.

Anonymus Byzantine recommended attacking a town in autumn, with the enemy engaged in gathering grapes or celebrating outside the town walls. The greater part of townsfolk being out of town, an opportunity would arise to capture numerous prisoners whose relatives would then surrender the town of their own free will, or pay tribute in exchange for the prisoners. As to a surprise night attack, he recommended undertaking it in winter, preferably during a feast when the inhabitants were either staying at home because of cold weather or were all drunk, and the guards would have lost vigilance.[363]

3. PITCH ONE OR MORE FORTIFIED CAMPS AND SURROUND THE CITY WITH SIEGE LINES.

The camp was surrounded with a moat, a rampart, and a wall with towers, all at a distance slightly surpassing the range of an arrow flight. This line of *circumvallation*, which Vegetius called *loricula*,[364] was earmarked to defend the camp against possible sorties of the garrison. To protect the rear the besiegers built another similar defense line, which was called the *contravallation line*. In front of the moat were wolf-holes—pits camouflaged on the top with pointed stakes driven into the bottom. Sometimes, so-called "lilies" were made, too. They were pits about 0.9 meter deep narrowing gradually toward the bottom. Smooth tree trunks as thick as a man's leg, pointed and seared on the top, were dug into the pit in such a way that they stuck no more than 10 centimeters above the surface. The upper part of the pit was covered with twigs and brushwood to hide the trap. There were also stakes about 30 centimeters long with iron spikes sticking up, which were driven into the ground; these were called *stimulus* ("spur"). When a warrior or his horse stepped on a "lily" or a *stimulus*, the man's or the animal's foot was seriously injured and neither could go on fighting. *Tribulus* ("garlic") served the same purpose. They were usually iron or bronze balls about 2 centimeters in diameter, having four spikes each. The 5-centimeter-long spikes stuck out in different directions so that whatever way a *tribulus* was thrown, one of the spikes would always be sticking up. In case of a field battle, a *tribulus* was made of four pointed stakes of the same length, which were joined in such a way that three of the stakes would rest on the ground and the fourth one always stuck up.[365]

The most complicated and fully described *circum-* and *contravallation lines* were built by Caesar at the siege of Alesia:

> Caesar, on learning these proceedings from the deserters and captives, adopted the following system of fortification: he dug a trench twenty feet [6 meters] deep, with perpendicular sides, in such a manner that the base of this trench should extend so far as the edges were apart at the top. He raised all his other works at a distance of four hundred feet [120 meters] from that ditch; [he did] that with this intention, lest (since he necessarily embraced so extensive an area, and the whole works could not be easily surrounded by a line of soldiers) a large number of the enemy should suddenly, or by night, sally against the fortifications; or lest they should by day cast weapons against our men while occupied with the works. Having left this interval, he drew two trenches fifteen feet [4.5 meters] broad, and of the same depth; the innermost of them, being in low and level ground, he filled

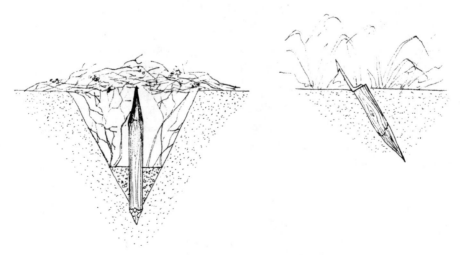

Left—a "lily," right—a *stimulus*.

with water conveyed from the river. Behind these he raised a rampart and wall twelve feet [3.6 meters] high; to this he added a parapet and battlements, with large stakes cut like stags' horns, projecting from the junction of the parapet and battlements, to prevent the enemy from scaling it, and surrounded the entire work with turrets, which were eighty feet [24 meters] distant from one another.

It was necessary, at one and the same time, to procure timber [for the rampart], lay in supplies of corn, and raise also extensive fortifications, and the available troops were in consequence of this reduced in number, since they used to advance to some distance from the camp, and sometimes the Gauls endeavored to attack our works, and to make a sally from the town by several gates and in great force. Caesar thought that further additions should be made to these works, in order that the fortifications might be defensible by a small number of soldiers. Having, therefore, cut down the trunks of trees or very thick branches, and having stripped their tops of the bark, and sharpened them into a point, he drew a continued trench everywhere five feet [1.5 meters] deep. These stakes being sunk into this trench, and fastened firmly at the bottom, to prevent the possibility of their being torn up, had their branches only projecting from the ground. There were five rows in connection with, and intersecting each other; and whoever entered within them were likely to impale themselves on very sharp stakes. The soldiers called these *cippi*. Before these, which were arranged in oblique rows in the form of a *quincunx*, pits three feet [0.9 meter] deep were dug, which gradually diminished in depth to the bottom. In these pits tapering stakes, of the thickness of a man's thigh, sharpened at the top and hardened in the fire, were sunk in such a manner as to project from the ground not more than four inches; at the same time, for the purpose of giving them strength and stability, they were each filled with trampled clay to the height of one foot [0.3 meter] from the bottom: the rest of the pit was covered over with osiers and twigs, to conceal the deceit. Eight rows of this kind were dug, and were three feet [0.9 meter] distant from each other. They called this a lily from its resemblance to that flower. Stakes a foot [0.3 meter] long, with iron hooks attached to them, were entirely sunk in the ground before these, and were planted in every place at small intervals; these they called spurs.

After completing these works, having selected as level ground as he could, considering the nature of the country, and having enclosed an area of fourteen miles [22.5 kilometers], he constructed, against an external enemy, fortifications of the same kind in every respect, and separate from these, so that the guards of

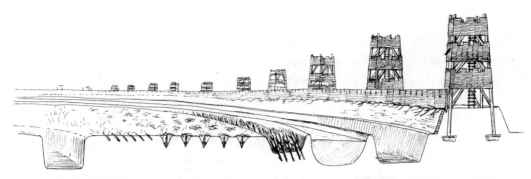

Defensive lines built by the Romans at the siege of Alesia. Reconstructed in accordance with the description by Caesar and archeological findings.

the fortifications could not be surrounded even by immense numbers, if such a circumstance should take place owing to the departure of the enemy's cavalry; and in order that the Roman soldiers might not be compelled to go out of the camp with great risk, he ordered all to provide forage and corn for thirty days.[366]

Complicated blockading lines were not employed as often in the Middle Ages. For a long-term siege, the besieged stronghold was usually surrounded with *bastilles*—wooden or stone siege towers or forts, which controlled the main approaches to the fortress. Those *bastilles* were seldom connected with each other by curtains or ramparts, and as a rule, they functioned on their own. At the siege of Orléans in 1428, the English built six square-shaped *bastilles* with rounded projections on the corners. Each of them held three cannon.[367] Fortunately for the French, the English never made them into an unbroken blockading line.

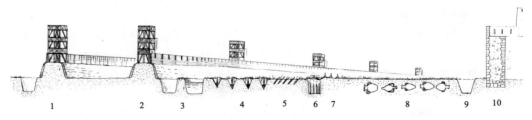

Circum- and *contravallation lines* and various traps:
1—a *contravallation line*; 2—a *circumvallation line*; 3, 9—ditches; 4—"lilies";
5—*stimulus*; 6—a wolf hole; 7—*tribulus*; 8—empty amphors dug into the ground;
10—fortress wall.

4. TRY TO CUT OFF THE ACCESS TO WATER IF THE FORTRESS IS SUPPLIED WITH WATER FROM OUTSIDE.

Thus, laying siege to the Cadurci town of Uxellodunum in 51 BC, Caesar turned the springs aside by means of underground canals and would not let the besieged get to the river, firing upon the approaches to it.[368] Clisthenes of Sicyon proved even more ingenious. While laying a siege to the town of the Crisaeans, he began with cutting off the town's access to water through the water pipe, and then, when the defenders started suffering from thirst, returned water to them—but it was poisoned with hellebore. The defenders, weakened by diarrhea, could no longer offer resistance.[369] If there was a river near the fortress and the fortress itself stood in a low place, it was possible to build a dam and direct the water of the river toward the fortifications in hopes of bringing down a section of the wall or a tower.[370]

5. ASSEMBLE SIEGE SHIELDS AND ENGINES.

6. START DIGGING AN UNDERGROUND TUNNEL.

In case the defenders should detect a tunnel and dig a counter-gallery, and the parties become engaged in underground fighting, Philon recommends that the men be armed with hunting stakes, Iberian javelins, and sharp sticks for urging on bulls. Even small throwing machines could turn out to be useful in an underground war, for which Philon advises using 3-span arrow-firers shooting bolts 69 centimeters long, and 2-mina stone-projectors shooting balls weighing about 0.9 kilogram. It was also advisable to try to "smoke" the enemy out of a tunnel. All these methods were equally fit for the attackers and the defenders,[371] but as to flooding a tunnel, only the defenders could do that.

7. FILL IN THE DITCH AND CHECK THE APPROACHES TO THE FORTRESS.

Prisoners and inhabitants of nearby villages were often used for filling in the moat. As a rule, they were brought to work by force; sometimes, however, they were paid for the work. For example, at the siege of Jerusalem the Crusaders' leaders offered to pay a penny for every three stones thrown into the ditch. Surprisingly heroism was manifested even at such operations. At the siege of Acre a woman was badly injured when filling in the ditch. Knowing that she was dying, the woman wished her body to be thrown into the ditch to help the common cause.

Before an assault, the besiegers had to check all the approaches to the fortress. If the defenders had dug empty earthenware crockery into the ground, heavy siege engines would come down and sink in it as the crockery broke down and the earth subsided. Therefore, the soil had to be examined with iron-tipped poles, or crowbars, or borers specially made for this purpose. Wolf-holes were sought with the help of a hoe, and then filled in. Iron spikes, or "garlics," scattered about and covered with earth could be torn out with a sharp rake, but one could also ignore them just by wearing shoes with wooden soles.[372]

8. TRY TO DESTROY THE WALLS WITH STONE-PROJECTORS, OR AT LEAST KNOCK MERLONS AND WOODEN GALLERIES OFF A WALL.

Apart from this main task, stone-projectors could inflict heavy losses on the defenders and even sow panic among them. From the following description of the siege of Montferrand (1137), one can easily imagine how hard it was for the defenders to stand their ground under such fire.

> Millstones and huge rocks hurled from the machines fell into the midst of the citadel, shattered the houses within, and caused intense fear to the refugees there. Great fragments of rock and all kinds of whirling missiles were hurled with such violence against them that there was no longer any place of security within the walls where the feeble and wounded might be hidden. Everywhere was danger, everywhere hazard, everywhere the specter of frightful death hovered before their eyes. Apprehension of sudden destruction and sinister foreboding of disaster ever attended them.[373]

9. BRING RAMS OR BORERS UP TO THE WALL AND TRY TO PULL DOWN A PART OF THE WALL.

During this operation throwing machines and archers incessantly fired upon the upper part of the wall so that the defenders could not counteract the attackers. The greatest effect was reached when the latter managed to bring a siege tower close to the wall and, firing from its upper floors, drive the defenders off the wall, which meanwhile had been shaken loose with the help of a ram. It is true that successful undermining could replace both a battering ram (or borer) and a siege tower.

If a section of the wall was built near deep water and the defenders had not taken the trouble to fill it with sharp stones, the assailants could try to bring the wall down with the help of a ship's battering ram.[374]

10. MAKE AN ATTACK ON THE WALL WITH THE HELP OF AN ASSAULT LADDER.

This method was preferable, provided the wall had already been partly broken by means of a ram, by mining, or with stone-projectors. A direct assault on a wall without special preparation, and with defenders offering brave resistance, was too expensive for the offense. Of course, on some occasions all siege operations were confined to such an assault; it happened either because of the offenders' inability to lay a "regular" siege, or lack of time or money. At this stage the walls were usually approached under the cover of a *tortoise* made with shields closed up over the heads and to the sides of the soldiers.

11. MAKE DISTRACTING MANEUVERS WHILE AN ASSAULTING PARTY IS CLIMBING THE WALL.

A fortress was often assaulted simultaneously on different sides so as to make the defenders scatter their forces. The storm on all directions but one usually served to distract the enemy's attention. If the assailants had enough forces at their disposal, it was advisable not to engage them

Assault with the use of a siege tower, a battering ram, an undermining, a *tolleno*, throwing machines (*perrière* and *trebuchet*), and *mantlets*.

all at once, but to bring them into battle in turns so that fresh forces continually entering the battle ensured the attack did not weaken.[375]

To give support to the storming troops, all men shooting bows, slings, crossbows, and hand firearms were mobilized. They were often put on a specially built siege tower, as it was much easier to bring fire to bear upon the defenders of the walls from above.

• TWENTY-FOUR •

METHODS OF DEFENSE

THE MAIN STEPS TAKEN BY THE DEFENSE:

1. PREPARE FOR A DEFENSE.

A detailed description of preparatory measures is given by Vegetius.[376] Philon[377] and Aeneas Tacticus also pay great attention to the preparation for the defense. All three of them wrote in ancient times, but we can claim with confidence that similar measures were taken in the Middle Ages as well.[378] Of course, it sometimes happened that the defenders did not have time for preparation and the attackers managed to seize a town or castle unawares, but this was an exception rather than the rule.

The first thing to do at the approach of an enemy was to try to bring into the town all food supplies, wine, vinegar, poultry, and forage for the horses. If the town had sufficient stores of fodder and forage, pigs and cattle were driven into the town; if it did not, the animals were slaughtered and the meat salted. Everything that could not be taken away was burned or destroyed. Moreover, Aeneas Tacticus and Philon recommend poisoning water in wells and reservoirs.[379]

Draft cattle and slaves were forbidden entry into the town. For the duration of a siege, they were to be handed over to friends who were not affected by the war. If there were no such friends, the cattle and slaves were handed over to mere acquaintances; it was done publicly and with the help of those in authority, who recorded all that was given away for safety.[380]

Asphalt, sulfur, tar, and oil were stored for incendiary purposes. Iron and wood were stored for manufacturing and repairing arms and various machines. Vegetius attaches great attention to the gathering and storage of stones. He recommends finding round stones in the river, as they are heavier and better fit for throwing. Small stones were thrown out of slings or just by hand; bigger ones, from *onagers*; and the biggest (round so that they could roll) were lifted onto the walls and thrown down from there. Big wooden wheels were also made, and smooth-finished logs were prepared to be thrown down on the attackers. It was necessary to have a store of sinew and horsehair, as torsion engines were useless without them. History records several instances where the lack of sinew for throwing machines forced women in a besieged town to cut off their own hair for this purpose. Women's hair was considered to be a very good material for torsion springs, but it seems to have been rarely used because of its relative shortage.

The approaches to the most vulnerable parts of a fortress were supplied with wolf-holes, empty large clay pots dug into the ground, and scattered-about "garlic."[381] Wolf-holes were the simplest traps for men and engines—but they were the easiest to discover. Empty large clay pots—which crashed only under the heavy weight of siege engines and caused the earth to sink—were much more difficult to detect.

2. BUILD THROWING MACHINES AND OTHER NECESSARY TOOLS IF LACKING.

The use of throwing machines for the defenders is obvious enough. Philon repeatedly underscores their necessity for the destruction of the siege weapons of the assailants (siege towers, movable sheds, etc.). He recommends employing 30-mina (13.1 kilogram) caliber stone-projectors against siege towers and movable sheds, and placing 10-mina (4.4 kilogram) caliber stone-projectors on the fortifications to be used against enemy throwing machines. In addition, he advises that one 10-mina stone-projector and two arrow-firers should be put in each street in case the enemy manages to break into the town.[382] In many medieval miniatures one can see throwing machines used by defenders as well. They were often placed by the gate. Stationary great crossbows and *espringals* were usually put in the towers. According to some miniatures, light man-powered stone-projectors could also be positioned on tower tops. Great and heavy stone-projectors with counterweights (*trebuchet*) were placed behind the walls.

3. ORGANIZE BATTLE-WORTHY POPULATION AND TAKE MEASURES AGAINST DESERTERS AND TRAITORS.

Various measures of organizing the defense in a besieged town are most fully illuminated in Aeneas Tacticus's treatise, which gives us a clear notion of the activities of the inhabitants of a besieged town in the 4th century BC. The treatise offers a detailed description of patrolling and carrying the sentinel service, gate guarding, agreed-upon signals, methods of revealing deserters, and so on. Aeneas Tacticus's views on the main points in the organization of defense can be reduced to the following: In case of danger, each phila of the citizens was charged with a certain section of wall to defend, the size of the latter depending on the size of the phila. Moreover, the stronger men were picked out in each phila and sent to patrol or guard public places. If there were allies or mercenaries, they were also distributed to different sections of the defense.[383]

However, to avoid an overthrow, the strength of the latter never exceeded or equaled the strength of the town militia. Mercenaries and allies were billeted in different houses of rich inhabitants and not allowed to gather together.[384]

Guards were to be changed often, and consist of a great number of people. No single sentinel was to know beforehand in what part of the town he would stand guard next time. Even the officers were not to have the same men under their command permanently. It was also recommended that a password be changed as often as possible so that if a traitor learned it, he could not make use of it. Moreover, it was advisable that, on giving the password, one should confirm it with a gesture (e.g., taking off a hat or a helmet, or putting a hand on the hilt of a sword), thus depriving the traitor of the opportunity to use an overheard password.[385] All of these measures were aimed at preventing traitors from committing an overthrow or letting the enemy in.

For patrolling along the foot of the wall, Aeneas recommends a detachment two *lochoi* (pl., from *lochos*) strong. Men should be fully equipped and wear identification marks in order to be easily recognized. He also believes that the first guard should be sent for patrolling without supper, as people become more placid and less responsible after a meal.[386] To repulse an assault on the wall, Aeneas recommends dividing the defenders into three parts so that one part would fight while another would rest, and the third one would prepare to enter the battle.[387] Thus, fresh forces would regularly enter the fighting.

At the time of a siege, no unsanctioned gatherings were permitted, and public meetings were only held in previously allotted places. Communal meals were also forbidden; people were to eat at home. Exceptions were only made for weddings and funeral banquets, of which the authorities were to be informed beforehand. Even the soothsayer was forbidden to make sacrifices without a representative of the authority. All those who had extra weapons were to record this fact in a special record. Dispatched and arriving letters were opened and inspected by censors.[388] Accusatory reports to the authorities were encouraged in every way possible; moreover, the informer was ceremonially rewarded with a certain sum of money.[389]

Particular attention is paid in the treatise to gate guarding. Aeneas advises enlisting the services of only wealthy citizens to guard the gates. It was even better if these people had some sort of commitment in the town—like a wife and children—making them much more difficult to bribe than a bachelor or a poor citizen. The Bosporan tyrant Leukon is said to have dismissed from the guard everyone who had lost all his money at dicing or was too much taken in by some other vice.[390]

Traitors most often were the ones who opened a gate for the enemy. The gate was closed with a bar that went horizontally back and forth between sockets in the wall. In the closed position the bar was fixed with a transverse catch. The latter also slipped into a special socket in the wall; then, a cylindrical pin was driven into the bar at its junction point with the catch. This pin could be unhooked with a special device called a *balanagra*, and if traitors managed to get a *balanagra* or make a copy of it, nothing could stop them from opening the gate. It was exactly in this way that the town of Heraea was captured in 236 BC.[391]

There were other means of taking the pin out without a *balanagra*. For instance, one could make a cut in the pin, tie a piece of thread to it, and pull the pin out. A thin net could also be used, into which the pin was placed. Sometimes traitors poured fine sand into the opening and shook the bar quietly, allowing the sand to get under the pin. As a result, the pin stuck out a little and could be pulled out.[392] To avoid these troubles, Aeneas Tacticus recommended that the gate be locked only by the commander himself, and that no one else be trusted with the *balanagra*. As a last resort, traitors would try to saw the bar in two, though the noise could bring the guard running to the gate. To muffle the noise, the bar was coated with oil, or a sponge was tied to the saw and the bar. Aeneas advised that the full length of the bar be bound with iron as a countermeasure.[393]

In order to not be taken unawares by a surprise night attack, Vegetius recommended keeping strong, keen-nosed dogs on the towers; they could smell an approaching enemy and inform their masters by barking. Aeneas advised tying the dogs on the outside of the wall.[394] Geese are known to be no less alert. In fact, it was precisely their cackle that saved the Romans besieged in the capital from a surprise night attack of the Gauls.[395]

If deserters could not be prevented, they had to be killed. Most interesting are cunning tricks used by Carthaginian generals. When Hamilcar Barca saw too many Gauls from his auxiliary troops desert to the side of the Romans, he ordered a detachment of faithful Gauls to feign desertion. The Roman detachment that came out to meet them was fully destroyed by the Gauls. Hamilcar's stratagem made the Romans regard true deserters with more suspicion, which led to a sharp decrease in their number. Similarly, the Carthaginian general Hanno had no luck with the Gauls during his campaign on Sicily in 261 BC. He suddenly learned that 4,000 Gaul mercenaries, having received no salaries for several months, were going to desert to the Romans. Hanno sent them away on the pretext of allowing them to pillage the neighborhood territories. At the same time he sent a false deserter to inform the Romans that the Gauls had been sent to take booty and could be intercepted. The Romans laid an ambush and their crack detachment unexpectedly attacked the Gauls. Thus, Hanno got a double gain: the Gauls inflicted heavy losses to the Romans and were themselves killed. Hannibal was no less ingenious. On learning that some of his soldiers had deserted to the enemy and that there were spies in his camp, he declared that the deserters were acting on his order, stealing enemy plans. The spies took the

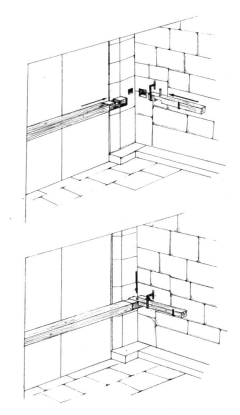

Construction of a gate lock.

information to the Romans who caught the deserters and cut off their arms. Few of the Carthaginian soldiers dared to desert to the Romans henceforth.[396]

4. RATION FOOD AND DEPRIVE THE CIVILIANS OF IT, IF NECESSARY.

There existed various means of supplying a besieged town with food and water. If there was a well in the town or fortress, or a river flowing through it, the besieged had no problems with water supply. However, some towns were situated on the top of a hill or were supplied with water through water pipes, which could be stopped up by the besiegers. In this case cisterns were put in all public buildings and private houses to accumulate the rainwater that ran down from the roofs. Water distribution was strictly controlled, and no waste of it on secondary needs was allowed. To a town that stood at the seaside and suffered from shortage of salt, Vegetius recommended using sea salt. Water from the sea was poured into saucers and left to evaporate in the sun. If the besiegers did not let the besieged come close to the water, sand was gathered on the beach and washed with freshwater. After the water had evaporated, the saucers were covered with salt.[397]

Food supplies presented a more serious problem. If these were insufficient, 100 percent nutrition was guaranteed only for battle-worthy men, as well as strong and hardy women who could be of use on the walls to repel an attack. Everyone else—the elderly and the sick, as well as children—received no more food than was necessary to preserve their lives. More often than not, however, food was still in short supply. As a last resort, many civil populations were driven outside the gate on the chance that the besiegers would let them go. The hope would usually come true: sick and old people and children were allowed to pass through the siege lines. In 1346 Edward III, having laid a siege to Calais, let a group of civilians go, and even supplied them with food for the journey. At Rouen, however, Henry V refused to give any food, or permission to pass through the siege lines, to the poor citizens. As a result, they all died of hunger on the no-man's-land between the two armies.[398]

5. APPOINT MONITORS TO DETECT UNDERMINING WORK.

Resonant copper vessels or shields, as well as bells, were used to detect undermining work. These were carried all the way along the walls and put to the ground every now and then. In the place where an underground tunnel was being dug, vibration caused a ringing of copper objects. Vessels with water were sometimes put along the wall. In this case, the vibration caused the water to ripple, thereby signaling the presence of a tunnel.

6. MAKE SPECIAL PREPARATIONS TO DISCOVER WHAT SECTION OF THE WALL WILL BE ASSAULTED.

Tar, water, and sand were quickly brought to this place and heated in big cauldrons. Stones, logs, and sometimes quicklime were brought onto all the walls beforehand, so that in case of a sudden attack they were ready to be thrown on the enemy. It was also necessary to store sacks with chaff, which could be hung from the wall to lessen the force of a ram blow. It was possible to weaken the force of the blows of the balls shot from stone-projectors by suspending nets, packed full of seaweed, or paneling gathered from planks made of date-palm and covered with a softening stuffing.[399] Double mats or Cilician goat carpets were hung between merlons as protection from arrows.[400] Mats and carpets hanging loose from the walls weakened the force of projectiles to a large degree. An additional wall could be erected beyond a vulnerable section of the fortress wall. It was advisable that the additional wall was constructed in a V-shape, with the tip directed inside the town; thus, the enemy breaking through the main wall would find themselves under fire from both sides.[401]

7. MAKE NUMEROUS SORTIES, IF POSSIBLE.

Sorties were made in an effort to fulfill the following goals: to destroy enemy siege engines; to strike a sudden blow on the enemy from a flank or rear; and to constantly harass the besiegers to maintain tension. Properly organized sorties were of great use for the besieged. However, sometimes they could bring deplorable results, as in the siege of Le Mans in 1099. During this battle, the garrison made a sortie, but was not able to retire in time and the besiegers rushed into the fortress. The town was captured, and the garrison just managed to hide in the citadel.[402]

8. USE SPECIFIC METHODS TO FIGHT THE SIEGE WEAPONS OF THE ATTACKERS (SEE TABLE 7).

Aeneas Tacticus recommended stretching thick awnings or sails behind the wall that was being fired on from stone-projectors. Not only did these awnings protect men from flying stones, but they also allowed the besieged to increase their stores of stones, as the stones did not break into small pieces and were easily gathered from the awnings.[403]

While increasing the height of the wall facing a siege tower, Philon recommended preserving the merlons and building up the wall in such a way as to create two parapetted levels. In this case, when the enemy threw a bridge from a siege tower onto the wall, it could easily be set alight from the lower level. A battering ram designed for destroying siege weapons of the assailants could also be more effectively operated from this level.[404]

Apart from traditional objects such as stones, logs, and so forth, which could be thrown down from the wall on the assailants, history also records references to fairly exotic ones. For example, Philon mentions some wheels with sickles, which, when rolling down a slanting surface, hit many an enemy. The same author recommends pouring *naphtha* (probably petroleum) down on the ascending attackers and then setting fire to them with torches. It seems hardly probable, however, that either method was widespread. At least, Philon himself says that *naphtha* was not accessible everywhere.[405]

Table 7. Methods the besieged used against various siege weapons.

Siege weapon	Conditions required	Fighting methods used by the besieged
Assault ladders	Walls no higher than 10 meters.	1. Pushing ladders off the wall. 2. Throwing down heavy objects (stones, logs, etc.); pouring boiling water, hot oil, or scorching sand down onto the besiegers.
Movable sheds (*mantlets, vineae, tortoises,* etc.)		1. Destruction with the help of throwing machines or cannon. 2. Setting fire with incendiaries. 3. Throwing down heavy objects like stones, etc.
Battering ram	Stone walls; no ditch at all, or one which has been filled in.	1. Destruction with the help of throwing machines or cannon. 2. Setting fire with incendiaries. 3. Catching the ram head with a loop or tongs and turning it over. 4. Destroying the ram or the ram *tortoise* with heavy objects like stones, logs, etc. 5. Suspending sacks of chaff down the wall to soften the ram's blow.
Borers	Brick walls; no ditch, or one which has been filled in.	The same as against a battering ram.
Siege towers	Hard, flat ground; no ditch, or one which has been filled in.	1. Destruction with the help of throwing machines or cannon. 2. Setting fire with incendiaries. 3. Increasing the height of a wall. 4. Rendering the surface in front of a wall impassable for a siege tower (e.g., boggy soil or hidden trap-pits). 5. Breaking a siege tower with a ram put on the wall.

Siege weapon	Conditions required	Fighting methods used by the besieged
Undermining	1. Relatively soft ground. 2. No moat with water. 3. A dry ditch that is not very deep.	1. Deepening the dry ditch. 2. Digging a counter-gallery followed by a hand-to-hand underground battle, flooding the tunnel, or "smoking out" the sappers.
Embankments (*agger*)	The fortress should not stand on a mountain peak or be washed by the sea on all sides.	1. Burning down the wooden framework of the *agger*. 2. Digging an underground tunnel and taking all the earth from the *agger* to the town.
Throwing machines		1. Destroying by stone-projectors or cannon. 2. Suspending softening canopies that lessen the force of the blows of projectiles from the walls.

9. FIGHT IN THE STREETS IF THE ENEMY HAS MANAGED TO RUSH INTO THE TOWN.

Having rushed into the town, the attackers often turned their efforts to plunder and were sometimes completely destroyed by the defenders. So to be successful, the defenders were advised to never yield to panic. By occupying all high places, such as towers, walls, and the roofs of houses, and shooting fire on the enemy from their slings, bows, and crossbows—or just throwing down tile and stones—they could inflict heavy losses on the enemy. To ensure the complete and utter defeat of the assailants, coordinated actions of detachments of armed defenders were needed; part of their mission was to destroy the enemy in the streets. The attackers, wishing to avoid desperate resistance on the part of the citizens, often left one of the gates open, thus giving the besieged an opportunity to run away.

As a rule, a town captured by storm was doomed to a dismal fate. Plunder went on every-where, usually accompanied by slaughter, taking prisoners and turning them into slaves, or re-settling the inhabitants elsewhere. The main factor that determined the cruelty of the attackers was the strength of the resistance. The longer and harder the besieged fought, the more deplorable their fate if they capitulated. If a town yielded at once, the townsfolk and sometimes the town valuables were spared, and only laid under indemnity. If many besiegers had perished during the assault on the town, or a commander was wounded, all the townsfolk might be slaughtered and the town itself razed to the ground. Alexander the Great serves as a typical example. Each time he was wounded during a siege, the town would be completely destroyed. Practically no other factors, including the nationality of the besieged, were taken into account; financial gain and political considerations took precedence over everything else. When analyzing the actions of the aforementioned Alexander the Great after the capture of a town, one cannot conclude that he treated his fellow tribesmen with any more mercy than he granted the Persians and other "barbarians."

TWENTY-FIVE

STRATAGEMS

Asiege was always a fairly costly enterprise—not only because of human losses, but also due to the huge sum required to put one into effect. Therefore, it is not surprising that the generals tried to avoid sieges in every way possible, often resorting instead to various ruses and tricks.

STRATAGEMS USED BY THE BESIEGERS

The main stratagems used by the besiegers can be summed up as follows:

1. USING TREACHERY.

The easiest way to capture a fortress was with the help of a traitor, who would open the gate or sow panic among the besieged. This method was the most popular stratagem employed by besiegers. There was probably no commander who would not try to avail himself of this opportunity. The usual way was to try to bribe the guards or some of the influential townsfolk. If that failed, false deserters would be sent into the fortress. For example, at the end of the 6th century BC, being unable to seize Gabii, the Roman King Tarquinius Superbus whipped his son and sent him to the enemy. Complaining of his father's cruelty, the young man persuaded the defenders to allow him to fight his loathsome parent. Having been made a commander, he betrayed the besieged and handed the town over to his father.[406] The Persian King Darius acted in the same way at the siege of Babylon. He maimed his retainer Zopyrus's face to such a degree that when the latter deserted to the besieged, the Babylonians had no doubt of the sincerity of his hatred for the king, made even more convincing when Zopyrus would constantly run ahead in battle and cast javelins at the king. Having bided his time, Zopyrus eventually helped the Persians to seize Babylon.[407]

2. TAKING A FORTRESS BY SURPRISE.

On laying a siege to the powerful Ligurian town of Lueria, Domitius Calvinus began regularly taking his troops out of the camp and around the town walls, after which he would bring the troops back to the camp. The defenders gradually got so used to the procedure that they paid no attention to the Romans. Then the day came when straight from the march, the Romans rushed to assault. Their vigilance weakened, the defenders failed to get themselves ready quickly enough for the defense, and the town fell.[408] This story highly resembles the biblical story of the Jericho trumpets (see Chapter 2, "Ancient Judea" p. 9).

During the siege of Sicyon, the Milesian general Thrasybulus constantly attacked the town from land. When the defense threw all their force to this sector, Thrasybulus's fleet seized the harbor by a surprise attack.[409]

One night the Athenian general Alcibiades brought his troops unnoticed to Cyzicus and ordered his trumpeters to blow near another section of the walls. The defenders were in abundance, quite sufficient for repulsing attacks on all the walls, but they gathered together to defend the section that they thought to be assaulted. Then Alcibiades seized the town from another side, facing practically no resistance.[410]

Pericles acted with even more cunning. Preparing for an assault on a Peloponnesian fortress that could only be approached from two sides, he had one of the approaches cut off by a ditch and then began to fortify the other. Being reassured as to the former side, the besieged only prepared to defend the latter, where fortifications were being built. Meanwhile, Pericles's army secretly made small bridges, threw them over the ditch, and broke into the fortress on the unguarded side.[411]

3. Penetrating into the Fortress under the Guise of Friendship.

The easiest way to gain entrance was to make one's soldiers change into the clothes of the besieged. This is what the Arcadians did when they learned that the besieged Messenian fortress was expecting reinforcements. They not only had to dress the same as the besieged, but they also had to manufacture arms that were similar to the enemy's as well. Taken for allies and let into the fortress, they captured it in no time. The same trick was used by Hannibal to seize a number of Italian towns: when approaching a town, he would send ahead the soldiers who knew Latin, dressed as Roman soldiers. [412]

The besiegers often penetrated a town under the guise of being merchants or foragers. This was not easy, as merchants and foragers were not supposed to carry arms, so the latter had to be hidden. Still, it was exactly by means of this stratagem that the Lacedaemonians captured the town of Tegea in Arcadia in 240–239 BC. Soldiers dressed as merchants were let into the town, where they proceeded to open the gate for their troops. The fortress of Suenda in Cappadocia fell because of a similar trick: soon after a team of actual foragers left the town, they were captured, and the drivers killed. Enemy soldiers dressed in their clothing penetrated the fortress, and let in the besiegers.[413]

Probably the most difficult task was undertaken by Epaminondas, whose soldiers changed into women's clothes as a method of gaining entry. A feast was under way at the time, and many townswomen were walking outside the fortress walls. (Presumably, the enemy was supposed to be still fairly far away; otherwise, this fact is hard to explain.) The Theban general ordered his soldiers to dress as women and mingle in the crowd. Toward evening, the women were let in, the disguised soldiers among them; the soldiers quickly slaughtered the guards and opened the gate for the besiegers. [414]

4. Decreasing the food stores of the besieged.

In the first place, the offense would blockade the food transport into the town. As a rule, attempts were also made to burn down the town's provision stores with the help of a spy or traitor. However, there were commanders who contrived to have the besieged themselves take provisions out of a fortress and waste it. For example, Fabius Maximus, having emptied the Campanian fields, took his troops away for the time of sowing. The besieged spent what was left of the corn for sowing. Then Fabius Maximus returned and easily took the town, which was left without food.[415] Dionysius I acted even more perfidiously in order to capture Regium in 391 BC. First, he feigned the signing of an armistice agreement, and then asked the town to supply his troops with provisions. When the stores of bread were in this way exhausted, he attacked the town and seized it easily.[416]

Another means of draining food stores of the besieged was to increase the town's population. Preparing to besiege Leucadia, which abounded in food products, King Alexander of Epirus first seized some small nearby fortresses and allowed their inhabitants to flee to Leucadia. As a result, provisions that could have lasted for a long time were soon eaten.[417] True, this stratagem could only be applied in cases where town leaders lacked sound judgment. It should be remembered that garrison commanders often took reverse measures, as well (i.e., not allowing too many mouths to feed inside a fortress); they would even send away all civilians who were unfit for fighting. In this respect, the defenders of ancient towns were usually more compassionate than their descendants in the Middle Ages.

5. Feigning retreat.

To feign retreat in order to lure the besieged out of a fortress is a very ancient and frequently used stratagem. The Bible says that the Hebrews resorted to this at the siege of the Canaanite town of Ai (see Chapter 2 p. 10). Marcus Cato (234–149 BC) acted similarly at the siege of a town of the Lacetani. Having taken away his main forces, he threw just an auxiliary detachment of the unbelligerent Suessetani in an assault upon the walls. The defenders made a sortie and, easily putting them to flight, rushed in pursuit. Then Cato led his main forces out of the ambush and captured the town with practically no fighting.[418] During the siege of a Sardinian town, Lucius Scipio, wishing to lure out the defenders, broke off an already launched attack and pretended to retreat. The besieged thoughtlessly rushed to pursue the enemy; meanwhile, a Roman detachment, hidden in an ambush nearby, took the town.[419] Feigned retreat of a besieging army combined with the use of ambushes is also recommended by Byzantine military treatises as a fairly effective means of inflicting casualties upon the enemy or capturing a fortress.[420]

STRATAGEMS USED BY THE BESIEGED

The main stratagems used by the besieged can be summed up as follows:

1. INCREASING THE VIGILANCE OF SENTINELS.

At the siege of Athens by the Lacedaemonians (408 BC), the Athenian general Alcibiades told those on guard that they were to wait for him to light a signal fire from the acropolis, and, on seeing it, to light a fire in return. The guard would keep vigil all night in tense expectation until the danger was past. This is, of course, the softest means of keeping the guards awake. Many a commander would simply execute all sentinels caught sleeping at their posts.[421]

2. SUPPLYING PROVISIONS.

When Hannibal laid siege to the town of Casilinum (presently, Capua) in 216 BC, the Romans helped the besieged by sending barrels of flour down the river. When Hannibal had a chain stretched across the river in order to hinder the practice, the Romans began to send down nuts.[422] Similarly, Hirtius sent barrels of salt down the river to the Mutinians, who were being besieged by Antonius; later, he sent cattle down the river as well.[423]

3. CREATING FALSE APPEARANCES OF ABUNDANCE OR SHORTAGE.

It was often vitally important for a besieged town to create the impression of having food in abundance or numerous troops at its disposal, so that the enemy would lose hope of starving the town out or taking it by storm, and lift the siege. Or the enemy could alter their tactics, sometimes serving the purpose of those in defense.

The soldiers of the Milesian general Thrasybulus were exhausted by a long siege laid by the Lydians, who hoped to reduce them to surrender by starvation. When the Lydians sent in their envoys, Thrasybulus ordered his men to bring all the bread that was left to the forum and pretend that the town was giving itself a feast. The envoys returned to their camp fully assured that the town was not to be starved out.[424]

Another example can be found in a siege laid by the Athenians against the Spartans. When the besieged only had enough food left to last for two days, a messenger from Sparta arrived. The Athenians did not let him pass into the town, but allowed him to stand in front of the wall and speak to the besieged so that he could be heard by both sides. The messenger addressed the commander of the garrison, saying: "The Lacedaemonians order you to rest assured and expect reinforcement as soon as possible." He received the following answer: "Do not be in a hurry with the help; I have got provisions for another five months." The Athenians decided that the siege was going to be a long one, and as winter was approaching, they broke camp and left.[425] Nothing can be more impressive, however, than the heroism of starving Romans besieged by the Gauls on the Capitoline hill in 390 BC. Starved to the last degree, they began to throw bread at the enemy. Thus pretending to have food in abundance, they managed to hold out till they were given a helping hand.[426]

Wishing to appear as if they had numerous troops at their disposal, the Romans, besieged by Hannibal in Rome in 211 BC, sent reinforcements through an unguarded gate to their army in Spain. At the same time, in order to show self-confidence, they put on sale the field on which Hannibal's army was encamped; moreover, they put it on sale at its prewar price.[427]

The inhabitants of Sinope, being in want of men, marched women dressed up as men along the walls in sight of the besiegers. Instead of helmets and shields they were "armed" with pots and copper vessels. They were not allowed to fire, though, as a firing woman was recognizable from a long distance, according to Aeneas Tacticus. Aeneas also gave general recommendations as to how to make patrols appear more numerous than they were—two soldiers marching side by side were to carry their spears on different shoulders, the right-hand one on his right shoulder and the left-hand soldier on his left shoulder. Thus, from afar it would appear they had twice as many soldiers.[428]

In some cases, however, the besieged purposely created the false impression of being weak. For instance, when Pompey was preparing to assault the town of Asculum, its defenders brought only a small group of old and sick people onto the walls. The Romans decided that the garrison was weak and became careless. Then the besieged made a sortie and put the Romans to flight. Similar stratagems were used in Gaul by Julius Caesar and his legate, Titurius Sabinus.[429]

4. Creating a desperate situation on purpose so as to make the defenders fight more courageously.

At the approach of the enemy, Cleitarhus brought all his troops out of the town, locked the gate, and threw the keys ostentatiously over the wall. Realizing that they were deprived of any possibility of retreat into the town, his soldiers fought bravely and carried the day.[430] Mempsis, in his fight with Aribbeus, purposely created a still graver situation: not only did he bring the troops out, but also ordered women and children and all their property to be brought out as well. Aribbeus was so frightened by these preparations that he retreated without ever entering a battle.[431]

Not all stratagems fall under these classifications, however. Some of them were distinguished by such boldness that they cannot be included in any of the aforementioned groups—they were truly unique. The most famous, of course, is the legend of the Trojan Horse (see Chapter 5, "Greece" p. 28). Other examples include the work of Theban commander, Pelopidas; in 369–368 BC, he was preparing to capture two towns situated about 20 kilometers from each other. Camping by one town, he ordered that four horsemen should ride from the side of the other town, arriving at his camp wearing garlands, as if they were messengers of victory. Moreover, he ordered his men to set fire to the forest that lay between the two towns in order to create the impression of a burning town. He also had a number of people brought from that side, ostensibly prisoners. The besieged surrendered, concluding that they were now alone and without any hope of help. Thereafter, Pelopidas added the garrison of the surrendered town to his troops, and with this enlarged force approached the second town, whose inhabitants decided that resistance was useless and soon yielded. Thus, by the use of sheer subterfuge, Pelopidas took two towns without a fight.[432]

In 201 BC Philip V besieged the Rhodian town of Prinassus in Asia Minor. As hard as he tried, the Macedonian king could not seize the town, so he ordered his men to dig a tunnel. However, the rocky bottom of the ditch was too hard, and would not give way. Philip resorted to a ploy, whereby his sappers descended into the tunnel and pretended to be digging vigorously. At night, a group of soldiers brought a lot of earth from another place and piled it high in front of the entrance to the tunnel. On waking up, the defenders saw a great heap of earth and decided that the tunnel was close to completion. Fearing imminent attack, they capitulated. When they learned later that they had been taken in by the ruse, they bitterly deplored their foolishness.[433]

During his Egypt campaign, the Persian King Cambyses had the well-fortified fortress Pelusium (presently, Tineh) lying in his way. Its siege, which took place in 525 BC, was a bloody one. The Egyptians resisted stubbornly, and all the efforts of the Persians to seize the fortress were in vain. Cambyses ordered his men to place dogs, sheep, cats, and ibises, sacred to the Egyptians, in front of the troops launching the assault. The Egyptians stopped firing for fear of hurting the animals, and the Persians captured the fortress.[434]

GREEK MEASUREMENTS

1 dactyl			=	1.93 cm
1 palm	=	4 dactyls	=	7.7 cm
1 span	=	12 dactyls	=	23.1 cm
1 foot	=	16 dactyls	=	30.8 cm
1 cubit	=	24 dactyls	=	46.2 cm
1 mina			=	437 g
1 talent	=	60 minas	=	26.2 kg

ROMAN MEASUREMENTS

1 digit (*digitus*)			=	1.85 cm
1 inch (*uncia*)			=	2.46 cm
1 cubit	=	24 digits	=	44.4 cm
1 foot (*pes*)			=	29.6 cm
1 pound (*libra*)			=	327.5 g
1 talent	=	80 pounds	=	26.2 kg

APPROXIMATE LIFE SPANS OF SOME ANCIENT AND MEDIEVAL AUTHORS

Aeneas Tacticus	mid-4th century BC
Albertus Magnus	AD 1193 (1206)*–1280
Ammianus Marcellinus	AD 330–400
Anonymus Byzantine	probably the 10th century AD
Anonymus Reformer (author of *De rebus bellicis*)	second half of the 4th century AD
Apollodorus	2nd century AD
Appian	2nd century AD
Arrian	end of the 1st–2nd century AD
Athenaeus Mechanicus	probably the 2nd century AD
Roger Bacon	AD 1214–1292 (1294)*
Biton	3rd century BC
Caesar	100–44 BC
Christine de Pisan	AD 1364–1430
Dio	second half of the 2nd–first half of the 3rd century AD
Diodorus	1st century BC
Frontinus	AD 40–103
Giles of Rome	AD 1246–1316
Herodotus	5th century BC
Heron	AD 60–150

*   Parenthesis is used when the exact date of birth or death is not known and opinions of historians differ.

Homer	8th century BC
Josephus	1st–beginning of the 2nd century AD
Livy	59 BC–AD 17
Mariano Taccola	AD 1381–1453 (1458)*
Murda al-Tarsusi	12th century AD
Philon	3rd century BC
Plutarch	AD 46–126
Polyaenus	2nd century AD
Polybius	2nd century BC
Procopius	6th century AD
Pseudo-Maurice	late 6th–early 7th century AD
Quintus Curtius	1st century AD
Tacitus	AD 55–120
Thucydides	5th century BC
Vegetius	second half of the 4th–beginning of the 5th century AD
Vitruvius	1st century BC
William of Tyre	AD 1130–1190
Xenophon	second half of the 5th–first half of the 4th century BC

* Parenthesis is used when the exact date of birth or death is not known and opinions of historians differ.

GLOSSARY

LIST OF ABBREVIATIONS:

Ar–Arabic, Arabian, Arab
Fr–French, Old French
Germ–German
Gr–Greek, Ancient Greek
It–Italian
Lat–Latin
LL–Late Latin
ML–Medieval Latin
Pers–Persian
Sp–Spanish
Turk–Turkish

alakatia	Gr; a light man-powered beam-sling stone-thrower propped on one pillar. Like *arradah*, it could be seated on a wheeled cart and conduct all-around fire.
algarrada	Sp; from Ar: *al-arradah*; a light man-powered stone-thrower on one supporting post.
ampela	See *vinea*.
aqqar	Ar; apparently, the most powerful hand crossbow ("two-foot crossbow"). It was pulled on a special stand or by means of a winch.
arcuballista	Lat: "bow-ballista"; heavy crossbow on a stand, whose string was stretched by means of a windlass. Synonyms—Fr: *arbalète è tour*; ML: *balista ad tornum*; Germ: *windenarmbruste*; variants: *baliste grosse, bariste de torno, baliste a torno, amgna ballista*.
arradah	Ar; a light man-powered beam-sling stone-thrower, more often than not having a support of one pillar. Like the Chinese "whirlwind stone-thrower," it could fire in 360 degrees. Sometimes it was placed on a wheeled cart.

ballista, *pl. ballistae*	Lat; the term was used by the Romans for a torsion-powered double-armed stone-projector (it is in this sense that the term is used in this book). In the Middle Ages the term was used for big, heavy, tension-powered crossbows (giant crossbows), and sometimes for hand crossbows.[435] Synonyms—Fr: *baliste*; Gr: *ballistra*.
ballista *fulminalis*	Lat; a certain *ballista* which was generally used during the defense of a fortress. It is only mentioned by the Anonymus Reformer (4th c. AD). Its structure remains unclear; it might have been a great crossbow (*arcuballista*) with an all-metal bow, or a light torsion-powered arrow-firer like *cheiroballistra*.
baroballistic *throwing* *machines*	From Gr: *baros* ("weight, heaviness"); throwing machines that used counterweights or the muscular force of men.
bastille	1. Siege tower or siege fort in Medieval Europe built on the most vulnerable approaches to a fortress (from the point of view of the approach of relieving forces or sorties on the part of the besieged); 2. The French term for the best-fortified part of a town (citadel).
belfry	Siege tower.
biffa	Fr; a *trebuchet* with one or two mobile counterweights (the same as *couillard*). This term might have been used for a hybrid throwing machine with a small counterweight and stretching ropes.
blida	Germ; the name for the *trebuchet* in German and Scandinavian lands. It comes from *biffa*, and thus possibly refers to a *trebuchet* with a mobile counterweight only. Synonyms: *bidda, bleda, bliden*.
bombard	From Gr: *bombos*—"droner," "rumbler"; a large-caliber cannon of the 14th and 15th centuries.
bombardelle	Small cannon of the 14th and 15th centuries.
borer, drill	Siege machine for drilling holes in a wall, which proved especially effective against brick walls. Like the battering ram, it was placed inside a shed (*tortoise*). Gr: *trypanon*; Lat: *terebra*.
bricole, brigola	Throwing machine with two symmetrically placed counterweights (Mariano Taccola). The term first occurs in the early 13th century in Genoa. In France it was possibly used for a hybrid machine (with a counterweight and stretching ropes).[436] Synonyms: *bricola, briccola, brichola, brigolo*.
carroballista	Lat; a light arrow-firer (possibly *cheiroballistra*) sitting on two- or four-wheeled cart drawn by mules or horses.
cat	The nickname used in the Middle Ages for a mobile shed.

catapult	Lat: *catapulta*; from Gr: *katapeltes*—a throwing machine. Initially (at least until mid-1st century AD), the term stood for a torsion-powered arrow-firer only; later on, a stone-projector was often called by the term.
charkh	Pers; stationary fortress crossbow fairly moderate in size. It could shoot bolts, stone balls, and "eggs" filled with an incendiary mixture. Synonyms—Ar: *jarkh*; Turk: *carh*.
cheiroballistra	Gr: ("hand *ballista*"); an improved *scorpion*. Unlike the latter, it had a metal framework (*peritreton*) and a sighting mechanism. The *cheiroballistra* appeared about AD 100. The term is analogous with Lat: *manuballista*.
chelandria	From Gr: *chalandron*; a fairly small, light Byzantine ship specially adapted to throwing Greek fire.
chelone	Gr: a *tortoise* (a mobile shed).
circumvallation (line of)	Line of fortifications built by the besiegers to prevent the besieged from breaking out of a fortress and to provide defense against possible sorties.[437]
contravallation (line of)	The external circular fortification lines erected by the army of the besiegers for protecting their rear.[438]
corona muralis	Lat; a reward—a garland awarded to the warrior who was the first to climb the fortress wall during a siege.
corona vallaris	Lat; a reward—a garland awarded to the warrior who was the first to mount the rampart during an attack on the enemy camp.
couillard	Fr; a *trebuchet* with two symmetrical movable counterweights.
cuniculum	Lat; an "underground way," or undermining (mining gallery); the name is derived from the name of a hare's burrow (Vegetius).
dabbabah	Ar; a wheeled *tortoise* covered with boards and raw hides.
demolishing raven	The term cited by Vitruvius apparently meaning the same as Vegetius's pole with a sickle (*falce*). Lat: *corvus demolitor*.
digging tortoise	*Tortoise* used by sappers to destroy a wall at the base.
Einarm	Germ: "one arm"; mono-armed tension-powered stone-thrower using the energy of one or more bent boards or steel springs. Existence in reality is highly questionable.
epibathra	Gr; an assaulting bridge of a siege tower.
espringal	Medieval torsion-powered two-armed throwing machine (13th–15th centuries). Sometimes, although much rarer, the term was also used to describe large stationary crossbows. Later on, it came to denote a small fortress gun (15th–16th centuries). Synonyms—E: *springal*, *springald*; It:

	spingarda; Fr: *espringale, espringarde*; SouthFr: *spingula, espingola*; SouthGerm: *springolf, selbschoß*; NorthGerm: *notstalle, noytstelle*.
euthytone	Gr: arrow-firer.
exostra	Lat; an assaulting bridge which could be pulled out at the center of a siege tower (*helepolis*).
falarica, phalarica	Lat; an incendiary missile resembling a spear. It was supplied by a hard iron head about 90 centimeters long; near the tube of the head it was covered with an incendiary mixture (sulfur, resin, etc.). It was hurled by a *ballista* or by hand.
falce	Lat; a siege contrivance for demolishing walls. It consisted of a pole with a hook at the end. The term *falce* is used by Vegetius and Caesar. Describing apparently the same contrivance, Vitruvius calls it a "demolishing raven" or "crane."
fascine	A bunch of brushwood.
fire wheel	Hoops clad with tow and soaked in resin; they were put on fire and thrown at the enemy.
gabion	Woven basket filled with earth, used in building field fortifications and providing protection from bullets and balls of the enemy.
gastraphetes	Gr: "belly-bow"; an ancient Greek crossbow. The force of tension was 70 to 90 kilograms; it fired short (40–60 cm) bolts with faceted metal heads. Sometimes the term *gastraphetes* was also used for non-torsion-powered throwing machines on stands (e.g., Biton).
grazing fire	Casting shells over open sights or at an elevation angle of less than 20 degrees.
great (giant) crossbow	The same as *arcuballista*.
Greek Fire	Incendiary mixture whose exact composition is not known. It was used in naval and siege warfare from the 7th century AD. As there are no precise criteria as to what the term "Greek Fire" stood for, in this book it is used in a broad sense, i.e., not only for a fire-throwing weapon but also for complex incendiary compositions cast by throwing machines.
helepolis, elepolis	Gr: "city-taker"; a wheeled wooden siege tower housing archers and crossbowmen, siege devices (e.g., battering rams) and throwing machines. At the time of the Roman Empire and medieval Byzantium, the term seems to have been sometimes applied to other siege engines, too, including throwing machines and battering rams.

jarkh	See *charkh*.
karwah	Ar; a large wheelless siege shield. It consisted of a framework filled with cotton and covered with hides.
laisa	A light portable shed used in the Byzantine Empire from about the 10th century. The construction is not clear; it is only known that there were different versions and sizes of it.[439] It may have been a common name for light sheds varying in size from a simple siege shield to the *vinea*.
lambdarea, labdarea	Gr; the name of a Byzantine man-powered beam-sling engine stone-projector with a lambda (Λ) shaped framework.
lithobolos	The full Greek name is *catapeltes lithobolos*, but the first word (*catapult*) was often omitted. It is a throwing machine of the ancient Greeks, adapted for projecting stones.
loricula	Lat: a diminutive from *lorica* ("armor, fence, enclosure"); a line of *circumvallation* (according to Vegetius).
luba, lu'ab	Ar; mentioned by al-Tarsusi alone, it is a small man-powered stone-thrower (*manjaniq*) on a prop of one pillar, easily turnable from one side to another (the construction is probably analogous with that of *arradah*).
malleolus	Lat; an incendiary arrow consisting of a cane staff with a little box, made of iron wire, fastened a little beneath the arrowhead. The box was filled with an incendiary mixture; then, a match was inserted and it was set on fire.
manganon, manganikon, magganika	Each of these is a common name of beam-sling throwing machines (man-powered or with a counterweight) in the Byzantine Empire. It is also possible that the terms were used in even a broader sense to denote military machines in general.
mangonel	Medieval European name of beam-sling stone-throwing machines (man-powered). Synonyms—ML: *manganum*; Fr: *mangonneau*; Sp: *manguanel, manganillas*.
manjaniq	Ar; the name for stone-throwers (man-powered or with a counterweight). Different versions of *manjaniq* were distinguished according to the construction of their framework ("Arab," "Turkish-style," "Frankish-style," "Persian," and others). Spanish names of stone-throwers such as *almajenech* and *almanganiq* derived their names from *manjaniq*.
mantlet, mantelet	Mobile (wheeled) or portable wooden siege shield.
manuballista	Lat: "hand *ballista*"; late Roman name for a light arrow-firer.
metalla, metella	Woven basket filled with stones and balanced between two merlons of a wall so that the besiegers themselves would turn it over on their heads.

ANCIENT AND MEDIEVAL SIEGE WEAPONS

midfa madfaa Ar: "firearm" (cannon or hand firearm). It is possible that in the 15th century the term was used to denote small cannon transported by camel (analogous with Persian *zanburak*).

monankon From Gr: *monankones* ("one-handed"); a throwing machine having one throwing arm (beam). The term was used both for the ancient and the early medieval *onager* and the medieval stone-throwers (man-powered or with a counterweight).

mortar Short-barreled large-caliber cannon casting balls in a high plunging trajectory.

musculus Lat; a siege shed, according to Vegetius, similar to *vinea* but smaller in size. According to Caesar, however, *musculus* are large-sized structures not unlike *tortoises*.

naffatun Ar: "naphtha troops"; a special unit in Muslim armies whose task was to attend to *Greek Fire* and other incendiary mixtures.

naphtha, naft The initial meaning was petroleum, but later on, the term came to stand for incendiary mixtures based on petroleum or oil, and even mixtures containing no petroleum at all (*Greek Fire*).

neuroballistic throwing machines From Gr: *neuron* ("tendon, nerve"); throwing machines using the energy of resilient bodies or twisted ropes.

onager Lat: "wild donkey"; a neuroballistic torsion-powered one-arm stone-projector, possibly invented about 200 BC; however, reliable information about its existence only refers to the 4th century AD. Its employment in the Middle Ages (with the exception of early medieval Byzantium), as well as the existence of wheeled models and those with spoons instead of a sling, is hardly probable. The machine was used in sieges only.

organon Gr: ("machine, engine"); any machine; the term was also used as a common name of throwing machines.

oxybeles The full Greek name is *catapeltes oxybeles*, but the first word (*catapult*) was often omitted. An ancient Greek throwing machine, the tension model appeared about 375 BC. It was mainly used for hurling bolts, but two varieties existed that fired small stone projectiles. A mechanism based on the principle of a windlass was used for stretching the string. Biton calls these stationary machines, as well as the first hand crossbows, *gastraphetes*, but in this book, to avoid confusion, we apply the term *gastraphetes* only to ancient Greek hand crossbows. Somewhat later (between 353 and 341 BC), a torsion-powered version of this machine appeared.

palintone Gr: a stone-projector.

pavis, pavise	A large shield often used in sieges, which appeared in the 15th century. More often than not it was lavishly decorated with heraldic emblems and religious inscriptions.
pedrero	From Sp: *pedro*, "stone"; a short-barreled cannon firing stones.
peritreton	Gr; the framework of a throwing machine, where torsion-springs were fixed.
perrière, perier	Stone-thrower; today the term is usually used with reference to a man-powered beam-sling engine (it is in this sense that the term is used in this book). In the Middle Ages, however, it could denote other models of stone-throwers as well. Synonyms—Fr: *pierrière*.
petraria	LL: "stone-thrower"—in the Middle Ages the term could mean any stone-thrower. Synonyms: *petrobolos, petrarhea*.
petrobolos	Gr: ("stone-projector"); the throwing machine, stone-projector, is probably just a synonym of *lithobolos*, although the name *petrobolos* might stand for the larger models as compared with *lithobolos*.
plunging fire	Casting shells at an elevation angle of 20 to 45 degrees.
pluteus	Lat; a mobile woven siege shield on three wheels, used in ancient warfare; in the Middle Ages its functions were taken over by *mantlets*.
polybolos	Gr: a repeating arrow-firer invented by Dionysius of Alexandria about mid-3rd century BC.
qaws al-lawab	Ar; great stationary crossbow.
qaws al-rijl	Ar; a hand crossbow later on adapted for firing "eggs" filled with an incendiary mixture.
ribaudequin, ribauld	Cannon of the 14th and 15th centuries consisting of several small barrels fastened together and placed on a two-wheeled cart. It fired volleys and was used to defend gates and breaches in a wall.
sambuca	1. Broad ladder placed in a roofed tunnel. It could be used in land and naval warfare. In the first case, the structure sat on a wheeled cart; in the second, on ships, tied in pairs; 2. Assaulting bridge of a siege tower (*helepolis*).
scorpion	Originally the term stood for a Roman torsion-powered two-armed arrow-firer (a small *catapult*), used in sieges and as field artillery. Later on (possibly from mid-1st century AD and certainly by the 4th century AD), the term was used for a stone-projector of a thoroughly different construction (*onager*). Lat: *scorpio*.
shabakah	Ar; a siege shield described by al-Tarsusi, consisting of a framework with a network stretched on it, and roofed with felt and hides.
sow	See *cat*.

271

stimulus	Lat; a barbed stake driven into the ground and camouflaged.
tension-powered throwing machines	Throwing machines that used the energy of wood under tension.
testudo	Lat: "tortoise"—see *tortoise*.
tetrareai	Byzantine man-powered beam-sling stone-thrower with a four-side framework.
tolleno	Lat; a siege contrivance—a basket with besiegers which was delivered to the top of a wall by means of a crane-type lifting mechanism.
tormentum	Lat; a common name of throwing machines used by ancient Romans. According to Ammianus Marcellinus, the name is associated with twisting torsion-springs.[440]
torsion-powered throwing machines	Throwing machines using the energy of twisted rope made of tendons or hair.
tortoise	1. Mobile shed, wheeled as a rule, which was used for the defense of warriors who were operating a battering ram or a borer; destroying a wall at the foot; or filling up a ditch; 2. Roman fighting order with warriors protecting themselves with shields at the front, on the sides, and above; the formation was used in assaulting fortifications.
toxoballistra	Large Byzantine stationary crossbow of the 10th and 11th centuries; it shot big bolts and stone balls.
trabucium	A *trebuchet* with a fixed counterweight.
trebuchet	A counterweight beam-sling engine. Synonyms: *trabuchellus, trabucchi, trabuchus, trabuco,* etc.
tribulus, tribolus	Lat: "tortoise" "garlic;" iron or bronze balls about 2 centimeters in diameter, with four 5-centimeter-long spikes. The spikes jutted in different directions, so that whatever way a tribulus was hurled, one spike invariably jutted upwards.
tripantium	A *trebuchet* having one part of a counterweight fixed and the other part movable.
tzagra, tzangra, tzarch	The name of a crossbow which appeared in Byzantium in the 11th century; probably there were both hand and stationary versions.
veuglaire	Germ: Vögler; a breech-loaded cannon of the 14th and 15th centuries.
vinea	Lat; a shed made of poles and brushwood and covered with raw hides.

zahhafah   Ar; a kind of the *dabbabah tortoise* but seemingly bigger, having a cover made of sheets of iron and a turret.

zanburak   A heavy fortress stationary crossbow. Later on, this term came to denote a small cannon transported by camel.[441] Pers: *kaman-i zanburak*; Turk: *semberek*; Ar: *qaws al-zanburak*.

zarraq   Ar; a siphon for casting *Greek Fire*. Apparently synonyms of this term include *naffata* and *mukhula*.

ziyar,   Ar; a throwing machine described by al-Tarsusi, employing the energy of
qaws al-ziyar   torsion-springs and composite arms. Although the construction is not very clear, we know it was used for throwing bolts and pots of *naphtha*.

ENDNOTES

1   Gravet, C., *Medieval Siege Warfare*, p. 3.

2   *Medieval Warfare. A History*, p. 164.

3   Kern, P. B., *Ancient Siege Warfare*, p. 20.

4   The Bible, Joshua 2:1–15.

5   The Bible, Joshua 6:2–21.

6   Kern, P. B., *Ancient Siege Warfare*, p. 31.

7   The Bible, Joshua 7:2–5.

8   The Bible, Joshua 8:3–22.

9   Kern, P. B., *Ancient Siege Warfare*, p. 36.

10 Yadin, Y., *The Art of Warfare in Biblical Lands*, pp. 275–284.

11 The Bible, 2 Samuel 20:15.

12 Kern, P. B., *Ancient Siege Warfare*, p. 17.

13 Kern, P. B., *Ancient Siege Warfare*, p. 18.

14 A. K. Nefedkin (*Boevye kolesnitsy i kolesnichie drevnih grekov* (*Fighting Chariots and Charioteers of Ancient Greeks*), pp. 106–107) believes that charioteers usually dismounted and conducted fire standing on the ground. Meanwhile shield-bearers protected them with a large shield. However, all the advantages offered by a chariot are lost in this case, and it is not clear why these elite units of charioteers should be exposed to danger when it would have been quite easy to use common archers for this purpose.

15 Shaw, I., *Egyptian Warfare and Weapons*, p. 65.

16 Kern, P. B., *Ancient Siege Warfare*, p. 43.

17 Kern, P. B., *Ancient Siege Warfare*, p. 43–44.

18 Kern, P. B., *Ancient Siege Warfare*, p. 54.

19 Herodotus, 1.84.

20 Herodotus, 1.191. True, some historians believe that Gerodot made a mistake and the siege he depicts refers to the second conquest of the city by Darius I; as to Cyrus, he took Babylon without a battle. But we will adhere to the data of the source.

21 Herodotus, 1.162.

22 Xenophon, *Cyropaedia*, 7.4.1. Although this work of Xenophon's is considered more of a military-historical novel rather than a reliable account of historic events, in this particular instance, the author could probably be believed.

23 Herodotus, 4.200.

24 Aeneas Tacticus, 37.7.

25 Sekunda, N., *Greek Hoplite 480–323 BC*, pp. 46–47.

26 Polyaenus, 2.1.10.

27 Homer, *Odyssey*, 8.492–515.

28 A good selection of descriptions of the Trojan Horse in the sources, as well of different theories on what the Trojan Horse might have been, can be found in: Fields, N., *Troy c. 1700–1250 BC*, p. 51–2. The author believes that the Trojan Horse was a drill analogous to the simplest ancient Egyptian or Assyrian battering rams.

29 Warry, J., *Warfare in the Classical World*, p. 23.

30 Herodotus, 7.154.

31 Thucydides (1.98) doesn't mention a long siege, but Herodotus (7.107) says that Eion surrendered only when there was no more food in the town.

32 Plutarch, *Pericles*, 27.

[33] Thucydides, 1.116.

[34] Diodorus, 22.28.

[35] Plutarch, *Pericles*, 27.

[36] Herodotus, 9.70.

[37] Thucydides, 6.44.

[38] Thucydides, 3.17.3.

[39] Thucydides, 2.75–78.

[40] Thucydides, 4.100

[41] Thucydides, 4.115.

[42] Kern, P. B., *Ancient Siege Warfare*, p. 122; Winter, F. E., *Greek Fortifications*, p. 235.

[43] Arrows for crossbows and throwing machines are usually called bolts.

[44] Kern, P. B., *Ancient Siege Warfare*, p. 179–183.

[45] Kern, P. B., *Ancient Siege Warfare*, p. 167.

[46] Aeneas Tacticus, 10.20

[47] Aeneas Tacticus, 14.1.

[48] Aeneas Tacticus, 17.4–6.

[49] Aeneas Tacticus, 22.7.

[50] Aeneas Tacticus, 10.6.

[51] Aeneas Tacticus, 10.4–5.

[52] Aeneas Tacticus, 10.9–10.

[53] Aeneas Tacticus, 25.1–4.

[54] Aeneas Tacticus, 32–37.

[55] Aeneas Tacticus, 16.5–8.

[56] Aeneas Tacticus, 39.1–4.

[57] Polyaenus, 2.38.2.

[58] Diodorus, 16.74–76.

[59] Arrian, 5.23.6–5.24.4

[60] Arrian, 4.18.4–4.19.4

[61] Arrian, 2.27.3.

[62] Kern, P. B., *Ancient Siege Warfare*, p. 218.

[63] Kern, P. B., *Ancient Siege Warfare*, pp. 201–202.

[64] Arrian, 6.9.1–6.11.1.

[65] Diodorus, 17.45.3.

[66] Diodorus, 17.44.1.

[67] Livy, 1.43.3.

[68] Livy, 2.17.1.

[69] Livy, 4.22.2–6.

[70] Livy, 4.47.5; 4.59.4–6.

[71] Plutarch, *Camillus*, 2.

[72] Livy, 5.5.6.

[73] Livy, 6.9.2.

[74] Livy, 6.8.9–10.

[75] Livy, 8.16.8.

[76] Polybius, 28.11.1–2.

[77] Livy, 10.41.14.

78 Polybius, 1.17–19.

79 Kern, P. B., *Ancient Siege Warfare*, p. 258.

80 Polybius, 1.24.12.

81 Diodorus, 23.9.5.

82 Polybius, 1.42.8–13; Diodorus, 24.1.1.

83 Polybius, 8.3–7; Livy, 24.33.9–24.34.16; Plutarch, *Marcellus*, 14–19.

84 Livy, 26.45.6.

85 Livy, 28.3.5.

86 Livy, 36.23.5–10.

87 Livy, 28.19.16.

88 Livy, 29.1.12–13.

89 Livy, 4.49.9–4.50.6.

90 Livy, 4.53.9–13.

91 Polybius, 10.16.

92 For instance, following the seizure of Carthage, the Romans took 120 very big *catapults*, 281 *catapults* of a smaller size, 23 big and 50 smaller *ballistae*, as well as a large number of big and small *scorpions* [Livy, 26.47.5–6].

93 Livy, 31.46.10.

94 Livy, 38.3.9–38.7; Polybius, 21.26–32.

95 Caesar, *Gallic War*, 7.22–28.

96 Caesar, *Gallic War*, 7.69–89.

97 Caesar, *Gallic War*, 2.32–33.

98 Marsden, E. W., *Greek and Roman Artillery. Historical Development*, p. 184.

99 Tacitus, *An.*, 13.39.

100 Josephus, *Jewish War*, 3.7.23.

101 Ammianus Marcellinus, 19.5.2.

102 Ammianus Marcellinus, 20.11.6–32.

103 Ammianus Marcellinus, 21.12.4–19.

104 Ammianus Marcellinus, 24.4.2–31.

105 Ammianus Marcellinus, 24.2.9–22.

106 War elephants were more than once used at the sieges of fortresses in Asia and the Far East, especially in India. They were more often than not employed as a live battering ram at an attack on a gate. For a more detailed description of how war elephants were used in siege warfare in India, see: Nossov, K. S., *Zamki i kreposti Indii, Kitaya i Yaponii* (*Castles and Fortresses of India, China and Japan*), p. 19–21.

107 Ammianus Marcellinus, 19.5.1–19.8.4.

108 Procopius, *Goth.*, 4.14.35–37.

109 Ammianus Marcellinus, 20.7.2.

110 Caesar, *Gallic War*, 2.6.

111 Caesar, *Gallic War*, 3.21.

112 Caesar, *Gallic War*, 2.12.

113 Caesar, *Gallic War*, 2.30–31.

114 Caesar, *Gallic War*, 3.21.

115 Caesar, *Gallic War*, 7.22–28.

116 Caesar, *Gallic War*, 5.42.

117 Ammianus Marcellinus, 16.2.1–2.

118 Ammianus Marcellinus, 29.6.12; 31.6.4; 31.8.1.

119 Ammianus Marcellinus, 31.15.2–15.

120 Procopius, *Goth.*, 1.24–26.

121 Procopius, *Goth.*, 2.12.1–25.

122 Procopius, *Goth.*, 4.35.9.

123 Belousov S.V., "Ob osade i oborone krepostei . . .", pp. 164–165, 167 (f. 7).

124 "De castrametatione," 27.

125 Galleries of *vineae* are mentioned by Procopius (*Goth.*, 2.19.6–7).

126 "De castrametatione," 27. This is also mentioned by the author of the "Strategicon" (10.1).

127 "De castrametatione," 21.

128 "De castrametatione," 21.

129 "Strategicon," 10.1.

130 "De velitatione bellica," 21.

131 Nicolle, D., *Medieval Siege Weapons (2), Byzantium, the Islamic World & India AD 476–1526*, p. 5.

132 Kennedy, H., *Crusader Castles*, p. 104.

133 Kennedy, H., *Crusader Castles*, pp. 108–109.

134 Kennedy, H., *Crusader Castles*, pp. 100–101.

135 Partington, J. R., *A History of Greek Fire and Gunpowder*, p. 189.

136 Partington, J. R., *A History of Greek Fire and Gunpowder*, p. 22.

137 Partington, J. R., *A History of Greek Fire and Gunpowder*, p. 209.

138 *Medieval Warfare. A History*, p. 181.

139 Nicolle, D., *French Armies of the Hundred Years War*, pp. 34–35.

140 Bradbury, J., *The Medieval Siege*, p. 292; *Medieval Warfare. A History*, p. 158.

141 Bradbury, J., *The Medieval Siege*, p. 245.

142 Bradbury, J., *The Medieval Siege*, p. 246.

143 Bradbury, J., *The Medieval Siege*, p. 244.

144 Polybius, 9.19.6–7.

145 Bradbury, J., *The Medieval Siege*, p. 275.

146 Vegetius, 4.30.

147 Bradbury, J., *The Medieval Siege*, p. 275.

148 Bradbury, J., *The Medieval Siege*, p. 275.

149 Anonymus Byzantine, 261.

150 Anonymus Byzantine, 213. Anonymus Byzantine obviously borrowed the passage describing leather ladders, as well as nets with hooks, from Philon [see: Philon, "Poliorketika," 4.73–75].

151 Bradbury, J., *The Medieval Siege*, p. 276.

152 Anonymus Byzantine, 256–258.

153 Apollodorus, 176–185.

154 Diodorus, 17.43–45.

155 Josephus, *Jewish War*, 3.7.28. Josephus ascribes the invention of this weapon to himself; this, however, is not true.

156 Taccola, 9R.

157 Vegetius, 4.6.

158 Anonymus Byzantine, 261.

159 Bradbury, J., *The Medieval Siege*, p. 280.

160 Bradbury, J., *The Medieval Siege*, p. 276.

161 Tacolla, 28v, 30R, 57v, 75R, 99v, 102R and others.

162 Vegetius, 4.13–15.

163 Apollodorus, 142; Anonymus Byzantine, 208; Vegetius, 4.15.

164 Vegetius, 4.13–16.

165 Caesar, *Civil Wars*, 2.10.

166 Philon, "Poliorketika," 4.34.

167 *Tortoise* (*testudo*) was also used in another sense, meaning a battle formation with soldiers covering themselves with shields at the front, on the sides, and above (see below).

168 Vitruvius, 10.14.1–3; 10.15.1. Athenaeus, 16–19.

169 Anonymus Byzantine, 259–260.

170 Anonymus Byzantine, 207. Apollodorus, 140–141. The descriptions of all these mobile sheds are rather vague. Duncan Campbell (Campbell, D. B., *Greek and Roman Siege Machinery*, 399 BC–AD 363, pp. 30 and 46) suggests a reconstruction of a beaked *tortoise* having vertical sides. In my opinion, however, descriptions like "in the form of the front part of a ship turned upside down and put on the ground" and "wedge-shaped" better fit structures with inclined sides forming a roof. Besides, this construction better protects those who are inside from the projectiles of the besieged, given that arrows shot from bows, as well as stones, could follow a plunging trajectory.

171 Nicolle, D., *Medieval Siege Weapons (2), Byzantium, the Islamic Worlds & India AD 476–1526*, pp. 39–40, 47.

172 Vitruvius, 10.13.1.

173 Vitruvius, 10.13.2. However, one should not rely upon Vitruvius's evidence here, either.

174 Vitruvius, 10.13.6. Athenaeus, 13–14. Unlike Vitruvius, Athenaeus speaks of a three-tier turret having throwing machines on the two upper tiers and a tank of water on the bottom one.

175 Vitruvius, 10.15.2–7. Athenaeus, 21–26. Anonymus Byzantine, 230–232.

176 Apollodorus, 155.

177 This is the way the description given by Apollodorus [154] and Anonymus Byzantine [226, 228] can be understood. On the other hand, a fairly short description of a ram-*tortoise* by Philon ["Poliorketika," 4.40] may bring us to the conclusion that it lacks this element.

178 For a general description of the structure of a ram-*tortoise*, see Apollodorus [154–159] and Anonymus Byzantine [225–230].

179 Apollodorus, 159–161.

180 Anonymus Byzantine, 228.

181 Apollodorus, 154. Anonymus Byzantine, 226–227.

182 Apollodorus, 155. Anonymus Byzantine, 228.

183 That is why the conclusion drawn by Duncan Campbell (Campbell, D. B., *Greek and Roman Siege Machinery, 399 BC–AD 363*, p. 42) to the effect that a triangle cross section of ram-*tortoises* was characteristic of Roman engines of this type, seems somewhat too categorical.

184 Apollodorus, 185–188. Anonymus Byzantine, 249–254.

185 Procopius, *Goth.*, 4.11.27–32.

186 Procopius, *Goth.*, 4.14.4–5.

187 According to Polyaenus [6.3] even logs were made of lead.

188 Vegetius, 4.23.

189 Vitruvius, 10.13.7. Athenaeus, 14–15.

190 Apollodorus, 148–152. Anonymus Byzantine, 220–224.

191 Vitruvius, 10.13.3–5.

192 Athenaeus, 11–12.

193 Anonymus Byzantine, 238–247.

194 According to Plutarch (*Demetrius*, 21), the height of a tower equals 30.3 meters; according to Athenaeus (27), it is 39.2 meters high; however, a calculation which takes into account the width of the foot, top, and side beams (45 meters) gives a result (44.5 meters) which is close to Diodorus's figure (45 meters).

195 Plutarch, *Demetrius*, 21.

196 Apollodorus, 166.

197 There is evidence that in the period of the Roman Empire and in medieval Byzantium, the term *helepolis* was sometimes used to denote any giant siege engine: siege towers, battering rams, or throwing machines. However, for the sake of clarity in this book, we retain the term "helepolis" only for the siege tower.

198 For a detailed description of the structure of siege towers, see Apollodorus (164–174), Anonymus Byzantine (238–247).

[199] Athenaeus, 11–12.

[200] Demetrius Poliorcetes's tower, whose basis consists of four vertical beams each nearly 100 cubits (45 meters) long, made with a declivity inside, is an exception. However, this construction is clearly weaker than the one described above: such a long beam, inclined like that, could easily break up, which would cause an inevitable collapse of the tower. Diodorus possibly made a mistake in describing this tower.

[201] Athenaeus, 12.

[202] Athenaeus, 34.

[203] Campbell, D. B., *Greek and Roman Siege Machinery, 399 BC–AD 363*, p. 37.

[204] Vegetius, 4.17.

[205] Vegetius, 4.17. Josephus, *Jewish War*, 3.7.30.

[206] Biton, W 55.

[207] Athenaeus, 32–33. Anonymus Byzantine, 268–269.

[208] Bradbury, J., *The Medieval Siege*, p. 247.

[209] Apollodorus, 173–174. Anonymus Byzantine, 247–248. Philon, "Poliorketika," 4.34–35.

[210] Philon's recommendation that machines be covered with metal sheets extends not only to siege towers but also to *tortoises* and other siege machines ["Poliorketika," 4.34].

[211] Philon, "Poliorketika," 4.57.

[212] Apollodorus, 174. Anonymus Byzantine, 247.

[213] Apollodorus, 168.

[214] Vegetius, 4.21.

[215] Apollodorus, 170–173.

[216] Bradbury, J., *The Medieval Siege*, p. 242.

[217] William of Tyre, 15.18. Cited from: Kennedy, H., *Crusader Castles*, p. 103.

[218] Vitruvius, 10.16.7.

[219] Vegetius, 4.20.

[220] Plutarch, *Demetrius*, 40.

[221] Bradbury, J., *The Medieval Siege*, pp. 247–248.

[222] Vegetius, 4.19.

[223] Vegetius, 4.20.

[224] Polybius, 8.6.2–11.

[225] Anonymus Byzantine, 271.

[226] Athenaeus, 27–28.

[227] Biton, W 57–60.

[228] Anonymus Byzantine, 266.

[229] Fields, N., *Troy c. 1700–1250 BC*, p. 53.

[230] Procopius, *War with the Persians*, 2.27.1–17.

[231] Apollodorus, 143–147. Anonymus Byzantine, 214–218.

[232] Partington, J. R., *A History of Greek Fire and Gunpowder*, p. 172.

[233] Taccola, 52v and 51v accordingly.

[234] Partington, J. R., *A History of Greek Fire and Gunpowder*, p. 173.

[235] Kennedy, H., *Crusader Castles*, p. 104.

[236] Kennedy, H., *Crusader Castles*, pp. 104–105.

[237] Kennedy, H., *Crusader Castles*, p. 105.

[238] Polybius, 5.100.

[239] Diodorus, 18.70.5.

[240] Herodotus, 4.200.

[241] Livy, 38.3.9–38.7; Polybius, 21.26–32.

[242] Bradbury, J., *The Medieval Siege*, p. 273.

[243] Bradbury, J., *The Medieval Siege*, p. 273.

[244] Kennedy, H., *Crusader Castles*, p. 106.

[245] Partington, J. R., *A History of Greek Fire and Gunpowder*, p. 171.

[246] Vitruvius, 10.16.11.

[247] Vitruvius, 10.16.10.

[248] Aeneas Tacticus, 37.2–4.

[249] Livy, 38.7.10–13. Polybius, 21.28.

[250] Marsden, E. W., *Greek and Roman Artillery. Historical Development*, p. 12.

[251] Occasional mentions of shooting a bow at a distance of 300 to 400 meters should be considered more an exception than the rule. This range of fire was only reached by excellent archers, using special light arrows at that.

[252] Marsden, E. W., *Greek and Roman Artillery. Historical Development*, pp. 10–11.

[253] Biton calls these non-torsion-powered throwing machines, as well as the first hand crossbows, *gastraphetes* [Biton, W 61 & W 65], but we, for clarity's sake, will use the term "*gastraphetes*" only to denote hand arrow-firers.

[254] Biton, W 61–67.

[255] Biton, W 45–51.

[256] For an arrow-firer: Philon, "Belopoeica," 54.25–55.5. For a stone-projector: Philon, "Belopoeica," 51.15–20.

[257] Campbell, D. B., *Greek and Roman Artillery, 399 BC–AD 363*, pp. 19, 21.

[258] The table is based on the calculation of the diameter of the torsion-spring according to the above formulas for arrow-firers and stone-projectors; the height of the torsion-spring was established for arrow-firers as 6.5 diameters and for stone-projectors as 9 diameters of the torsion-spring, the length and width of the engine as 25 and 14 diameters (for arrow-firers) and 30 and 15 diameters (for stone-projectors), respectively. Philon, *Belopoeica*, 51.15–25; 53.15–20; 54.25–55.5. Campbell, D. B., *Greek and Roman Artillery, 399 BC–AD 363*, pp. 11, 13–14, 18, 20. Marsden, E. W., *Greek and Roman Artillery. Historical Development*, pp. 34–36, 44–47.

[259] Philon, "Belopoeica," 67.28–73.20.

[260] Philon, "Belopoeica," 77.9–78.26.

[261] Philon, "Belopoeica," 73.21–77.8.

[262] Heron, "Cheiroballistra."

[263] The opinion exists that Heron's *cheiroballistra* used lamellar bronze springs instead of bunches of sinew. Marsden (*Greek and Roman Artillery. Technical Treatises*, p. 209) has convincingly proved the absurdity of such conclusions, however.

[264] Marsden, E. W., *Greek and Roman Artillery. Historical Development*, pp. 17–43.

[265] Vitruvius, 10.10–11.

[266] Philon, "Poliorketika," 91.36. Marsden, E. W., *Greek and Roman Artillery. Technical Treatises*, p. 249.

[267] Apollodorus, 188.

[268] Ammianus Marcellinus, 23.4.4–7.

[269] Vegetius, 2.25; 4.9; 4.22, etc.

[270] Sometimes Ammianus Marcellinus's description is understood so that the buffer was not a part of the machine, but a huge sloping buffer placed in front of it on a heap of turf or a brick platform (e.g., D. B. Campbell, *Greek and Roman Artillery, 399 BC–AD 363*, pp. 32, 42–43, and 47). However, I think that Ammianus Marcellinus's sentence following the description of a buffer (". . . if we put this machine right on a stone wall, it will shake loose everything beneath it, not by its weight but by the force of concussion") leaves no doubt but that what is meant in this case is just a bedding that softened recoil under the entire machine when placed on a stone wall.

[271] Marsden, E. W., *Greek and Roman Artillery. Historical Development*, p. 188.

[272] Ammianus Marcellinus, 23.4.1–7.

[273] Marsden, E. W., *Greek and Roman Artillery. Historical Development*, p. 189.

[274] Vegetius, 2.25.

[275] *TC* 104–5, 163–4.

[276] Anonymus, *De Reb. Bell.*, 7.

[277] Anonymus, *De Reb. Bell.*, 18.1–6.

[278] Marsden, E. W., *Greek and Roman Artillery. Technical Treatises*, p. 245.

[279] Vegetius, 4.22.

[280] It is commonly believed that the term "*scorpion*" came to be used in this sense in the 4th century, or not long before it. However, Josephus's description of an episode that took place during the siege of Jotapata in AD 67 [*Jewish War*, 3.7.23] gives one the impression that the terms "*scorpion*" and "*catapult*" stood already at that time for stone-projectors. ("The functioning of *scorpions* and *catapults* killed many at a time; the burden of masses of stones disgorged by it brought down parapet of the wall, broke up corners of towers.") The passage is unclear enough, as both before and after this moment he describes the operations of *ballistae*—stone-projectors. However, given the absence of a mistake on his part, we are led to believe that already in the second half of the 1st century AD, the term "*scorpion*" stood not for an arrow-firer but for a stone-projector, which was powerful enough to cause the destruction of a wall. Bearing in mind the aforementioned words of Ammianus Marcellinus, this stone-projector could only be an *onager*, which confirms the version that *onagers* appeared much earlier than the 4th century AD. It is also well known that the term "*catapult*" in time came to denote a stone-projector instead of an arrow-firer; it is used more than once in this sense by Ammianus Marcellinus.

[281] Josephus, *Jewish War*, 5.6.

[282] E. W. Marsden (*Greek and Roman Artillery. Historical Development*, p. 179) maintains that there were only fifty-five machines, i.e., one century in a cohort had an *onager*, the others, *carroballistae*.

[283] Vegetius, 2.25.

[284] Tacitus, *Ann.*, 12.56.

[285] Livy, 26.47.5–6.

[286] Polyaenus, 2.38.2.

[287] Marsden, E. W., *Greek and Roman Artillery. Historical Development*, p. 171. E. W. Marsden speaks of ten 3-span *catapults*, but in this case the summing up gives 9.5 tons, not 9 tons.

[288] The last reliable mention of the *onager* is to be found in Procopius (*Goth.*, 1.21.19) and refers to 537–8.

[289] So far the only reconstruction of a *ziyar* has been suggested by David Nicolle and drawn by Sam Thompson (Nicolle, D., *Medieval Siege Weapons (2), Byzantium, the Islamic World & India AD 476–1526*, p. 25). It is a pity, however, that this excellent reconstruction is not without some inaccuracies which do not quite agree with al-Tarsusi's text and drawings, e.g., the position of arms (the broader part ought to be in the center), as well as the fastening of the arms and torsion-springs. The reconstruction rather conforms to the European *espringal* of a later period.

[290] It should be noted that other opinions exist. T. Wise (Wise, T., *Medieval Warfare*, p. 165) and C. Oman (Oman, C., *The Art of War in the Middle Ages*, Vol. 2, p. 46) believe that an *espringal* was a great crossbow and R. Payne-Gallwey thinks that it might be a one-armed arrow-firer that employed the energy of a resilient board. The last assertion is a mistaken one in my view. But on the whole, this confusion as regards terminology is a result of fairly widespread usage of the term *espringal* in the Middle Ages—this term, in different places and at various times, has been used for a stationary crossbow, a torsion-powered machine, and even small cannon. In this book, however, for the sake of clarity we shall only use the term *espringal* to denote a two-armed torsion-powered arrow-firer.

[291] This fact does not appear absolutely unquestionable if we remember that it was considered that such fastening of torsion-springs (Mark I type) in antique *catapults* did not guarantee sufficient twisting and was promptly given up.

[292] Procopius, *Goth.*, 1.21.14–19.

[293] E. W. Marsden (Marsden, E. W., *Greek and Roman Artillery. Technical Treatises*, p. 247) believes that Procopius described an engine of the *cheiroballistra* type, while C. Oman (Oman, C., *The Art of War in the Middle Ages*, Vol. I, p. 138) thinks that it was just a common great crossbow and that Procopius's description of the trigger mechanism was simply inaccurate.

[294] For a more detailed description of these crossbows, see: Kirpichnikov, A. N., *Metatel'naya artilleriya Drevnei Rusi* (*Throwing machines of Ancient Russia*) // *Materialy i issledovaniya po arheologii SSSR*, No 77, Moscow, 1958, pp. 7–51; Nossov, K. S., *Russkiye kreposti i osadnaya tehnika VIII–XVII vekov* (*Russian Fortresses and Siege Warfare, 8–17 cc.*), pp. 88–91.

[295] Nicolle, D., *Medieval Siege Weapons (2), Byzantium, the Islamic World & India AD 476–1526*, pp. 20–23.

[296] *Perrière* literally means "stone-projector." Like "*espringal*", the term "*perrière*" did not have a strictly limited range of meanings in the Middle Ages, and could be used to describe any stone-projector; in this book, however, for the sake of clarity, this term will denote a man-powered beam-sling stone-projector without a counterweight.

[297] De Vries, K., *Medieval Military Technology*, pp. 133–4.

[298] Personally, I think that neither their being mounted on a wheeled cart not their ability to turn from one side to another is a sufficient argument in favor of a torsion-powered machine, the *carroballista* type. Man-powered stone-projectors possessing similar capacities were well known in China (see discussion below on *arradah*).

[299] Nicolle, D., *Medieval Siege Weapons (2), Byzantium, the Islamic World & India AD 476–1526*, p. 14.

[300] Possibly, it is to *arradah* that al-Tarsusi gives the name of *luba*; the former being widespread, it may account for al-Tarsusi's unwillingness to describe *luba* in detail. The term "luba" is not found except in al-Tarsusi, and we hardly can describe this name as widespread.

[301] Nicolle, D., *Medieval Siege Weapons (2), Byzantium, the Islamic World & India AD 476–1526*, p. 8.

[302] Nicolle, D., *Medieval Siege Weapons (2), Byzantium, the Islamic World & India AD 476–1526*, pp. 14–15.

[303] Gravet, C., *Medieval Siege Warfare*, p. 52.

[304] The reconstruction of such a machine made by Payne-Gallwey (*The Book of the Crossbow*, p. 319) had a 1.5-meter-high resilient lever made of ash and launched crossbow bolts at a distance of 145 meters.

[305] L'vovskii, P.D., "Osnovaniya ustroistva metatel'nyh mashin. Nevroballisty" ("The basis of the construction of throwing machines. Neuroballistae") // *Sbornik issledovanii i materialov artilleriiskogo istoricheskogo museya*, issue I, pp. 26–54.

[306] Josephus, *Jewish War*, 5.6.3. In this passage, Josephus again says that *scorpions* threw stones. It has already been mentioned above (see footnote 280) that, perhaps as early as the 1st century AD, a shifting of meanings took place and *scorpion* came to stand for a stone-projector instead of a small arrow-firer. This episode once more emphasizes the fact that only this stone-projector could have been the *onager*, as only the *onager* and a very big *ballista* were powerful enough to throw such heavy balls, weighing talents (if it is not an exaggeration).

[307] The Bible, Psalm 7:13.

[308] Aeneas Tacticus, 35.1.

[309] Partington, J. R., *A History of Greek Fire and Gunpowder*, p. 20.

[310] Thucydides, 4.100.

[311] Aeneas Tacticus, 33.1–2.

[312] Polyaenus, 6.3.

[313] Partington, J. R., *A History of Greek Fire and Gunpowder*, p. 5.

[314] Ammianus Marcellinus, 23.4.14–15.

[315] Vegetius, 4.18.

[316] Livy, 21.8.10–12.

[317] Partington, J. R., *A History of Greek Fire and Gunpowder*, p. 5.

[318] Apollodorus, 153. Anonymus Byzantine, 219.

[319] Philon ["Poliorketika," 3.39–40], who wrote as far back as the 3rd century BC, mentions *naphtha*, which, if available, he recommends dispersing on the assailants who are climbing scaling ladders to storm a fortress. Then he recommends a burning torch be thrown at them. He suggests that siege towers and other siege engines that have approached the wall be burned in a similar way. Apparently, it is one of the earliest, if not *the* earliest, mention of petroleum in siege warfare.

[320] Ammianus Marcellinus, 23.6.37–38.

[321] This and the two quotations that follow it are cited according to the following work: Arendt, V. V., *Grecheski Ogon'* (*Greek Fire*) // *Trudy instituta istorii nauki i tekhniki*, series I, volume 9, pp. 165–167 and 170.

[322] Leo, *Taktika*, 19.57. Partington, J. R., *A History of Greek Fire and Gunpowder*, p. 15.

[323] Partington, J. R., *A History of Greek Fire and Gunpowder*, pp. 22, 203, 207.

[324] Among other works written in support of this version, James Partington's "*A History of Greek Fire and Gunpowder*" is probably the most noteworthy one.

[325] V. V. Arendt's "*Grecheski Ogon'* (*Greek Fire*)" is probably the most interesting work written in support of this version.

[326] These three quotations and the recipe for *Greek Fire* are given according to: Partington, J. R., *A History of Greek Fire and Gunpowder*, pp. 48–50, 54.

[327] Partington, J. R., *A History of Greek Fire and Gunpowder*, pp. 58–59.

[328] An excellent discussion on the history of saltpeter is to be found in the chapter "Saltpeter" in J. R. Partington's book, *A History of Greek Fire and Gunpowder*. Also see pp. 22 and 32 of this book.

[329] Nicolle, D., *Medieval Siege Weapons (1), Western Europe AD 585–1385*, p. 41.

[330] Gravet, C., *Medieval Siege Warfare*, p. 30.

[331] Aeneas Tacticus, 34.1.

[332] Partington, J. R., *A History of Greek Fire and Gunpowder*, p. 5.

[333] Partington, J. R., *A History of Greek Fire and Gunpowder*, p. 5.

[334] References to cannon in 1313 in Ghent and in 1324 in Metz are now considered to be later additions.

[335] Partington, J. R., *A History of Greek Fire and Gunpowder*, p. 101.

[336] The table is made on the basis of the data given in: Partington, J. R., *A History of Greek Fire and Gunpowder*, pp. 324–327.

[337] Smith, R. D., "The reconstruction and firing trials of a replica of a 14th-century cannon" // *Royal Armories Yearbook*, Vol. 4, 1999, p. 86–94.

[338] Partington, J. R., *A History of Greek Fire and Gunpowder*, p. 191.

[339] Partington, J. R., *A History of Greek Fire and Gunpowder*, pp. 193, 196.

[340] Oman, C., *The Art of War in the Middle Ages, AD 1278–1485*, Vol. 2, pp. 216, 222.

[341] Partington, J. R., *A History of Greek Fire and Gunpowder*, p. 154.

[342] Bradbury, J., *The Medieval Siege*, p. 283.

[343] Apollodorus, 161–4; Anonymus Byzantine, 232–8.

[344] Vegetius, 4.21.

[345] Vegetius, 4.13. Vitruvius, 10.13.3.

[346] An event of the year 364 BC. Polyaenus, 3.10.15.

[347] Vitruvius, 10.13.8.

[348] Bradbury, J., *The Medieval Siege*, p. 281.

[349] Aeneas Tacticus, 39.6.

[350] Livy, 44.9.5–7.

[351] Livy, 44.9.9.

[352] Ammianus Marcellinus, 26.8.9.

[353] Bradbury, J., *The Medieval Siege*, p. 280.

[354] Athenaeus, 37.

[355] Athenaeus, 38. Anonymus Byzantine, 205.

[356] Anonymus Byzantine, 206.

[357] Polybius, 8.3–8.

[358] Procopius, *Goth.*, 1.21.19–22.

[359] Thucydides, 2.70.2; Kern, P. B., *Ancient Siege Warfare*, p. 117.

[360] Nossov, K.S., *Rytsarskie turniry (Knights' Tournaments)*, p. 48.

[361] Caesar, *Gallic War*, 2.13; 2.15; 7.11.

[362] Gravet C., *Medieval Siege Warfare*, p. 19.

[363] Anonymus Byzantine, 213. Similar recommendations are to be found in: Philon, "Poliorketika," 4.2–4.

[364] Vegetius, 4.28.

[365] Procopius, *Goth.*, 3.24.15–18.

[366] Caesar, *Gallic War*, 7.72–74.

[367] Bradbury, J., *The Medieval Siege*, p. 173; Yakovlev, V. V., *Istoriya krepostei (History of Fortresses)*, p. 67.

[368] Frontinus, 3.7.2.

[369] Frontinus, 3.7.6.

[370] Philon, "Poliorketika," 4.8.

[371] Philon, "Poliorketika," 4.31–33.

[372] Anonymus Byzantine, 210–212.

[373] Kennedy H., *Crusader Castles*, p. 106.

[374] Philon, "Poliorketika," 4.29. On the counteraction to this operation and the defense of the harbor, see Philon, "Poliorketika," 3.51–59.

[375] Philon, "Poliorketika," 4.26.

[376] Vegetius, 4.7–9.

[377] Philon devotes a whole chapter (2) to it in his work, "Poliorketika."

[378] For instance, similar admonitions are also cited by the author of "Strategicon" who wrote at the end of the 6th century AD [X, 2–4].

[379] Aeneas Tacticus, 8.4; Philon, "Poliorketika," 2.53.

[380] Aeneas Tacticus, 10.1–2.

[381] Philon, "Poliorketika," 1.76–77.

[382] Philon, "Poliorketika," 3.3; 3.26; 3.67–71.

[383] Aeneas Tacticus, 3.1–3.

[384] Aeneas Tacticus, 12.1–2.

[385] Aeneas Tacticus, 22.4–8; Philon, "Poliorketika," 3.35–38.

[386] Aeneas Tacticus, 26.1–2.

[387] Aeneas Tacticus, 38.1.

[388] Aeneas Tacticus, 10.4–7.

[389] Aeneas Tacticus, 10.15.

[390] Aeneas Tacticus, 5.1–2.

[391] Polyaenus, 2.36.

[392] Aeneas Tacticus, 18.3–6.

[393] Aeneas Tacticus, 19.1; 20.1–2.

[394] Aeneas Tacticus, 22.14.

[395] Vegetius, 4.26.

[396] Frontinus, 3.16.2–4.

[397] Vegetius, 4.11.

[398] Bradbury, J., *The Medieval Siege*, pp. 157, 309.

[399] Philon, "Poliorketika," 3.3–4.

[400] Vegetius, 4.6.

[401] Philon, "Poliorketika," 3.18.

[402] Gravet, C., *Medieval Siege Warfare*, p. 25.

[403] Aeneas Tacticus, 22.9–10.

[404] Philon, "Poliorketika," 3.14–17.

[405] Philon, "Poliorketika," 3.39; 3.49–50.

[406] Frontinus, 3.3.3.

[407] Herodotus, 3.154–8.

[408] Frontinus, 3.2.1.

[409] Frontinus, 3.9.7.

[410] Frontinus, 3.9.6.

[411] Frontinus, 3.9.9.

[412] Frontinus, 3.2.3–4.

[413] Frontinus, 3.2.8–9.

[414] Frontinus, 3.2.7.

[415] Frontinus, 3.3.1.

[416] Frontinus, 3.4.3.

[417] Frontinus, 3.4.5.

[418] Frontinus, 3.10.1.

[419] Frontinus, 3.10.2.

[420] "De castrametatione," 26.

[421] Frontinus, 3.12.1.

[422] Frontinus, 3.14.2.

[423] Frontinus, 3.14.3–4.

[424] Frontinus, 3.15.6.

[425] Polyaenus, 2.18.

[426] Frontinus, 3.15.1.

[427] Frontinus, 3.18.1–2.

[428] Aeneas Tacticus, 40.4–7.

[429] Frontinus, 3.17.6–8.

[430] Polyaenus, 5.24.

[431] Polyaenus, 7.30.

[432] Frontinus, 3.8.2; Polyaenus, 2.4.1.

[433] Polyaenus, 4.18.1.

[434] Polyaenus, 7.9. Describing this siege, Polyaenus mentions *catapults*, throwing arrows, and stones. However, no other source confirms such an early appearance of throwing machines. Polyaenus, who wrote in the 2nd century AD, by which time throwing machines had already been long known, must have misunderstood the author whose story he was rendering.

[435] D. Nicolle (*Medieval Siege Weapons (1), Western Europe AD 585–1385*, p. 9) believes that the term *ballista* in medieval Europe also stands for *onager*. However, as mentioned above, the author of this book believes that *onager* was not used in the Middle Ages and, consequently, the term *ballista* could not be used in this sense.

[436] Christine de Pisan obviously draws a distinction between *bricole* and *couillard* (see Table 1). Thus, at least in France, these terms were not synonymous.

[437] See the footnote to the *contravallation line* (footnote 438).

[438] The terms *contra-* and *circumvallation lines* are not to be found in the work of any of the ancient or medieval authors and came to be used later for the description of siege lines. The Latin word *circumvallo* meant "to surround, besiege, encircle," and did not necessarily imply a line of defense, although it could mean "enclose by a rampart." The term *contravallatio* only appeared later and is not used by ancient authors. The Romans seem to have had no special terms for the designation of internal and external siege lines. We only know that Vegetius's [4.28] name for the defense line designed to oppose the sorties of the besieged is *loricula*.

[439] Nicolle, D., *Medieval Siege Weapons (2), Byzantium, the Islamic World & India AD 476–1526*, pp. 39, 47.

[440] Ammianus Marcellinus [23.4.7] speaks of this term concerning the *onager*, but apparently it was used about other torsion-powered machines as well.

[441] About the later meaning of the term *zanburak*, see: Partington, J. R., *A History of Greek Fire and Gunpowder*, pp. 196 and 205.

BIBLIOGRAPHY

Primary Sources

Abbo, *Le Siège de Paris par les Normands*, Paris, 1942.

Aeneas Tacticus, *How to Survive under Siege*, Oxford, 1990.

Ammianus Marcellinus, *The Later Roman Empire, 354–378*, Harmondsworth, 1969.

Ammianus Marcellinus, *The Roman History*, Saint-Petersburg, 2000.

Anonymus Byzantine, "Instruktsii po poliorketike" ("Siegecraft instructions") / in the book: *Grecheskie poliorketiki. Vegetsii*, Saint-Petersburg, 1996.

Anonymus Reformer, *De rebus bellicis*, Lipsiae, 1984.

Apollodorus, "Poliorketika" / in the book: *Grecheskie poliorketiki. Vegetsii*, Saint-Petersburg, 1996.

Appian, *Roman History*, London & New York, 1912–1913.

Arrian, *Anabasis Alexandri*, Cambridge & London, 1976–1983.

Athenaeus Mechanicus, "O mashinah" ("On machinery") / in the book: *Grecheskie poliorketiki. Vegetsii*, Saint-Petersburg, 1996.

Biton, "Construction of War Engines and Artillery" / in the book: Marsden, E. W., *Greek and Roman Artillery. Technical Treatises*, Oxford, 1999.

Caesar, *The Civil Wars*, New York, 1869.

Caesar, *The Gallic War*, New York, 1869.

Comnena, Anna, *The Alexiad*, Harmondsworth, 1969.

Comnena, Anna, *The Alexiad*, London, 1928.

"De castrametatione" // in the book: *Dva vizantiiskih voennyh tractata kontsa X veka*, Saint-Petersburg, 2002.

"De velitatione bellica" // in the book: *Dva vizantiiskih voennyh tractata kontsa X veka*, Saint-Petersburg, 2002.

Diodorus of Sicily, *Library of History*, Cambridge & London, 1933–1967.

Froissart, Jean, *Chronicles*, Harmondsworth, 1968.

Frontinus, *Stratagems*, Saint-Petersburg, 1996.

Frontinus, *The Strategems and the Aqueducts of Rome*, London & New York, 1925.

Gregory of Tours, *The History of the Franks*, Harmondsworth, 1974.

Herodotus, *The History*, Cambridge, 1960–1963.

Herodotus, *The History of Herodotus*, London, 1914.

Heron, "Belopoeica" / in the book: Marsden, E. W., *Greek and Roman Artillery. Technical Treatises*, Oxford, 1999.

Heron, "Cheiroballistra" / in the book: Marsden, E. W., *Greek and Roman Artillery. Technical Treatises*, Oxford, 1999.

Homer, *Iliad*, Chicago, 1951.

Homer, *Odyssey*, New York, 1968.

Josephus, *The Jewish War*, Cambridge & London, 1961.

Kyeser, Conrad, *Bellifortis*, 2 vols., Dusseldorf, 1967.

Livy, *The History of Rome*, London, 1905.

Philon, "Belopoeica" / in the book: Marsden, E. W., *Greek and Roman Artillery. Technical Treatises*, Oxford, 1999.

Philon, "Poliorketika" / in the book: Lawrence, A. W., *Greek Aims in Fortification*, Oxford, 1979.

Plutarch, *Plutarch's Lives*, London & New York, 1919–1920.

Polyaenus, *Stratagems*, Saint-Petersburg, 2002.

Polybius, *The Histories*, Cambridge & London, 1927–1954.

Procopius, *War with the Goths*, Moscow, 1950.

Procopius, *War with the Persians. War with the Vandals. The Secret History*, Saint-Petersburg, 2001.

Pseudo-Maurice, "Strategicon" / in the book: *Iskusstvo voiny*, Saint-Petersburg, 2000.

Quintus Curtius Rufus, *History of Alexander*, Cambridge, 1946.

Taccola, Mariano, "Machines et Stratagemes de Taccola, Ingenieur de la Renaissance" / in the book: E. Knobloch, *L'Art de la Guerre*, Paris, 1992.

Tacitus, *The Complete Works*, New York, 1942.

Thucydides, *History of Peloponnesian War*, Cambridge & London, 1975–1976.

Vegetius, "De Re Militari" / in the book: *Grecheskie poliorketiki. Vegetsii*, Saint-Petersburg, 1996.

Vegetius, *Flavius Renatus, Epitoma Rei Militaris*, New York, 1990.

Vitruvius, *Ten Books on Architecture*, Cambridge, 1999.

William of Tyre, *Chronicon*, 2 vols., Brepols, 1986.

William of Tyre, *A History of Deeds Done Beyond the Sea*, 2 vols., New York, 1943.

Xenophon, *Cyropaedia*, Cambridge & London, 1914.

Xenophon, *Hellenica*, Cambridge & London, 1918–1922.

Secondary Sources

Arendt, V. V., "Grecheski ogon'" ("Greek Fire") // *Trudy instituta istorii nauki i tekhniki*, series I, volume 9, Moscow & Leningrad, 1936, pp. 151–204.

Avdiev, V. I., *Voennaya istoriya Drevnego Egipta* (*Military History of Ancient Egypt*), Vol. 1, Moscow, 1948.

Avdiev, V. I., *Voennaya istoriya Drevnego Egipta* (*Military History of Ancient Egypt*), Vol. 2, Moscow, 1959.

Baatz, D., *Bauten und Katapulte des römischen Heeres*, Stuttgart, 1994.

Belousov, S. V., "Ob osade i oborone krepostei v voennom dele germantsev IV–VI vekov" ("On the siege and defense of fortresses in the warfare of German tribes in the 4th–6th centuries") // in the book: *Antichnost' i srednevekov'e Evropy*, Perm, 1996.

Boeheim, W., *Enciklopediya orujiya* (*Encyclopedia of Weapons*), trans. from Germany, Saint-Petersburg, 1995 (first published: *Handbuch der Waffenrunde*, Leipzig, 1890).

Bradbury, J., *The Medieval Siege*, Woodbridge, 1996 (first published 1992).

Buttery, A., *Armies and Enemies of Ancient Egypt and Assyria*, Goring-by-Sea, 1974.

Campbell, D. B., illustrated by B. Delf, *Greek and Roman Artillery, 399 BC–AD 363*, Oxford, 2003.

Campbell, D. B., illustrated by B. Delf, *Greek and Roman Siege Machinery, 399 BC–AD 363*, Oxford, 2003.

Connolly, P., *Greece and Rome at War*, London, 1981.

Contamine, P., *Voina v srednie veka* (*Warfare in the Middle Ages*), trans. from Fr., Saint-Petersburg, 2001 (first published: *La Guerre au Moyen Age*, Paris, 1980).

Corfis, I. A. and M. Wolfe, eds. *The Medieval City under Siege*, Woodbridge, 1995.

Delbrück, H., *Istoriya voennogo iskusstva v ramkah politicheskoi istorii* (*Geschichte der Kriegskunst im rahmen der politischen Geschichte*), trans. from Germ., in 4 volumes, Saint-Petersburg, 2001.

De Vries, K., *Medieval Military Technology*, Peterborough, Ontario, 1992.

Drachmann, A. G., *The Mechanical Technology of Greek and Roman Antiquity*, Copenhagen, 1963.

Duffy, C., *Siege Warfare, The Fortress in the Early Modern World 1494–1660*, London & New York, 1997.

Ellenisticheskaya tehnika (Hellenistic Engines), collection of articles ed. by Academician I. I. Tolstogo. The USSR Academy of Sciences' Publishing House, Moscow & Leningrad, 1948.

Ferrill, A., *The Origins of War, From the Stone Age to Alexander the Great*, London, 1986.

Fields, N., illustrated by D. Spedaliere & S. Sulemsohn Spedaliere, *Troy c. 1700–1250 BC*, Oxford, 2004.

Garlan, Y., *Recherches de Poliorcétique Grecque*, Paris, 1974.

Gravet, C., illustrated by R. Hook & C. Hook, *Medieval Siege Warfare*, Oxford, 1996 (first published 1990).

Griffith, P., *The Viking Art of War*, London & Mechanicsburg, 1995.

Guhl, E.; Koner, W., *The Romans. Their Life and Customs*, Twickenham, 1994.

Heath, I., *Armies of the Dark Ages 600–1066*, Goring-by-Sea, 1976.

Heath, I., illustrated by A. McBride, *Byzantine Armies 1118–1461*, Oxford, 1995.

Jurga, R. M., *Machiny wojenne*, Krakow & Warszawa, 1995.

Kagay, D. J. and L. J. A. Villalon, eds. *The Circle of War in the Middle Ages*, Woodbridge, 1999.

Kaufmann, J. E.; Kaufmann, H. W., *The Medieval Fortress*, London, 2001.

Keen, Maurice, ed., *Medieval Warfare. A History*, Oxford, 1999.

Kemp, P., *The History of Ships*, London, 1978.

Kennedy, H., *Crusader Castles*, Cambridge, 2001.

Kern, P. B., *Ancient Siege Warfare*, London, 1999.

Kirpichnikov, A. N., *Metatel'naya artilleriya Drevnei Rusi (Throwing machines of Ancient Russia) // Materialy i issledovaniya po arheologii SSSR*, No 77, Moscow, 1958, pp. 7–51.

Kozlenko, A. V., *Voennaya istoriya antichnosti (Military History of Antiquity)*, Minsk, 2001.

Kuchma, V. V., *Voennaya organizatsiya Vizantiiskoi imperii (Military Organization of Byzantine Empire)*, Saint-Petersburg, 2001.

Lawrence, A. W., *Greek Aims in Fortification*, Oxford, 1979.

Le Bohec, Ya., *L'armée Romaine sous le haut-empire*, Paris, 1989.

Lendle, O., *Schildkröten. Antike Kriegsmaschinen in poliorketischen Texten*, Wiesbaden, 1975.

Lendle, O., *Texte und Untersuchungen zum technischen Bereich der antiken Poliorketik*, Wiesbaden, 1983.

Liebel, J., *Springalds and Great Crossbows*, Leeds, 1998.

L'vovskii, P. D., "Osnovaniya ustroistva metatel'nyh mashin. Nevroballisty" ("The basis of the construction of throwing machines. Neuroballistae") // *Sbornik issledovanii i materialov artilleriiskogo istoricheskogo museya*, issue I, Leningrad & Moscow, 1940, pp. 26–54.

MacDowall, S., illustrated by G. Embleton, *Late Roman Infantryman, AD 236–565*, Oxford, 1994 (first published 1969).

Marsden, E. W., *Greek and Roman Artillery. Historical Development*, Oxford, 1999 (first published 1969).

Marsden, E. W., *Greek and Roman Artillery. Technical Treatises*, Oxford, 1999 (first published 1971).

Mursia, U., *Storia delle armi*, Milano, 1964.

Nefedkin, A. K., *Boevye kolesnitsy i kolesnichie drevnih grekov (XVI–I veka do n.e.)* (*War Chariots and Charioteers of the Ancient Greeks (16–1st centuries BC)*, Saint-Petersburg, 2001.

Nicolle, D., *Arms and Armour of the Crusading Era, 1050–1350*, London & Mechanicsburg, 1999 (first published 1988).

Nicolle, D., illustrated by A. McBride, *French Armies of the Hundred Years War*, Oxford, 2000.

Nicolle, D., illustrated by S. Thompson, *Medieval Siege Weapons (1), Western Europe AD 585–1385*, Oxford, 2002.

Nicolle, D., illustrated by S. Thompson, *Medieval Siege Weapons (2), Byzantium, the Islamic World & India AD 476–1526*, Oxford, 2003.

Nicolle, D., *Medieval Warfare, Source Book, Volume 1: Warfare in Western Christendom*, London, 1995.

Nossov, K. S., *Russkiye kreposti i osadnaya tehnika VIII–XVII vekov* (*Russian Fortresses and Siege Warfare, 8–17 cc.*), Saint-Petersburg & Moscow, 2003.

Nossov, K. S., *Rytsarskie turniry* (*Knights' Tournaments*), Saint-Petersburg, 2002.

Nossov, K. S., *Zamki i kreposti Indii, Kitaya i Yaponii* (*Castles and Fortresses of India, China and Japan*), Moscow, 2001.

Oman, C., *The Art of War in the Middle Ages, AD 378–1278*, Vol. 1, London & Mechanicsburg, 1998 (first published 1885).

Oman, C., *The Art of War in the Middle Ages, AD 1278–1485*, Vol. 2, London & Mechanicsburg, 1998 (first published 1885).

Partington, J. R., *A History of Greek Fire and Gunpowder*, Baltimore & London, 1999 (first published 1960).

Payne-Gallwey, R., *The Book of the Crossbow*, New York, 1995 (first published 1903).

Prestwich, M., *Armies and Warfare in the Middle Ages, The English Experience*, New Haven & London, 1999 (first published 1996).

Rogers, R., *Latin Siege Warfare in the Twelfth Century*, Oxford, 1992.

Schramm, E., *Die antiken Geschütze der Saalburg*, Berlin, 1918.

Schramm, E., "Poliorketik" / in the book: J. Kromayer and G. Veith, *Heerwesen und Kriegführung der Griechen und Römer*, Munich, 1928.

Sekunda, N., illustrated by A. Hook, *Greek Hoplite 480–323 BC*, Oxford, 2000.

Shaw, I., *Egyptian Warfare and Weapons*, Princes Risborough, 1991.

Shokarev, Yu. V., *Istoriya orugiya: Artlleriya (History of Weapons: Cannon)*, Moscow, 2001.

Smith, R. D., "The reconstruction and firing trials of a replica of a 14th century cannon" // *Royal Armories Yearbook*, Vol. 4, 1999, pp. 86–94.

Soedel, W.; Foley, V., "Ancient Catapults" // *Scientific American*, March, 1979.

Stone, G. C., *A Glossary of the Construction, Decoration and Use of Arms and Armor in All Countries and in All Times*, New York, 1999 (first published 1934).

Toy, S., *Castles, Their Constructions and History*, New York, 1985 (first published 1955).

Veis, G., *Istoriya civilizacii. Temnye veka i Srednevekov'e, IV-XIV veka (The history of civilization. The Dark Ages and the Middle Ages, the 4th–14th centuries)*, trans. from Germ., Vol. 2, Moscow, 1999.

Velishskii, F., *Istoriya civilizacii. Byt i nravy drevnih grekov i rimlyan (The history of civilization. Everyday life and customs of Ancient Greeks and Romans)* trans. from Czech, Moscow, 2000.

Wagner, E., *European Weapons and Warfare 1618–1648*, London, 1979.

Warry, J., *Warfare in the Classical World. An illustrated encyclopedia of weapons, warriors and warfare in the ancient civilisations of Greece and Rome*, London, 1995 (first published 1980).

Winter, F. E., *Greek Fortifications*, Toronto, 1971.

Wise, T., *Medieval Warfare*, London, 1976.

Yadin, Y., *The Art of Warfare in Biblical Lands*, London, 1963.

Yakovlev, V. V., *Istoriya krepostei (History of Fortresses)*, Moscow & Saint-Petersburg, 2000.

INDEX

A

Abel Beth Maacah, siege of, 11
Achilles, 28
Acre, siege of, 73, 184, 197, 239
Adad-Nirari II, 22–23
Adrianople, siege of, 55
Aduatuci, 54
Aeneas Tacticus
  on defense, 243, 244, 245, 246, 249, 257
  on incendiary weapons, 189, 190, 203
  on lassos, 224
  life span, 263
  on sappers, 131
  siege warfare treatise of, 36–37
  on undermining, 26
Agesilaus II, 27
Agger (embankments). *See also* Embankments
  (agger), 44, 119–21
Agrigentum, siege of, 44
Ai, siege of, 10, 255
Alakatia, 164, 265
Albertus Magnus, 205, 206, 263
Alcibiades, 254, 256
al-Din, Fakhr, 166
Alesia, siege of, 49, 236–38
Alexander, King of Epirus, 255
Alexander the Great, 91
  and *lithobolos*, 136
  tactics of, 38–41, 96, 103, 252
Alexiad (Comnena), 195
Algeciras, siege of, 209
Alicante, siege of, 209
al-Mutasim, Caliph, 165
al-Tarsusi, Murda
  incendiary mixture of, 201–2
  life span, 264
  on *luba*, 165

  on *manjaniq*, 169–70
  on *shabakah*, 88
  treatise by, 61, 155–56
Alum, 203
Ambracia, siege of, 48–49, 131, 189
Amenemhat's Tomb, Beni Hasan, 4, 5
Amida, siege of, 108
Ammianus Marcellinus
  on barbarians, 55
  on incendiary arrows, 190, 192
  on Late Empire, 50, 51
  life span, 263
  on *onagers*, 150, 152, 281n270, 282n280
Ampela. See also Vinea, 83
Anonymus Byzantine
  on attacking, 235
  on battering rams, 93, 95, 96
  on borers, 99, 100, 101, 102
  on Greek fire, 196
  on ladders, 76, 77
  life span, 263
  on *sambucas*, 117–18
  on siege towers, 103, 105, 106
  on *tortoises*, 83, 86, 87, 123, 125
Anonymus Reformer, 151, 263
Apollodorus
  on battering rams, 92, 93, 96, 111
  on borers, 99
  on ladders, 77, 78
  life span, 263
  on siege towers, 104, 109, 110
  on *tortoises*, 83, 87, 123, 124
Apollonia, siege of, 131
Appian, 263
Appius Claudius, 45
Aqqar, 161, 265
Aquileia, siege of, 51

Aquilonia, siege of, 44
Arab world, 61–64
  Greek fire, 196–97
  incendiary weapons, 62–64
  influence in Europe, 66
  mobile sheds, 88
  throwing machines, 161–62, 164–66, 169
  use of cannon, 208–9
Archaic Period (Greek), 29
Archers
  in Assyria, 15, 17, 19
  in Egypt, 3, 8
  and *gastraphetes*, 134
Archimedes, 45, 228
Arch of Septimius Severus, 93, 94
Arcuballista, 150, 265
Aribbeus, 258
Ariminum, siege of, 55
Armaments. *See* specific weapons
Arpad, siege of, 22
Arradah, 61, 63, 165–66, 265
Arrian, 39, 263
Arrow-firers. *See also* Throwing machines,
    44, 187
  in Arab world, 61, 161–62
  in Byzantine Empire, 57
  in Middle Ages, 65, 66, 155
  names for, 150
  polybolos, 143, 144
  resilient board, 181, 182–84, 188
  Roman, 145, 151–52
  sizes of, 139–41, 146–48
  torsion-powered, 136–37, 144
Arrows. *See also* Arrow-firers
  in cannons, 207–8
  incendiary, 190–91
Artillery. *See also* Cannon; Throwing machines,
    67, 210
  ribaudequins, 216
Art of War (al-Din), 166
Asculum, siege of, 257
Ashurbanipal, 21, 189
Ashurnasirpal II, 14, 20, 91
Assaulting bridge, 106, 110

Assault ladders. *See also* Scaling ladders,
    241, 250
Assur. *See* Assyria
Assyria, 13–23
  battering rams, 14–20, 22, 91
  embankments, 15, 17, 119–20
  incendiary weapons, 189
  kings' role in sieges, 21–22
  ladders, 20, 76
  passive sieges, 22–23
  sapping work, 13–14, 19, 20–21, 123
  siege shields, 19, 20, 21, 81
  siege towers, 13, 14, 103
Athenaeus Mechanicus, 77, 103, 227
  on borers, 99
  life span, 263
  on *sambucas*, 118
  on siege towers, 105, 106–7
Athenians, tactics of. *See also* Greece,
    31–32
  against Spartans, 257
Athens, siege of, 256
Attack, methods of. *See also* specific siege
    engines, 233–42
  breaching walls, 240–42
  cut access to water, 239
  filling moat, 239–40
  propose capitulation, 234–35
  siege lines, 235–38
  surprise, 235
  tunnels, 239
Attalus, King of Pergamum, 48
Auberoche, siege of, 179
Augustodunum (Autun), assault on, 54–55
Augustus, Octavian, 49–50
Avaricum, siege of, 49
Axes, 3, 7

B
Babylonia, 13
  siege of Babylon, 25, 253
Bacon, Roger, 205, 206, 263
Balanagra, 246
Baldwin II, King, 128

Ballista, 50, 136, 151, 187, 266,
    286n435
   ballista fulminalis, 151–52, 266
   in Middle Ages, 65
   number of, 154
   range of, 150, 188
   size of, 147
   tension-powered, 160–61
   use of, 153
Balls
   cannon, 213, 221, 222
   for throwing machines, 137–42
Banyas, siege of, 112–13
Barca, siege of, 26, 129
Barcelona, siege of, 226
Baroballistic machines, 187, 266
Barrels, cannon, 217–18, 219, 220
Barud. See also Saltpeter, 208
Baskets
   as cover, 88
   stone-filled, 79
Bastilles, 67–68, 238, 266
Battering rams, 89–97, 240, 241
   Assyrian, 13, 14–20, 22
   defense against, 97, 250
   Egyptian, 5, 7, 8
   Greek, 31, 32, 91
   in Judea, 11
   in Middle Ages, 67
   origins of, 90–91
   ram-*tortoise*, 91–94, 96
   Roman, 44
   on ships, 41, 96
   and siege towers, 110–11
   suspended from ladders, 94–96
   Trojan Horse, 29
Battles, vs sieges. *See also* specific
   battles, 1
Baybars, Sultan, 62
Bayeux, siege of, 71
Beam-sling machines. *See also* Throwing
   machines, 57, 59, 155, 164–65
   perrière, 166–68
   trebuchet, 171–81

Beaucaire, siege of, 202
Belek, 128
Belfrey, 111, 266
Beni Hasan, drawings at, 4, 5–6,
   90–91
Bergamo, siege of, 226
Bezabde, siege of, 51
Bible
   battles in, 9–11
   incendiary weapons in, 189
Biffa, 176, 266
Birds, use of, 191
Biringucio, Vanoccio, 127
Biton, 135, 136, 263
Black powder. *See also* Gunpowder, 202
Blockade. *See also* Attack, methods of,
   233–34
   in early Middle Ages, 66
   Roman, 44
Boeotians, fire machine, 32, 189–90
Bohemond, 76
Bombards. See also Cannon, 71, 209, 211,
   213, 266
   balls for, 222
   loading and shooting, 214–15
Booty, sharing, 47–48
Borers. *See also* Battering rams, 99–102,
   240, 266
   defense against, 250
Boucicaut, Marshal, 76
Boulogne, siege of, 75
Bows, 7
Brasidas, 32–33, 234
Brick walls, 96–97, 99
Brigola, 176, 266
Bristol, siege of, 191
Bückse (jar), 209
Burgos, siege of, 71
Byzantine Empire, 57–59
   crossbows, 162
   crude oil, 191–92
   Greek fire, 57, 58–59, 193–96
   throwing machines, 163–64
   trebuchet, 171

C

Caesar, Julius, 46, 234
   in Gaul, 49, 53–54, 257
   life span, 263
   tactics of, 236–38, 239
Caesarea, citadel of, 129
Calamandrinus, 73
Cales, siege of, 44
Callinicus, 58, 193
Cambyses, King, 258
Camillus, 43, 44
Campbell, Duncan, 279n170, 279n183
Canaan, battles in, 9–10
Cannon, 69–72, 205–22
   in Arab world, 64, 208–9
   balls for, 221, 222
   barrels of, 217–18, 219, 220
   breech or muzzle-loading, 216–17
   de Milemete's, 205, 207–8
   development of, 69–70
   gunpowder for, 202, 205, 206–7, 220, 222
   loading and shooting, 214–15
   and siege towers, 113
   sizes of, 210–14
   vs throwing machines, 188
Capitulation, 234–35
Carlisle, siege of, 178
Carolstein, siege of, 179
Carroballista, 150, 151, 152, 153, 266
Carthaginians, 30
   battering ram, 89
   First Punic War, 44–45
   Second Punic War, 46
   war with Greece, 34–36
Casilinum, siege of, 256
Castles, 1, 67, 68
   weapons for defense/offense of, 70–71
Cat, 87, 266
Catapults, 38, 136, 150, 153, 267, 282n280
   arrow-shooting, 50
   on ships, 154
   washers, 141
Cato, Marcus, 255–56

"Causia," 84
Charias, 91, 103, 104
Chariots, 275n14
   in Assyria, 19, 21
   in Egypt, 4
Charkh, 161, 267
Charon of Magnesia, 135
Cheiroballistra, 148, 151, 152, 187, 267, 281n263
   accuracy of, 145
   moving, 153
Cherbourg, siege of, 71
Chester, siege of, 80
China, throwing machines in, 57, 162–63, 166
Circumvallation line, 58, 235, 238, 267, 286n438
   in Assyria, 23
Cleitarhus, 257–58
Clisthenes of Sicyon, 239
Coal, 202, 205
Colossus of Rhodes, 73
Comnena, Anna, 195
Companion Cavalry, 39
Constantine VII Porphyrogenitus, 196
Constantinople, siege of, 59, 76, 113, 129
Contravallation line, 58, 235, 238, 267, 286n438
Corned powder, 220
Corona muralis, 47, 267
Corona vallaris, 47, 267
Cortés, Hernando, 72
Couillard, 176, 267
Cover. See Siege shields
Cranes, 223, 228–29
Crassus, 54
Crema, siege of, 80
Crossbow, great, 157, 160–62, 163, 187, 282n290
   as defense, 244
   gastraphetes, 34, 133
   jarkh, 169
   range of fire, 281n251

Crowbars
  in Assyria, 20
  in Egypt, 3, 7
Crusades, 61–62, 66–67
  Greek fire, 196–97
  siege towers, 112–13, 115
  testudo, 226
  undermining, 128
Ctesibius of Alexandria, 142, 143
Cuniculum, 124, 267
Cyrus, 25–26, 106

D
Darius, King, 253
David, King, 10–11
Da Vinci. *See* Leonardo da Vinci
Dax, siege of, 71
Defense, methods of, 243–52
  against battering rams, 97
  cranes, 228–29
  against embankments, 120–21
  by Germanic tribes, 56
  organizing population, 244–47
  preparation for, 243–44
  protecting walls, 248–49
  rationing food, 247–48
  against scaling ladders, 78–80
  screens/scorching sand, 40
  against siege towers, 114–15
  sorties, 249
  against specific weapons, 250–51
  stratagems of besieged, 256–58
  street fighting, 251–52
  throwing machines, 244
  against undermining, 129, 131, 248
"De Machinis" (Taccola), 126
Demetrius Poliocretes, 41
  siege towers, 104–5, 106, 108, 110, 113–14,
    280n200
Deserters, 246–47
  false, 253
Diades, 91, 224
  borer, 99
  siege towers, 103–4, 106

Dio, 263
Diodorus, 31, 44
  life span, 263
  on scorching sand, 40, 78–79
Diognetus, 113
Dionysius I, 91, 103
  methods of, 34–36
  throwing machines, 133
Dionysius of Alexandria, 143
Dogs, use of, 246
Domitius Calvinus, 253
Dortmund, siege of, 69–70
Dura-Europos (Syria), 129
Durazzo, defenders of, 189

E
Edessa, siege of, 120–21
Edward I, 108
Edward III, 216, 248
Egypt, 3–8
  battering rams, 90–91
  incendiary weapons, 189
  Middle Kingdom, 189, 508
  New Kingdom, 8
  Old Kingdom, 3–4
  siege towers, 103
Einarm, 181–84, 187, 267
Eion, siege of, 31, 275n31
Elephants, use of, 51–52, 277n106
Embankments (agger), 44, 119–21
  in Assyria, 13, 15, 17
  defense against, 120–21, 251
  in Persia, 25–26
Empire Period (Rome), 49–51
Engineers, 73
England, castles in, 1
Epaminondas, 255
Esarbaddon, 22
Espringals, 65, 66, 155, 158, 187, 267–68,
    282n290
  bolts for, 159–60
  for defense, 244
  range of fire, 188
Euphrates River, diverting, 25–26

Europe. *See* Middle Ages
Euthytone. See also Arrow-firers, 187, 268
Exostra (assaulting bridge), 106, 110, 268

F
Fabius Maximus, 255
Falarica, 190–91, 268
Falce, 54, 223–24, 268
Fascine, 88, 268
"Faule Mette," 213
Fidenae, siege of, 43
Fields, N., 275n28
Fire, and siege engines. *See also* Incendiary
        weapons, 17
Firearms. *See also* Cannon, 205
    ribaudequins, 216
    spread of, 209
Fire machines, 32–33, 189–90
Fire wheels, 202, 203, 268
First Punic War, 44–45
Food supplies
    attacks on, 255
    false appearances of, 256–57
    protecting, 243
    rationing, 247–48
Foot Companions, 39
Fortifications. *See also* specific fortifications, 1
    methods of capturing, 233
    modifications in, 62
Franks, 66
Fredegarius, 76
Frederick I Barbarossa, 80
Frederick II, 73
Froissart, 179
Frontinus, 263

G
Gabion, 88, 268
Gaius Valerius Potitus, 47
Gallic tribes, 53–54
Garlands, 47
Gastraphetes, 34, 36, 133–35, 187, 268,
        281n253
Gate, guarding, 245–46, 247, 253

Gate of Shalmaneser III, 18
Gauls
    defense methods of, 49
    siege tactics of, 54–56
Gaza, siege of, 39
Geese, use of, 246
Gelon, 30
Geoffrey V, 1, 198
Germanic tribes, tactics of, 54–56
Giblet, citadel of, 129
Giles of Rome, 176, 263
Gironville, siege of, 68
Glossary, 265–73
Golden Horde, 182, 198
Goths
    siege of Rome, 106
    tactics of, 55
Graecus, Marcus
    on Greek fire, 198–99, 203
    gunpowder, 205, 206
    on incendiary composition, 192
Greece, 27–41
    Alexander the Great's tactics, 38–41
    Archaic period, 29
    battering rams, 32, 91
    Demetrius' tactics, 41
    detecting undermining, 26
    Dionysius I's tactics, 34–36
    Greek measurements, 259
    Greek-Persian Wars, 30–32
    Hippocrates' tactics, 29–30
    incendiary weapons, 189
    Philip II's tactics, 37–38
    Second Peloponnesian War, 32–34
    siege of Troy, 28–29
    siege shields, 81, 83
    siege towers, 103
    strategy of devastation, 27
    torsion-powered throwers, 136
    treatise on siege warfare, 36–37
Greek fire, 193–203, 268
    in Arab world, 63, 196–97
    in Byzantine Empire, 57, 58–59,
        193–96

composition of, 198–202
in Europe, 66, 198
extinguishing, 203
Gunpowder, 202, 220
compositions of, 206–7, 222
first recipe for, 205
Guns. *See* Firearms

H

Halicarnassus, siege of, 136
Hamilcar Barca, 246
Hannibal, 46, 246–47, 254, 256, 257
Hanno, 246
Harald, 191
Hastings, Battle of, 1
Hatarikka, siege of, 23
Hebrews, tactics of, 9–11
Hector, 28
Hegetor, 91
Helepolis, 104, 108, 268, 279n197
assaulting bridge, 110
Henry V, 248
Heraclea, siege of, 46
Heraea, capture of, 246
Herodotus, 25, 29
life span, 263
on siege of Eion, 275n31
Heron, 264
Himera, siege of, 36
Hippocrates, sieges of, 29–30
Hirtius, 256
History of Outremer (William of Tyre), 168
Homer, 28, 263
Honnecourt, Villard de, 172
Hoplites, 27, 31–32
How to Survive under Siege (Aeneas), 36–37
Hugh of Provence, 196
Hundred Years' War, 76, 80, 108
Hypaspists, 39

I

Ibn Khaldun, 208
Igor, Prince, 195

Iliturgi, siege of, 46–47
Incendiary weapons, 62–64, 189–203
arrows, 190–91
and cannons, 209
compositions of, 191–93
extinguishing, 202–3
fire wheels, 202, 203
Greek fire, 193–203
Intef's Tomb, 5, 6, 103
Inti's Tomb, 3
Ishme-Dagan I, 13
Isidorus of Abydos, 135

J

Jaime I, 114
Jarkh, 61, 161, 169, 269
Jericho, siege of, 9–10
Jerusalem, siege of, 76, 239
Joab, 11
Josephus, 79, 152, 188, 282n280
life span, 264
Joshua, 9–10
Jotapata, siege of, 50, 79, 108, 189, 282n280
Judea, tactics of, 9–11
Julienne, sister of Constable du Guesclin, 80
Julius Caesar. *See* Caesar, Julius

K

Kafartab, siege of, 61–62, 126–27
Karwah, 88, 269
Khaemweset's Tomb, 4
Kharput, siege of, 128
Khety's Tomb, 6
Kyeser, Konrad, 188, 202
gunpowder recipe, 206

L

Lachish, siege of, 15, 17, 22
Ladders
assault, 241, 250
sambuca, 117–18
scaling, 4, 7, 20, 25, 75–80
Laisa, 269
Lambdarea, 164, 269

Lancers, Assyrian, 17, 19, 20
Lassos, 224
Le Mans, siege of, 249
Leo, Emperor, 193–94, 195–96
Leonardo da Vinci, 181, 183, 200
Leukon, 245
"Liber ignium ad comburendos hostes"
    (Graecus), 192
Liebel, Jean, 65, 159, 160
"Lilies," 235–36, 238
Lilybaeum, siege of, 44–45
Lithobolos, 136, 137, 187, 269
Liudprand, 195
Livy
    on commanders, 46
    on *falarica*, 191
    life span, 264
    on siege of Oreus, 48
    on siege of Veii, 43
    on *testudo*, 224–25
    on throwing machines, 44
Loricula, 235, 269
Luba, 165, 269, 283n300
Ludlow, defenders of, 224
Lueria, siege of, 253–54
L'vovskii, P. D., 188
Lydians, 25

M
Macedonian army. *See also* Greece, 39–40
Machine gun, 216
Maciejowski Bible, 228
Magganika, 164
Maghribi, 170
Makahil al-barud, 209
Malleolus, 190, 269
Malta, siege of, 113, 222
Manganikon, 164
Manganon, 57, 59, 164, 269
Manjaniq, 164–65, 169–70, 209, 269
    use in 7th–15th centuries, 61, 62, 63
Mantlet, 81–82, 88, 168, 241, 269
Manuballista, 145, 150, 152, 269
Marcellus, Marcus Claudius, 45

Mardian Hyroiades, 25
Marsden, E. W.
    on *ballista*, 151
    on *gastraphetes*, 134, 135
    on *quinquereme*, 154
    on Roman throwing machines, 50
    on torsion-powered throwing machines,
        145, 146, 148
Marwan II, 61
Masada, siege of, 105
Massilia, siege of, 84–85, 131
Measurements, 259, 261
"Media Fire," 191–92
Medieval Europe. *See* Middle Ages
Megalopolis, siege of, 129
Mehmed II, 210, 212
Memphis, seizure of, 22
Mempsis, 258
Mercenaries, 37
Mesopotamia, sieges in. *See also* Assyria, 13
Metalla, 79, 269
Mézos, Jean de, 73
Middle Ages, 65–72
    battering rams, 96
    cannon, 69–72, 205–22
    diversions during sieges, 234
    Greek fire, 198
    knowledge of weapons/methods,
        65–66
    siege lines, 238
    siege shields, 81
    siege towers, 111–13
    terms of capitulation, 234–35
    testudo formation, 226
    throwing machines, 155–84
Middle Kingdom (Egypt), 5–8
    incendiary weapons, 189
Midfa, 197, 209, 210, 270
Milemete, Walter de, 156
    cannon of, 205, 207–8
Miletus, siege of, 26
Mining galleries. *See also* Undermining, 126
Mitrailleuse, 216
Moats, filling in, 239–40

Mobile sheds. *See also* specific types of, 81–88, 279n170
  defense against, 250
  siege shields, 81–85
  tortoise, 85–87
Monankon, 270
Montferrand, siege of, 240
Montreuil-en-Bellay, siege of, 200
Mortar, 216, 270
  balls for, 222
Motya, siege of, 34–36, 103
Multan, citadel of, 40
Munqidh, Usamah B., 126–27
Musculus, 84–85, 270
Muslim world. *See* Arab world

N

Naphtha, 62–63, 192, 209, 270, 283n319
  for defense, 249
  and Greek fire, 193, 197
Naxos, siege of, 30, 31
Nefedkin, A. K., 275n14
Nekheb (El Kab), 4
Nets, 80
Neuroballistic machines, 186–87, 270
New Carthage, siege of, 46
New Kingdom (Egypt), 8
Nicaea, siege of, 226
Nicolle, David, 282n289
Noviodunum, siege of, 53

O

Odysseus, 28
Oil, hot, 79
Old Kingdom (Egypt), 3–4
Olga, Princess, 191
Oman, C., 282n290, n293
Onagers, 51, 152, 161, 187, 270, 282n280, 283n306
  and *arradahs*, 166
  and great crossbows, 163
  in Middle Ages, 155, 286n435
  number of, 153

  range of fire, 188
  structure of, 149–51
Onomarchus, general of the Phocians, 38, 154
Oreus, siege of, 48
Orléans, siege of, 68, 238
Orongis, siege of, 46
Oxen, 106
Oxybeles, 34, 36, 38, 150, 154, 187, 270
  origin of, 135

P

Palintone. See also Stone-projectors, 187, 270
Paris, siege of, 66, 80, 112, 226
Partington, James, 209
Pavise, 82–83, 271
Payne-Gallwey, R., 186, 282n290
Pelopidas, 258
Pelusium, siege of, 258
Pephrasmenos, 89
Pericles, 31, 254
Perinthus, siege of, 38
Peritreton, 136, 271
Perrière, 68, 162–68, 187, 241, 271, 282n296
  firing, 173–74
  origins of, 162–66
  rate/range of fire, 184, 188
  and *trebuchet*, 179–81
  types of, 167
Persia, 25–26
  Greek-Persian Wars, 30–32
Petra, siege of, 96
Petrabolos, 57, 163–64, 271
Petroleum, 191–92, 193, 198, 200
Philip II, tactics of, 37–38, 91, 103, 154
Philip V, 258
Philon
  on defense, 239, 243, 244, 249
  life span, 264
  on *naphtha*, 283n319
  on siege towers, 109, 149
Pickaxes, 20
Pillage, 47
Pisan, Christine de, 70, 263

Plan Carpin, Giovanni de, 198
Plataea, siege of, 31, 32, 33, 189
Plutarch, 31, 104, 264
Pluteus, 83, 87, 271
Polyaenus, 38, 190, 264, 286n434
Polybius, 46
  on ladders, 75
  life span, 264
  on Roman siege weapons, 44
  on *sambuca*, 117
  on undermining, 128
Polybolos, 143, 144, 271
Polyidus, 91
Pometia, siege of, 43
Porta, Baptista, 200
Pot de fer (iron pots), 209
Potidaea, siege of, 233
Powder. *See also* Gunpowder, 202
Procopius
  on *ballistra*, 160–61
  on Goths, 55
  life span, 264
  on siege of Edessa, 120–21
  on "wolf," 229
Pseudo-Maurice, 264

Q

Qarabugha, 170
Qaws al-lawab, 161, 271
Qaws al-rijl, 161, 271
Qaws al-rikab, 161
Quicklime, 198, 200
Quinquereme, 118, 154
Quintus Curtius, 264

R

Rahab, 9
Ramelli, 157, 180
Rams. *See* Battering rams
Ramses II, King, 8
Raven, demolishing, 223–24, 267
Reliefs, Assyrian, 14–21, 76, 81, 189
Resin, 189, 198
Retreat, feigning, 255–56

Rewards, 47
Rhodes, siege of, 41, 71, 73, 154
Ribaudequin, 216, 271
Ribauld, 216, 271
Richard I, 1, 73
Robert of Bellême, 235
Robert the Bruce, 178
Rock of Sogdiana, siege of, 39
Romanus, Emperor, 196
Rome, 43–52
  battering rams, 44
  defense tactics, 257
  embankments, 120–21
  Empire Period, 49–51
  First Punic War, 44–45
  Gallic War, 49
  incendiary weapons, 189, 190–91
  ram-*tortoise*, 93–94
  Roman measurements, 261
  sambucas, 117
  Second Punic War, 46–47
  sharing booty, 47–48
  siege by Goths, 55, 106
  siege of Ambracia, 48–49
  siege of Oreus, 48
  siege of Syracuse, 45–46
  siege shields, 83
  siege towers, 105–6
  testudo formation, 44
  throwing machines, 145, 151–52
  undermining, 43
Rouen, siege of, 71, 184, 248
Russia, crossbows in, 161

S

Sabirs, 96
Saladin, 61, 62
Saltpeter, 198, 199, 200, 202
  in powder, 205
Samaria, siege of, 22
Sambucas, 45, 117–18, 271
Samos, siege of, 31
Sanctuary of Athena, 144
Sand, scorching, 40, 79

Sangala, siege of, 39
Sapping work. *See also* Undermining, 123–29
   in Assyria, 13–14, 19, 20–21
Saracens, methods of, 61–62
Sardis, siege of, 25
Sargon II, 15, 16
Satricum, siege of, 44
Scala, Antonio della, 216
Scaling ladders, 75–80
   in Assyria, 20
   defenses against, 78–80
   height of, 75–76
   in Old Kingdom, 4, 7, 75
   in Persia, 25
   types of, 76–78
Schramm, General E., 185
Schwartz, Berthold, 205
Scipio, Lucius, 256
Scipio Africanus, 46–47
Scorpions, 50, 136, 150, 154, 187, 271
   in Empire Period, 151, 152
   moving, 153
   and *onagers*, 282n280, 283n305
   range of fire, 188
Screens, softening, 40
Seasons, and sieges, 234, 235
Second Peloponnesian War, 32–34
Second Punic War, 46–47
Selinus, siege of, 34
Sennacherib, King, 15, 18, 22
Servius Tulluis, 43
Shabakah, 88, 271
Shalmaneser III, 14–15
Shamshi-Adad I, 13
Shields. *See* Siege shields
Ships
   battering rams on, 41, 96
   and Greek fire, 195
   sambucas on, 117–18
   siege towers on, 106–7
   testudo formation on, 226
   throwing machines on, 154
Sicyon, siege of, 254

Siege engines. *See also* specific engines, 73
   Egyptian, 7–8
   and fire, 17
   in Middle Ages, 65–66
   miscellaneous, 223–29
   Persian, 26
   Roman, 43, 44, 51
Siege machines. *See also* specific machines, weapons
   Greek, 31–32, 34
   Roman, 45
Sieges. *See also* specific sieges, countries, 1
Siege shields, 81–88
   in Assyria, 19, 20, 21
   tortoises, 85–87
Siege towers, 103–15, 241, 279n197
   advantages of, 109–10
   in Assyria, 13, 14
   covering for, 108–9
   defense against, 114–15, 250
   Goths, 55
   Greek, 36, 38
   in Middle Ages, 67, 111–13
   Middle Kingdom, 6–7
   movement of, 106, 113–14
   Roman, 105–6
   structure of, 103–6
   watchtowers, 223
   weapons in, 110–11
Siege weapons. *See also* specific weapons
   Assyrian, 14
   for castles' defense/offense, 70–71
   incendiary, 189–203
   in Middle Ages, 67–72
   in Middle Kingdom, 7–8
Sighting mechanism, 145
   on cannon, 215
Sinon, 29
Slingers
   in Assyria, 19
   in Greece, 38
   in Middle Kingdom, 7
Soli, siege of, 26
Solomon, 11

Sorties, 249
Spartans. *See also* Greece, 27, 31, 32
Stephen V, Pope, 196
Stimulus ("spur"), 235–36, 238, 272
Stone-projectors. *See also* Throwing machines,
   57, 136, 187, 240, 282n280
   arradah, 61, 165–66
   for defense, 244
   Einarm, 181–84
   first use of, 40
   man-powered, 165–68
   in Middle Ages, 155
   petrobolos, 163–64
   sizes of, 139–41, 146–48, 153
Stratagems, 253–58
   of besieged, 256–58
   of besiegers, 253–56
   "strategy of destruction," 27, 58
Suenda, capture of, 254
Sulphur, 189, 198, 202, 205
Supplies, protecting, 243
Syracuse, siege of, 45–46, 117, 228

T
Taccola, Mariano
   "De Machinis," 126
   life span, 264
   on siege shields, 81–82
   on siege towers, 112
   on *trebuchet*, 178
Tacitus, 50, 264
Taktika (Emperor Leo), 195
Tarquinius Superbus, 253
Tegea, capture of, 254
Tension-powered machines. *See also* Throwing
   machines, 65, 187, 272
Testudo formation, 44, 224–26, 272
   hot oil on, 79
   use by Gauls, 53
Tetrareai, 164
Thebes, siege of, 29
Thessaloniki, siege of, 163
Thompson, Sam, 282n289
Thrasybulus, 254, 256–57

Throwing machines. *See also* specific machines,
   133–88, 241
   balls for, 137–42
   in Byzantine Empire, 57
   classification of, 186–88
   cranes, 228–29
   crossbows, 157, 160–62
   for defense, 244
   defense against, 45–46, 251
   espringals, 159–60
   Greek, 34, 38, 40
   manganon, 57, 59
   in Middle Ages, 61, 62, 63, 66, 68, 71–72,
      155–84, 168–70
   in modern era, 184–85
   moving, 153
   origins of, 34, 133–36
   perrière, 162–68
   polybolos, 143, 144
   range of fire, 188
   reconstructions of, 185–86
   with resilient board, 181–84
   Roman, 44, 48, 50, 51, 145
   on ships, 154
   and siege towers, 110
   sizes of, 139–42, 146–48
   terminology of, 150–52
   torsion-powered, 136–37, 142, 144,
      145–50, 155
   trebuchet, 170–81
   use by Goths, 55
   ziyar, 155–56, 158
Thucydides, 34, 189, 264
Thutmose III, 8
Tiglath-Pileser I, 13
Timotheos, 224
Titurius Sabinus, 257
Tolleno, 223, 241, 272
Tombs, Egyptian, siege art in, 3–8
Tormentum, 152, 272
Torsion-powered machines. *See also* Throwing
   machines, 65, 144, 187, 272, 281n258
   basis of, 136–37
   development of, 38